THE CHALLENGE OF CRIME
IN A FREE SOCIETY

Perspectives on the Report of the
President's Crime Commission

SYMPOSIA ON LAW AND SOCIETY

GENERAL EDITOR: LEONARD W. LEVY

Claremont Graduate School

THE CHALLENGE OF CRIME IN A FREE SOCIETY

Perspectives on the Report of the
President's Commission on Law Enforcement
and the Administration of Justice

HENRY S. RUTH, JR.   FRANK J. REMINGTON
LLOYD E. OHLIN   NORMAN ABRAMS
IRVING LANG   ELIOT H. LUMBARD
PETER BARTON HUTT   DEAN JOSEPH O'MEARA

With a Supplement on the Legal Implications
of Mass Urban Disorder

DA CAPO PRESS · NEW YORK · 1971

This volume consists of papers presented at the annual Notre Dame Law School
Symposium held on February 12, 1968, and first published in the *Notre Dame
Lawyer,* Volume 43, Number 6 (1968), and of a related student survey, "The
Long, Hot Summer: A Legal View," published in the same issue of the *Lawyer.*
The material contained herein is reprinted with the permission of the editors of
the *Notre Dame Lawyer* and, for the symposium, by arrangement with each
contributor.

Library of Congress Catalog Card Number 79-152126

SBN 306-70124-3

Published by Da Capo Press, Inc.
A Subsidiary of Plenum Publishing Corporation
227 West 17th Street, New York, N.Y. 10011
All Rights Reserved

Manufactured in the United States of America

CONTENTS

SYMPOSIUM

SURVEY

TO DUST SHALL YE RETURN?

*Henry S. Ruth, Jr.**

I. Introduction

"In this world, nothing can be said to be certain except death and taxes"[1] — and presidential commissions. Proponents of any commission argue that an executive should launch a broad action program only on the basis of a prior independent study of all relevant factors.

In April of 1931, Calvin Coolidge said:

> The use of fact-finding commissions is again being criticized. About twenty-five years ago agitation caused the Congress to prohibit spending public money for such purpose. . . .
> Some people are born with a complete set of ready-made opinions. Facts do not affect them. But no executive, from first selectman to President, can know everything necessary to discharge his office or be able to learn it from official sources. He must call on some body which can gather the information. Public duty requires it.[2]

Critics of these bodies note acidly that a commission is a cynical creature of politics, a method of buying time, or a device for calming the public in matters where agitation and aggressive concern are truly appropriate.[3] In the past few years numerous presidential commissions[4] have filed their reports on subjects

---

* Director, Criminal Justice Coordinating Council, Office of the Mayor, City of New York; former Associate Professor of Law, University of Pennsylvania Law School; former Deputy Director, President's Commission on Law Enforcement and Administration of Justice.

1 C. VAN DOREN, BENJAMIN FRANKLIN 773 (1938).
2 N.Y. Herald Tribune, April 16, 1931, at 1, col. 2-3.
3 In 1929, one writer noted:

> Washington has grown exceedingly cynical on the subject of special governmental commissions. Many such bodies have come into existence and passed away in recent years, leaving behind them voluminous unread reports and recommendations. . . . The establishment of a special commission to investigate or consider some great question of the hour is a tried and reliable device which makes it possible for an administration to offer the appearance of great activity without making any definite decision. . . . (N)ine times out of ten, when these conclusions and recommendations have been announced with all proper solemnity, that is the end of the subject. . . . Murphy, *The Sphinx Commission*, 10 COMMONWEAL 249 (1929).

In MacKenzie, *The Compromise Report on Crime*, NEW REPUBLIC, Feb. 4, 1967, at 15, the author wrote that the membership of the President's Commission on Law Enforcement and Administration of Justice was "chosen cross-sectionally the way the Warren Commission was chosen and partly for the same purpose: to calm the country down." The author concluded that President Johnson had "bought time with the commission study, and soon he must move, ready or not." *Id.* at 16.

4 Use of the term "presidential commission" is circumscribed to include only ad hoc commissions appointed for a specific term by an Executive Order. Of course, the President is connected with many other kinds of study groups. In January of 1968, there existed 193 committees, commissions, task forces, study groups, advisory councils, and interagency committees with some degree of presidential involvement. Letter from Joseph Laitin, Assistant to the Director, Bureau of the Budget, to Henry S. Ruth, Jr., Jan. 12, 1968.

For a discussion of the goals, problems, and functions of commissions and other study groups, see Bell, *Government by Commission*, THE PUBLIC INTEREST, Spring, 1966, at 3-9. For a description of the roles served by advisory committees in local government, see Schaller, *Is the Citizen Advisory Committee a Threat to Representative Government?*, 24 PUB. ADMIN. REV. 175 (1964). For an analysis of presidential commissions from 1900 to 1940, see C. MARCY, PRESIDENTIAL COMMISSIONS (1945). For Marcy's analysis of the future role of the commission device, see *id.* at 102-06.

ranging from the assassination of a president[5] to heart disease, cancer, and stroke.[6] In fact, it is fair to say that no major national problem has been immune from study by a temporary commission. It is hardly surprising, then, that in the midst of a bitter national debate on crime and criminal justice, President Johnson appointed his Commission on Law Enforcement and Administration of Justice. The purpose of this Article is to discuss briefly the background of this national crime commission, its method of operation, and the plans for implementation of its recommendations.

During its work from July of 1965 to June of 1967, the Commission had a full-time staff of approximately forty professionals and utilized the services of about four hundred fifty consultants and advisers.[7] Its publications include nine task force reports concerned with specific aspects of crime and criminal justice,[8] five field survey reports,[9] forty-one consultant papers,[10] and a general report, *The Challenge of Crime in a Free Society*, which summarizes all the Commission's conclusions and recommendations.

II. Background of the Commission

For various reasons, public concern about crime ascended rapidly during the first half of the 1960's. National crime rates during 1960-65 reflected an upward trend that was increasing faster than the previous long-term trend.[11] The number of serious offenses known to the police per 100,000 population for these five years rose twenty-five percent for violent crimes and thirty-six percent for property crimes.[12] The largest increases occurred in 1964, with

5 THE PRESIDENT'S COMMISSION ON THE ASSASSINATION OF PRESIDENT JOHN F. KENNEDY, REPORT (1964).

6 THE PRESIDENT'S COMMISSION ON HEART DISEASE, CANCER AND STROKE, A NATIONAL PROGRAM TO CONQUER HEART DISEASE, CANCER AND STROKE: REPORT TO THE PRESIDENT (1965).

7 A listing of the consultants and advisers is found in THE CHALLENGE OF CRIME IN A FREE SOCIETY, A REPORT BY THE PRESIDENT'S COMMISSION ON LAW ENFORCEMENT AND ADMINISTRATION OF JUSTICE, 313-25 (1967). [hereinafter cited as CRIME REPORT.] A listing of professional staff members is found at an unnumbered page following the foreword to the Crime Report.

8 The nine task force reports are entitled: THE POLICE, THE COURTS, CORRECTIONS, ORGANIZED CRIME, SCIENCE AND TECHNOLOGY, DRUNKENNESS, NARCOTICS AND DRUG ABUSE, JUVENILE DELINQUENCY AND YOUTH CRIME, and CRIME AND ITS IMPACT — AN ASSESSMENT. All were published in 1967. [hereinafter the task force reports will be cited as, for example, TFR ON THE POLICE.]

9 The five field survey reports are authored and titled as follows: BUREAU OF SOCIAL SCIENCE RESEARCH, FIELD SURVEY I: REPORT ON A PILOT STUDY IN THE DISTRICT OF COLUMBIA ON VICTIMIZATION AND ATTITUDES TOWARD LAW ENFORCEMENT; NATIONAL OPINION RESEARCH CENTER, FIELD SURVEY II: CRIMINAL VICTIMIZATION IN THE UNITED STATES: A REPORT OF A NATIONAL SURVEY; UNIVERSITY OF MICHIGAN SURVEY RESEARCH CENTER, FIELD SURVEY III: STUDIES IN CRIME AND LAW ENFORCEMENT IN THE MAJOR METROPOLITAN AREAS (volumes I and II); UNIVERSITY OF CALIFORNIA AT BERKELEY, SCHOOL OF CRIMINOLOGY, FIELD SURVEY IV: THE POLICE AND THE COMMUNITY (volumes I and II); NATIONAL CENTER ON POLICE AND COMMUNITY RELATIONS, SCHOOL OF POLICE ADMINISTRATION AND PUBLIC SAFETY, MICHIGAN STATE UNIVERSITY, FIELD SURVEY V: A NATIONAL SURVEY OF POLICE AND COMMUNITY RELATIONS. All the field surveys are dated 1967.

10 The forty-one consultant papers were published individually in June of 1967. Several other consultant papers were published as appendices in the task force reports.

11 CRIME REPORT 24.

12 *Id.*

forcible rape the leader among the violent crimes and motor vehicle theft the leader among property crimes.[13]

Other developments converged that year to heighten public interest and alarm. A wave of riots commenced in the summer of 1964 as disturbances erupted in New York City, Philadelphia, Chicago, Rochester, Paterson, Elizabeth, and Jersey City.[14] The Republican presidential candidate, Barry Goldwater, was decrying lawlessness and crime in the streets during the summer and fall of 1964.[15] A Gallup poll in 1963 revealed that many persons considered juvenile delinquency the second most important problem in their respective communities.[16] A 1964 Harris survey showed that the factor most often cited by persons as causing increased crime in their neighborhoods was the existence of " 'disturbed and restless teenagers.' "[17] Finally, those blaming restrictive court decisions for the rising crime rates acquired new fuel in June of 1964 with the Supreme Court's decision in *Escobedo v. Illinois*.[18] The mounting alarm mirrored a twofold concern: a belief by many that our system of criminal justice and law enforcement was not adequately performing its role and a public fear that criminality was a rapidly spreading force threatening basic public order and security.

The overwhelming involvement of the federal government in social betterment programs — a development that had created revolutionary changes in federal-state-city relationships during the past thirty or so years — had largely bypassed the problems of law enforcement and criminal justice. For Americans traditionally have desired hometown policing and hometown judicial systems with neither the appearance nor the reality of administrative control or influence from the higher levels of government. One need only mention the words "national police force" to reinforce this local law enforcement orientation.

But in the Fall of 1964 it became apparent in the United States Department of Justice that a suitable time for national action had arrived. All the factors cited above influenced the decision for action. To cite this decision as a political response to Barry Goldwater, as some may do, is to fall prey to a much over-simplified view of federal government operations. Such a view also does great injustice to the sincere, active, and abiding interest of the then Acting Attorney General, Nicholas Katzenbach, in creating an intelligent, informed public appraisal of the crime problem and in rescuing law enforcement and criminal justice from creaking concepts, machinery, procedures, and organization. Political considerations may properly be cited as a catalyst, but not as a founding father.

There were significant forerunners to a concentrated federal program in this area. The President's Committee on Juvenile Delinquency and Youth Crime

---

13 *Id.*
14 TFR ON CRIME AND ITS IMPACT — AN ASSESSMENT 118.
15 Candidate Goldwater, however, apparently did desire to suppress the racism and further public incendiarism that would have been engendered by emphasizing the riots; he refused to authorize the showing of a film documentary, prepared by his staff, that depicted looting and rioting by Negroes. T. WHITE, THE MAKING OF THE PRESIDENT — 1964, at 236, 332 n.9 (1965).
16 CRIME REPORT 49-50.
17 *Id.* at 49.
18 378 U.S. 478 (1964).

had been operating since 1961 and, through the Office of Juvenile Delinquency and Youth Development in the Department of Health, Education, and Welfare, was funding comprehensive, crime prevention-related programs in several major cities.[19] The President's Advisory Commission on Narcotic and Drug Abuse completed its report in 1963.[20] With impetus from the report of the Attorney General's Committee on Poverty and the Administration of Federal Criminal Justice,[21] the Department of Justice and the Vera Foundation in 1964 sponsored a national conference on bail practices[22] and appointed an executive board to assist in the development of bail programs in various states.[23] In August of 1964, Attorney General Robert Kennedy created a small Office of Criminal Justice in the Department of Justice.[24] One of the major functions of this office was to propose and aid in the implementation of reform measures in state and local criminal justice operations.

Thus, the stage was set when, in his January 1965 State of the Union message, President Johnson announced a forthcoming federal program touching upon all the problems of crime.[25] Details of this program were revealed in his first message to Congress on crime in March of 1965.[26] Included in the program were: proposed federal aid to state, local, and private criminal justice organizations; creation of a presidential commission on crime in the District of Columbia; and establishment of the President's Commission on Law Enforcement and Administration of Justice (National Crime Commission).[27]

The presidential mandate to the National Crime Commission apparently ran to all problems, and all institutions related to crime in any way. The message to Congress, the Executive Order creating the Commission in July of 1965,[28] and the President's remarks to the members at their first meeting in September

---

19   U.S. DEPT. OF HEALTH, EDUCATION, AND WELFARE, ANNUAL REP. 63-64 (1966). Both the Committee and the Office have since been abolished.
20   THE PRESIDENT'S ADVISORY COMMISSION ON NARCOTIC AND DRUG ABUSE, FINAL REPORT (1963).
21   THE ATTORNEY GENERAL'S COMMITTEE ON POVERTY AND THE ADMINISTRATION OF FEDERAL CRIMINAL JUSTICE, REPORT (1963).
22   NATIONAL CONFERENCE ON BAIL AND CRIMINAL JUSTICE, PROCEEDINGS AND INTERIM REPORT (1965).
23   Id. at xiv-xxxii. The Vera Foundation is now the Vera Institute of Justice.
24   The early planning for the National Crime Commission was undertaken by the Office of Criminal Justice. Four of the six members of the Office joined the Commission staff, including the executive director and deputy director of that staff.
25   I PUBLIC PAPERS OF THE PRESIDENT — LYNDON B. JOHNSON 1965, at 1 (1966). In the message, President Johnson stated: "I will soon assemble a panel of outstanding experts to search out answers to the national problem of crime and delinquency." Id. at 7.
26   LYNDON B. JOHNSON, COMMENTS ON CRIME: ITS PREVALENCE AND MEASURES OF PREVENTION, H.R. DOC. No. 103, 89th Cong., 1st Sess. (1965).
27   The proposed federal aid program was passed by the Congress in September of 1965 and became the Law Enforcement Assistance Act of 1965, 18 U.S.C. Ch. 201 (Supp. 1966). The Program has been administered by the Office of Law Enforcement Assistance in the Department of Justice. See DEPT. OF JUSTICE, 2D ANN. REP. TO THE PRESIDENT AND THE CONGRESS ON ACTIVITIES UNDER THE LAW ENFORCEMENT ASSISTANCE ACT OF 1965 (1967).
     The President's Commission on Crime in the District of Columbia was created in July 1965 to study all aspects of crime and criminal justice in the District. See Exec. Order No. 11234, 3 C.F.R. 326 (Comp. 1964-65). The Commission's report was forwarded to the President in December of 1966. It was entitled THE PRESIDENT'S COMMISSION ON CRIME IN THE DISTRICT OF COLUMBIA, REPORT AND APPENDIX (1966).
28   Exec. Order No. 11236, 3 C.F.R. 329 (Comp. 1964-65).

of 1965[29] blanketed the spectrum from the causes of crime to crime prevention, criminal justice agencies, and rehabilitation of released offenders in the community. Factual findings, conclusions, and recommendations were to be delivered to the President during the course of the Commission's work, with a final report due not later than the end of January of 1967. It seems clear that the President's 1965 crime program represented a compromise. A proposal limited to the creation of study groups would certainly have been greeted with a massive public yawn, if not outright indignation. As one periodical stated: "Commissions come cheap in Washington, and most often their reports turn out to be vague and anticlimactic."[30] And yet, the federal government and the public were probably not prepared for a massive, revolutionary program directed towards informed, truly responsible, and properly framed reform. Thus, the law enforcement assistance program was launched with a relatively small appropriations request. In a very meaningful sense, time was being bought, but more importantly a carefully formulated set of conclusions and recommendations, and opportunities for public education, were being created.

III. Prior National Crime Study

Any commission with a broad mandate and a short time limit does well at least to consider the adage that there is nothing new under the sun. Somewhere, at some time, persons have probably promulgated ideas, facts, theories, and proposals that collectively will form a major part of any commission's report. Existing enlightenment can be collected in a convincing package. A search for dramatic new concepts and proposals, for instant solutions, or for universal answers could, if a dominating factor, negate the utility and validity of any report. True creativity will necessarily be offered by a commission in only a few areas; its boldness and integrity is reflected primarily in its willingness to accept the existing ideas of progressive scholars and administrators who have been unable to influence or affect the existing system to any great degree.

In the discovery and sorting process, the past is not to be discounted. For example, in the 1880's, a Philadelphia police chief analyzed the crime problem in the following manner:

> What makes criminals, and how to deal with them, are two of the most intricate problems of social science. Their own good should be considered as well as that of society . . . . My own views are founded less upon theory, I think, than upon observation. I have noticed that when a man is convicted of crime, especially of any crime against the rights of property, he usually commits another offence within a short period of his release from prison. He serves his term, is released, and goes back into the world . . . . Does he reform and lead an honest life? On the contrary, he returns to his old associates, if he had any; if not, he finds some, and it is not long till he re-enters the prison for the second time a convict. There-

29 Remarks to the Members of the National Crime Comm'n, II PUBLIC PAPERS OF THE PRESIDENT — LYNDON B. JOHNSON 1965, at 982 (1966). See also, Statement by the President on Establishment of the National Crime Comm'n. Id. at 785. Excerpt of Letter to Members of National Crime Comm'n. Id. at 879. Remarks on Announcing Appointment of James Vorenberg. Id. at 901.
30 The Reporter, Sept. 23, 1965, at 18.

fore I am brought to the conclusion that while existing prison systems are useful to society by keeping dangerous men where they can do no mischief, they are of little use to the criminal. I see that they restrain him; I cannot see that they reform him. Records kept in this office show as many as eight convictions of the same criminal . . . .

But philanthropy may long rack its brain in search for a cure for crime; it would find much more satisfactory results from studying the prevention of its many causes; such as defective training, evil companions, mental incapacity, bad temper, strong drink, grinding poverty, and, for persistency in crime, difficulty in retrieving lost character, which a somewhat extended observation has led me to name as some of the chief causes of crime. I might add to them two others, which I have found prolific in bad fruit: difficulty in obtaining employment, and carelessness: carelessness on the part of owners of property, who leave temptation in the way of the needy, from the housekeeper who leaves the day's wash unguarded on the lines and the back gate open, to the board of bank directors who trust blindly their own property and that of others to the falsified books of some cashier, as needy in his way as the tramp that robbed the clothes line in his. To these causes I might add another: the opportunity to dispose of stolen goods, readily and without fear of detection or betrayal.[31]

Here is an early perception of today's "new" trends: recognition of the failure of institutional confinement as a rehabilitative device; emphasis upon the problem of recidivism; recognition of poverty, ineffective family training, and lack of job opportunities as basic conditions of crime; recognition of the necessity to resurrect or create individual self-respect; a proposal to concentrate upon crime prevention programs; recognition of the problem of white collar crime; awareness of the importance of a study of victims' contributions to crime (so-called victimology); and recognition of the need to explore the structured system for disposal of stolen goods.

In the search for answers to crime problems, the concept of a national study commission had precedent in President Hoover's National Commission on Law Observance and Enforcement (popularly known as the Wickersham Commission). Despite unique factors surrounding the chaos of prohibition and its enforcement, there are remarkable similarities between the commissions of 1929 and 1965. Although the public in the prohibition era did not seem to be concerned about the broad problems of crime nearly as much as the President himself was, his short assessment of that period rings a still-familiar tune. In April of 1929, President Hoover stated:

What we are facing today is . . . the possibility that respect for law as law is fading from the sensibilities of our people. . . .

Every student of our law-enforcement mechanism knows full well that it is in need of vigorous reorganization; that its procedure unduly favors the criminal; . . . that justice must be more swift and sure. In our desire to be merciful the pendulum has swung in favor of the prisoner and far away from the protection of society. The sympathetic mind of the American people in its over-concern about those who are in difficulties has swung

31   SPROGLE, THE PHILADELPHIA POLICE, 270-71 (1887).

too far from the family of the murdered to the family of the murderer.[32]

During the presidential campaign of 1928 Mr. Hoover promised that, if elected, he would appoint a law enforcement commission.[33] Its broad mandate was to carry beyond the problems of prohibition, although this fact was not readily apparent in either the Congressional authorization[34] or the President's Inaugural Address in March of 1929.[35]

The eleven-member Commission, with the exception of the president of Radcliffe College, was composed of lawyers and judges.[36] Drawn from ten states, its membership included Dean Roscoe Pound of the Harvard Law School; Newton Baker, a former Secretary of War; and a former Attorney General of the United States, chairman George W. Wickersham.[37] Public comment upon appointment of the Commission in May of 1929 reflected the seeming ambivalence of its mandate. Political motives were attributed to the President, and the ensuing emphasis by the Administration upon a broad crime study was ascribed by some to a desire to submerge the prohibition question.[38]

The President's address to the first meeting of the Commission in May of 1929 did not even mention prohibition.[39] Chairman Wickersham later observed that the most explicit definition of the Commission's undertaking appeared in the President's annual message to Congress in December of that year.[40] In that message the President declared:

> Under the authority of Congress I have appointed a National Committee on Law Observance and Enforcement for an exhaustive study of the entire problem of the enforcement of our laws and the improvement of our judicial system, including the special problems and abuses growing out of

32   Address by President Hoover, Associated Press Annual Meeting, April 22, 1929, in MYERS AND NEWTON, THE HOOVER ADMINISTRATION 384 (1936). When asked on a television show whether or not there was, in the 1960's, a growing disrespect for law, Professor Herbert Wechsler (a member of the National Crime Commission) stated:
> This is entirely a personal opinion, but my recollection of the 1920's, when I went to college was that my generation, the class of 1928 in college, hadn't the slightest respect for law indeed. Indeed, we didn't even believe there was a legal system. As a matter of fact, we were almost right about that. Meet the Press, Feb. 19, 1967, at 9 (Merkle Press 1967).

33   MYERS AND NEWTON, supra note 32, at 389.

34   Act of March 4, 1929, ch. 706, 45 Stat. 1613. The Act appropriated the sum of $250,000 to cover the fiscal years of 1929 and 1930 "[f]or the purposes of a thorough inquiry into the problem of the enforcement of prohibition . . . together with the enforcement of other laws." Id. The money was to be expended under the authority and by direction of the President, who was to report results and recommendations to Congress.

35   Inaugural Address of President Hoover, March 4, 1929, 71 CONG. REC. 4-5 (1929). As to the prospective appointment of a law enforcement commission, President Hoover spoke in terms of a searching investigation of only the federal system, including the problems of prohibition, and called for recommendations for reorganization of the administration of federal laws and procedures.

36   MYERS AND NEWTON, supra note 32, at 389-90; Wickersham, The Program of the Commission on Law Observance and Enforcement, 16 A.B.A.J. 654 (1930).

37   Wickersham, supra note 36.

38   For example, one writer stated that no one could agree as to why the Commission was appointed, but most of the given reasons were political. Murphy, The Sphinx Commission, 10 COMMONWEAL 249 (1929). See also, 156 OUTLOOK 85 (1930). But cf., Editorial, 15 A.B.A.J. 418 (1929), praising the President for visualizing "nothing less than a consideration of the whole problem of law observance and law enforcement."

39   Address of the President of the United States in Opening the First Session of the National Law Enforcement Commission, 71 CONG. REC. 3100 (1929).

40   Wickersham, supra note 36, at 654.

the prohibition laws. The commission has been invited to make the widest inquiry into the shortcomings of the administration of justice and into the causes and remedies for them.[41]

Whatever the President's intentions might have been, Chairman Wickersham never doubted the existence of a broad mandate.

Similarities in the background and work of the 1929 and 1965 commissions are striking. As with the origin of the 1929 Commission, professional concern about improving the framework and procedures of criminal justice produced important studies that preceded the appointment of the 1965 Commission. In the 1960's the American Law Institute had completed its Model Penal Code[42] and was constructing a Model Code of Pre-Arraignment Procedure.[43] The American Bar Association had launched a three-year project to develop minimum standards for criminal justice.[44] The International Association of Chiefs of Police was completing its Model Police Standards Council Act.[45] A federally-funded, three-year study of correctional manpower and training needs was just commencing.[46] The American Bar Foundation was completing a then fourteen-year-old project, Survey of the Administration of Criminal Justice in the United States, for detailed factual observation and analysis of police, court, and correctional procedures.[47] In 1930, Mr. Wickersham commented:

> Constant assertion has led to general acceptance of the statement that there are radical defects in our laws and their administration, especially in our criminal law and procedure. Within the last decade, Judicial Councils have been established in some nineteen (19) states; official Crime Commissions in thirteen (13) and unofficial Crime Commissions in at least two states and three cities; surveys of judicial establishments and the administration of criminal justice have been made and published in not less than five states and several cities. The American Law Institute . . . has been . . . preparing a model code of criminal procedure.[48]

---

41   72 CONG. REC. 21, 27 (1929).

42   MODEL PENAL CODE (Proposed Official Draft 1962).

43   THE MODEL CODE OF PRE-ARRAIGNMENT PROCEDURE (Tent. Draft No. 1, 1966) was in the drafting process when the National Commission commenced its work.

44   AMERICAN BAR ASSOCIATION, PROJECT ON MINIMUM STANDARDS FOR THE ADMINISTRATION OF CRIMINAL JUSTICE. The project's committees, staff, and reporters were most cooperative with the National Crime Commission staff. Minimum Standard Project publications include to date: FAIR TRIAL AND FREE PRESS, POST-CONVICTION REMEDIES, PLEAS OF GUILTY, APPELLATE REVIEW OF SENTENCES, SPEEDY TRIAL, PROVIDING DEFENSE SERVICES, JOINDER AND SEVERANCE, SENTENCING ALTERNATIVES AND PROCEDURES, and PRETRIAL RELEASE. All are tentative drafts, and all but the first (which was published in 1966) were published in 1967.

45   This project was completed in 1966 by the Advisory Council on Police Training and Education and the Professional Standards Division of the International Association of Chiefs of Police. The Model Police Standards Council Act represents proposed state legislation to establish a regulatory council that would create and administer standards for recruitment and training of local police. The act is reprinted in TFR ON THE POLICE 219-20.

46   The three-year Joint Commission on Correctional Manpower and Training was funded pursuant to the Correctional Rehabilitation Study Act, 29 USC § 42 (Supp. II, 1965-66), amending 29 U.S.C. § 42 (1964), and will make its report in 1968.

47   Raw material and drafts of chapters from the Survey Project were made available to the National Crime Commission by the American Bar Foundation. Survey publications to date include: LAFAVE, ARREST (1965); NEWMAN, CONVICTION (1966); and TIFFANY, MCINTYRE AND ROTENBERG, DETECTION OF CRIME (1967). Forthcoming publications will deal with prosecution and sentencing.

48   Wickersham, supra note 36, at 656.

Both commissions were also beset by an initial lack of real progress and by funding problems.[49] Both utilized full-time staffs and drew upon renowned scholars and practitioners as consultants and advisers. The broad areas of study were substantially similar. However the Wickersham Commission completed more comprehensive surveys of matters such as lawlessness in law enforcement and court processing of cases. The National Crime Commission's surveys, on the other hand, included a much broader range of subjects and reflected the improvements in methodology.

The Wickersham Commission filed fourteen reports during 1930 and 1931: two on prohibition; one each on prosecution, criminal procedure, the federal courts (progress report only), lawlessness in law enforcement, police, criminal statistics, cost of crime, penal institutions-probation-parole, causes of crime, crime and the foreign born, enforcement of the deportation laws, and the child offender in the federal system of justice.[50] In most cases, each report contained findings and the recommendations of the Commission itself, followed by findings and conclusions of advisory committees and individual consultants. There was no comprehensive general report such as that produced by the 1965 Commission. As one might surmise from the titles, the 1929 Commission concentrated to a much greater degree than the 1965 Commission on federal problems and procedures — prohibition enforcement and the eighteenth amendment, the federal court system, and children processed in the federal system. In addition, a report on crime and the foreign born was appropriate only because of the social conditions of that earlier time.

---

49   Chairman Wickersham wrote:
> Progress in our work at the outset was slow, because of the difficulty in securing men and women to do the necessary work of research and inquiry. By the end of the fiscal year 1930, we had some forty-five men and women, besides the regular paid office force, more or less engaged in work for us, none of whom were receiving compensation from the Commission!

> In addition, we have had the assistance of a few regularly paid scholars. In some cases we were indebted to colleges and universities for the services of members of their regular staff. Wickersham, *supra* note 36, at 657.

Although the Wickersham Commission had received a $250,000 appropriation at the beginning of its study in 1929, the unpopular prohibition report which it published in January of 1930 led to a move in Congress to withhold funds after June 1930. *Id.* at 654. The President then made a public statement on June 27, 1930:
> This deleted part of the appropriation is that devoted to investigation into the cause and remedy for crime in general and for the determination of the reform needed in our judicial and administrative machinery. . . .
> With growing crime of all kinds and with insistent recommendations from every bar association and public body concerned that we should have an accurate study of the reforms necessary . . . , that we should have some constructive program for decrease and control of crime as a whole, I cannot abandon the question for one moment or allow the work of this Commission to cease. I have asked the Commission to proceed with its full program of work and it has consented to do so.

MYERS AND NEWTON, *supra* note 32, at 444-45.

Six days later, Congress appropriated an additional $250,000 for the Commission for use until June 30, 1931. Act of July 3, 1930, ch. 846, 46 Stat. 862. *See also, Foreword, Reports on Law Enforcement*, 30 MICH. L. REV. 1, n.3 (1931); C. MARCY, *supra* note 4, at 18-19.

50   Report No. 1 consists of a Preliminary Report on Observance and Enforcement of Prohibition (Nov. 21, 1929) and an undated supplement thereto. H.R. Doc. No. 252, 71st Cong., 2d Sess. 5-25 (1930). The study of the federal courts was completed by the American Law Institute. ALI, A STUDY OF THE BUSINESS OF THE FEDERAL COURTS, PARTS I, II (1934).

In the areas where the two commissions overlapped the preceding one created paths that the 1965 Commission either repeated, expanded, or carried forward. In many areas the same theoretical and philosophical orientation prevailed. The studies and analyses of economic and social factors as conditions of crime are thus strikingly similar in the reports of both commissions.[51] However, President Hoover's Commission did not follow through with recommendations on many of these matters as did the Johnson Commission. In other areas, though, the two commissions did make similar recommendations, such as those with respect to: the need for a national inventory of the costs of crime;[52] the need for centralized criminal statistics;[53] the need for centralized prosecution systems at the state level;[54] the need for improved communications, coordination between departments, education, training, minority group representation, and crime prevention in the police world;[55] the failure of prisons, the need to strengthen probation and parole, and the assumption that community treatment for offenders is the appropriate disposition unless proved otherwise in individual cases;[56] the emphasis upon improving the discretionary, invisible administrative processing of offenders in the criminal justice system,[57] and the recognition that most offenders in the system are processed through without trial;[58] the shocking conditions in the lower courts and the need for the same procedures and services there that are found in the felony courts;[59] the need for counsel for all defendants facing more than the very lightest penalties;[60] the use of other procedures as alternatives to custodial arrest;[61] the appropriateness of indeterminate, as opposed to mandatory minimum, sentences.[62]

In general, then, it can be stated fairly that both commissions emphasized the same broad needs, i.e., crime prevention activities, development of alternative ways to deal with offenders, elimination of unfairness and injustices, the need for greatly improved personnel and other resources in the criminal justice system,

---

51 For example, the findings of Shaw and McKay in the 1929 Commission's Report on the Causes of Crime (vol. II) received great emphasis in TFR on CRIME AND ITS IMPACT — AN ASSESSMENT 60-76. Professor McKay also edited and wrote parts of a consultant paper for the 1965 Commission: SUBSEQUENT ARRESTS, CONVICTIONS, AND COMMITMENTS AMONG FORMER JUVENILE DELINQUENTS (McKay ed. 1967).

52 NATIONAL COMMISSION ON LAW OBSERVANCE AND ENFORCEMENT [hereinafter WICKERSHAM COMM'N], REPORT ON THE COST OF CRIME 449-53 (1931). TFR on CRIME AND ITS IMPACT — AN ASSESSMENT 42-59. In its recommendations, the 1931 report was somewhat narrow in stressing primarily the need to determine the cost factors of the nation's criminal justice machinery. The later commission placed additional emphasis upon ascertaining with some degree of precision various other cost impacts of crime.

53 WICKERSHAM COMM'N, REPORT ON CRIMINAL STATISTICS 5-18; TFR on CRIME AND ITS IMPACT — AN ASSESSMENT 123-37.

54 WICKERSHAM COMM'N, REPORT ON PROSECUTIONS 37-38; CRIME REPORT 147-49.

55 WICKERSHAM COMM'N, REPORT ON POLICE 1-10; CRIME REPORT 91-125.

56 WICKERSHAM COMM'N, REPORT ON PENAL INSTITUTIONS PROBATION AND PAROLE 170-74; CRIME REPORT 159-87.

57 WICKERSHAM COMM'N, REPORT ON PROSECUTION 6-29; TFR on THE COURTS 4-13.

58 WICKERSHAM COMM'N, REPORT ON PROSECUTIONS 59-73, 186-221; CRIME REPORT 130-31.

59 WICKERSHAM COMM'N, REPORT ON CRIMINAL PROCEDURE 46; WICKERSHAM COMM'N, REPORT ON PROSECUTIONS 45-221; CRIME REPORT 128-30.

60 WICKERSHAM COMM'N, REPORT ON PROSECUTIONS 27-33; CRIME REPORT 149-53.

61 WICKERSHAM COMM'N, REPORT ON CRIMINAL PROCEDURE 47; CRIME REPORT 132-33.

62 WICKERSHAM COMM'N, REPORT ON PENAL INSTITUTIONS PROBATION AND PAROLE 141-45; CRIME REPORT 142.

and detailed requirements for research to fill massive gaps in the current state of knowledge and information.

One can detect progress during the years between the two commissions. For example, at the time of the Wickersham report, police training was a virtually new phenomenon.[63] The third degree was said to be commonplace.[64] Probation and parole for adults lacked program content.[65] Community treatment alternatives that included elements of both regulation and community activity for the offender had not commenced to any noticeable extent. Government programs to aid those living in poverty areas were non-existent. Criminal code reform had not commenced. The procedural revolution of the Supreme Court as to police practices was yet to begin. Thus, a 1929 Commission member looking at all these things today would detect improvement.

On the negative side, it is also clear that major recommendations of the Wickersham Commission have never been implemented. The lack of individualized justice by the police, prosecutor, judge, and correctional officer is probably more of a problem today than it was in 1931. The lower courts looked the same in 1965 as they did then.[66] The decrepit prisons, condemned by the 1931 report, in many instances were merely thirty-four years older in 1965.[67] Jurisdictional fractionalization of police departments, prosecutive offices, courts, and corrections has persisted and created increasingly severe problems because of intervening social change. Public attitudes still concentrate upon a perceived moral decay, lack of respect for law, uncontrolled lawlessness, and criminal propensities allegedly related to race. We have no national inventory of the costs of crime and no national collection of statistics as to every stage of the criminal process. Administrative processing of offenders by police and prosecutors still represents an invisible anarchy suffering from lack of manpower, resources, information about offenders, and policy guidance.

Of course, an exhaustive comparison of the two commissions, and of the crime and criminal justice processes of their times, cannot be attempted here. Nor may absolute comparisons be appropriate. For progress connotes not only improvement in the way of doing things, but also an elevation of expectations and ideals. A prisoner not physically abused by the police in the 1930's would probably attribute improved fairness to the system then; today's concerns about fairness center around counsel in the police station and politeness and lack of compulsion during on-the-street questioning. But the Wickersham Commission

---

63 WICKERSHAM COMM'N, REPORT ON POLICE 4, 70-71.
64 WICKERSHAM COMM'N, REPORT ON LAWLESSNESS IN LAW ENFORCEMENT 1-6.
65 WICKERSHAM COMM'N, REPORT ON PENAL INSTITUTIONS PROBATION AND PAROLE 135-36, 167-68. In U.S. BUREAU OF PRISONS, THIRTY YEARS OF PRISON PROGRESS: 1930-1960, *Hearings Before the Subcomm. on National Penitentiaries of the Senate Comm. on the Judiciary,* 88th Cong., 2d Sess. 142, 144-45 (1964), the statement is made that when the Federal Bureau of Prisons took jurisdiction over the U.S. Probation Service in 1930, there were 4,280 probationers and eight probation officers.
66 *See* TFR ON THE COURTS 29-33, 120-38.
67 "Forty-three state penitentiaries or prisons, seven reformatories for men, and one institution for women that were opened between 1805 and 1900 still stand and are still in use in 36 states." MACCORMICK, ADULT CORRECTIONAL INSTITUTIONS IN THE UNITED STATES 7 (Consultant Paper 1967). The author points out that the design and construction of these institutions make mass treatment almost inevitable. *Id.* at 62-63.

did perceive many goals of their tomorrow and, for much of their guidance, that tomorrow has not yet appeared.

IV. Operations of the National Crime Commission

As with any presidential commission, the membership of the National Crime Commission was chosen by the President and his White House staff with the aid of suggestions from many private and governmental sources. If labels are desirable or have any validity, the membership reflected a somewhat conservative orientation, with an average age of over fifty years. Those who cry for public bodies to "tell it like it is" hardly anticipated a radical document from a present and former U. S. Attorney General, the then president and two former presidents of the American Bar Association, a former president of the American College of Trial Lawyers, a police chief, a prosecutor, a state attorney general, a former mayor of New York City, a former state secretary of internal affairs, a newspaper publisher, and three judges.[68] The four remaining members were the president of the League of Women Voters of the United States, the executive director of the National Urban League, the president of Yale University, and a distinguished law school professor who is co-reporter for the Model Penal Code. President Johnson appointed Attorney General Katzenbach as chairman of the Commission and James Vorenberg, a professor from Harvard Law School and director of the Office of Criminal Justice, as the executive director.

Aside from complicated and difficult administrative problems, the first task facing the Commission was to build a staff and to outline the full scope of the intended study. Although the Commission was created in July of 1965, appropriations were not available until the following November, and a full staff was not assembled until December.[69] By then, six of the eighteen months allotted to the Commission had passed. During this time, however, task forces were established to deal with the subjects of police, courts, corrections, and assessment of the crime problem. Later, other working groups were established to deal with juvenile delinquency, organized crime, narcotics and drug abuse, and drunkenness. Categorical subdivisions of study based upon less conventional lines were devised but abandoned as unworkable in light of time and cost factors. Early in 1966, the Institute for Defense Analyses was chosen to conduct broad

---

68 For biographical information about each Commission member, see CRIME REPORT 309-11. Attorney General Katzenbach became Undersecretary of State in September of 1966 but continued as chairman of the crime commission.

69 For a summary of Commission operations, see CRIME REPORT 311-12. The cost of the Commission can be set at approximately two million dollars. About one million dollars came from the joint appropriation for the national and District of Columbia commissions. One and one-half million dollars was authorized for the two commissions. S.J. RES. 102, Pub. L. No. 89-196, 79 Stat. 827 (1965). The combined appropriation for the two commissions was $900,000 for fiscal year 1966. Act of Oct. 31, 1965, Pub. L. No. 89-309, 79 Stat. 1151. And $550,000 was appropriated for fiscal year 1967. Act of Nov. 8, 1966, Pub. L. No. 89-797, 80 Stat. 1502. The remaining one million dollars consisted primarily of services and personnel loaned to the Commission by other agencies and research grants awarded to others by the Office of Law Enforcement Assistance for projects of mutual benefit to the Commission and to the Department of Justice. The greatest amounts of money were expended in the areas of assessment of the crime problem, science and technology, and the police; least money was expended upon drunkenness and organized crime.

inquiries into the possible contributions of science and technology to analysis of crime and criminal justice and to changing and improving society's approach to these problems. Each Commission member was assigned by the chairman to work closely with one or two of the particular task forces. The Commission then approved and added to work plans for each area of study at its first two meetings in September of 1965 and January of 1966. The young staff (two-thirds of whom were under thirty-eight years of age), with suggestions from Commission members and other sources, recruited consultants and advisers from every relevant discipline and agency to assist in the work. The staff itself included lawyers, police officials, correctional personnel, prosecutors, sociologists, psychologists, systems analysts, juvenile delinquency prevention planners, and professional writers and editors. Federal, state, and local agencies loaned personnel for appropriate part-time or full-time endeavors.

Much of the output of any study proceeds naturally from the fundamental precepts that form its base. For many reasons, the Commission and its staff primarily offered analysis and recommendations built upon existing foundations of criminal law and its enforcement. Primary emphasis was not placed upon studies of the appropriateness of the criminal sanction or of the traditional division of responsibility among entities broadly categorized as police, prosecutor, court, and corrections. Aside from the recommendation to remove drunkenness per se as a crime, the subject of overcriminalization produced only a general recommendation that states should reconsider their criminal laws pertaining to personal status and social morality.[70]

Other issues, critical in the eyes of many, also failed to receive primary attention: capital punishment, civilian review boards, a perceived decline in religion and traditional morality, the effect of court decisions upon crime and law enforcement, violence and the mass media, crime and pornography, the anatomy of riots, and electronic surveillance. Although all these subjects did receive attention, they did not receive primary attention and study. Some rose to the level of recommendations wherein the generality of context makes evident the underlying emotionalism and compromise. Others were dismissed as having no basis in fact or as simplified, emotional cloud-cover for complex questions. Lack of time and data also precluded productive analysis of some of these problems.

I do not think it appropriate for me, as a former staff participant in the Commission, to defend or condemn the approach taken. There are compelling reasons for and against the decisions not to carry many of these issues to definitive conclusions in a broad commission study. It should be recognized, however, that these decisions were not made by default or through lack of recognition.

---

70 The recommendation to remove drunkenness in itself as a criminal offense is found in CRIME REPORT 236. The recommendations on dangerous drugs and marijuana stated only the need for research upon which a framework of regulatory law could be based. *Id.* at 216, 225. There was no recommendation as to the substantive crimes connected with narcotics. But see the separate statement of four Commissioners. *Id.* at 302-03. As to gambling, abortion, vagrancy, disorderly conduct, and minor sexual offenses, the Commission said only that when states institute the recommended general criminal code reform, the kinds of behavior to be defined as criminal should be weighed carefully. *Id.* at 126-27. The whole problem of substantive law reform was considered in TFR ON THE COURTS 97-107. *See also,* J. SKOLNICK, COERCION TO VIRTUE: A SOCIOLOGICAL DISCUSSION OF THE ENFORCEMENT OF MORALS (Consultant Paper 1967); TFR ON ORGANIZED CRIME 114-26. A study of gambling and possible ramifications of its legalization was commenced but could not be completed in time.

Proper attention and heat were present in the decision-making process. Others must judge whether the gaps remaining after the Commission concluded its work doomed its study to failure or formed a prerequisite to the probability of positive achievement. Those who looked to the Commission for detailed pronouncements about the enforcement of individual and public morality through criminalization were profoundly disappointed.[71] Those, too, who sought confirmation of moral indignation at the state of lawlessness or desired immediate solutions or yearned for the reassertion of a punishment philosophy or expected identification of single-track, remediable causes of crime, must have written off the Commission's work as avoiding the real issues at hand.[72]

---

71 See, e.g., Packer, Copping Out, New York Review of Books, Oct. 12, 1967, at 17; Silver, Crime-American Style: The President's Commission, 86 COMMONWEAL 141 (1967); McCord, We Ask the Wrong Questions About Crime, N.Y. Times, Nov. 21, 1965, (Magazine) at 27. Professor Kadish prepared the substantive criminal law chapter in the Task Force Report on the Courts. TFR on THE COURTS 97-107. He subsequently stated:

> I could hardly come now either to praise it or to bury it. Still, it may be said that the controversial character of these issues, and the need to achieve consensus among nineteen Commissioners of highly differing backgrounds and orientation, quite understandably required some reduction in scope and muting in tone and conclusion of my original draft. I note this not in complaint. Indeed, that these distinguished citizens, who, as a group, can scarcely be charged with being immoderate or visionary, were prepared to raise substantial reservations concerning the overextension of the criminal law is itself an event of significance. Kadish, The Crisis of Overcriminalization, 374 ANNALS 157 (1967).

As to legalized gambling, my own view is that if a Commission device were to be used, a study devoted exclusively to that subject is necessary. Current writing and suggestions by scholars, practitioners, and public officials are extremely narrow, simplistic, naive, and unsophisticated.

72 Columnist James J. Kilpatrick wrote:

> What matters to the average citizen is not so much the abstract of statistical problems, or even the sociologists' long-range solution. His concern goes to the mugger, the rapist, the dope-crazed thief, the arrogant young punks who infest his streets. What can be done about them now? One of the commission's answers is to provide textbooks for slum schools that are written in slum English. Okay, okay. But what can be done tomorrow, next week, next month, to lock up the hoods and thieves?

The Washington Evening Star, Feb. 21, 1967, at 23, col. 4. An Anderson, South Carolina, newspaper wrote in an editorial:

> Those who were under the impression that the National Crime Commission was established to afford direction and support to immediate practical steps to curb crime must now be having second thoughts.
> Can you imagine even a nervous shoplifter, much less hardened killer-rapists, cringing under the threat of a set of "meaningful statistics"?
> Hardly!

Anderson Independent, March 11, 1966. The editorial was entitled: "If You Hoped for a Real Attack on Crime, Just Forget About It."

The lack of recommendations for immediate reduction in street crime probably caused the greatest public disappointment in the Commission's work. Although implementation of many recommendations of the Commission could have been commenced without cost the day after the report appeared, none of them would have caused immediate crime reduction. As to the long-range nature of the report, an urban affairs expert commented:

> The lay reader might respond, "yes, of course, but what do we do tomorrow morning that will reduce the chance of my wife having her purse snatched by some punk on the way to the supermarket?"

Not much, it appears. Wilson, A Reader's Guide to the Crime Commission Reports, THE PUBLIC INTEREST, Fall, 1967, at 65.

Reaction to the report, of course, depended a great deal upon the preconceptions, attitudes, and knowledge that the particular reader possessed before examining the documents. For example, Wilson stated that the great majority of the over two hundred recommendations seemed rather obvious and not very illuminating. Id. On the other hand, Congressman Rarick (D., La.) termed the National Crime Commission "the new anti-law-and-order front . . . against just about everything American. . . . Without any experience or testing of their revolutionary theories, they would destroy overnight 190 years of proven record." 113 CONG. REC. A2532 (daily ed. May 23, 1967).

What the Commission primarily concentrated upon was the measure of crime in our society today, the current responses thereto, and the formulation of directions for change. The reports had to be geared to serve divergent interests and levels of knowledge. Public education considerations required documents attractive to, and comprehensible by, the layman. Reform considerations required a presentation that would be persuasive to public officials and practitioners alike. The requirements of research in the future dictated goals of servicing the academic community and creating a useful educational tool for students. Integrity required that matters be presented as perceived despite what practical or political considerations might otherwise imply. An impossible task indeed, but one that required each person to concentrate upon this impossible possibility. No one could honestly claim in the end that compromises were not made.

Urban crime received the most intensive treatment. But the most difficult, as well as the most unmanageable, part of the study was crime prevention. As the general report states:

> Warring on poverty, inadequate housing and unemployment, is warring on crime. A civil rights law is a law against crime. Money for schools is money against crime. Medical, psychiatric, and family-counselling services are services against crime. More broadly and most importantly every effort to improve life in America's "inner cities" is an effort against crime.[73]

The Commission's study thus became concerned with practically every social program and every social service provided by the various branches of government. The most vexing problem centered around the degree of specificity that was necessary and practical in formulating findings and recommendations concerning schools, jobs, welfare, and community and family services. Consultants were requested to study the relationship between each of these problems and crime: crime and the inner city, crime and employment, crime and the family, and crime and the school. Examples of promising social programs were requested. The scarcity of ideas for direct deterrent and apprehension methods in controlling crime in the streets led to the science and technology study. This later broadened to include the entire criminal justice system. Emphasis was also placed upon gathering information that would demonstrate the diversity, complexity, and universality of crime in our society.

Extensive field studies were conducted in each area. Only a few can be mentioned here. In assessing the crime problem, the first national survey of unreported crime[74] and a detailed three-city survey of law enforcement practices[75] were completed. In the police task force, a survey of promising new procedures in 2,200 police departments was initiated.[76] A nationwide survey[77] and an

---

73 CRIME REPORT 6.
74 NATIONAL OPINION RESEARCH CENTER, FIELD SURVEY II, CRIMINAL VICTIMIZATION IN THE UNITED STATES (1967).
75 UNIVERSITY OF MICHIGAN SURVEY RESEARCH CENTER, FIELD SURVEY III, STUDIES IN CRIME AND LAW ENFORCEMENT IN THE MAJOR METROPOLITAN AREAS (1967).
76 POLICE PROCEDURES ADVISORY GROUP, REPORT ON POLICE FIELD PROCEDURES (Consultant Paper 1967). Responses from the various police departments offered astoundingly few ideas or programs geared to increased apprehension or deterrence.
77 NATIONAL CENTER ON POLICE AND COMMUNITY RELATIONS, FIELD SURVEY V: A

intensive two-city study[78] of police-community relations were completed. A national survey of corrections was conducted by the National Council on Crime and Delinquency.[79] Detailed observations of selected lower courts in various areas of the country were conducted.[80] A national juvenile court survey was conducted by the Department of Health, Education, and Welfare in conjunction with the Commission.[81] Information was collected from various agencies on organized crime, court processing of offenders, delinquency prevention programs, enforcement of drunkenness laws, and enforcement and other programs in the narcotics field. Federal departments made available extensive data. The science and technology study included the collection and analysis of data on the police apprehension process, the administration of court systems, police communications, command, and control, programed learning in corrections, and various criminal justice information systems.[82] The four hundred individual consultants and advisers produced facts as well as ideas.

The reports of the Commission reflect this literal mountain of data. But even so, in many areas the members and staff had to rely on initial samplings or traditional measuring devices as bases for conclusions. This naturally had a bearing on the accuracy of these conclusions. For example, there is much more crime than is reported to the police, but how accurate is a public sampling device for this purpose?[83] If there are twenty instances of excessive use of force by police in 5,339 police-citizen encounters observed in three cities, what nationwide projections can be made as to the extent of such brutality? If an experimental community program in California for youth offenders reduced the rate of recidivism further than that of a prison control group, what general conclusions are justifiable in formulating a corrections philosophy? Is there any correlation between the number of convictions of organized crime figures and society's degree of control over the influence of organized crime? If police response time to calls in one city separates out as the crucial factor in eventual solution of crime there, does this afford a basis for prime emphasis in recommended improvements in police procedures? Again, these are merely examples of the data problems. The collection of data as to each facet of crime and criminal justice was burdened by a fundamental lack of information, research, and statistics.

Also to be met were the untested assumptions: A college-educated policeman is better than an uneducated one. Police corruption has decreased con-

NATIONAL SURVEY OF POLICE AND COMMUNITY RELATIONS (1967).
    78 UNIVERSITY OF CALIFORNIA AT BERKELEY, SCHOOL OF CRIMINOLOGY, FIELD SURVEY IV, THE ·POLICE AND THE COMMUNITY (1967).
    79 National Council on Crime and Delinquency, *Correction in the United States*, TFR ON CORRECTIONS 115.
    80 *See, e.g.*, TFR ON THE COURTS 120.
    81 TFR ON JUVENILE DELINQUENCY AND YOUTH CRIME 77.
    82 These studies are printed as appendices in TFR ON SCIENCE AND TECHNOLOGY 83.
    83 See Biderman and Reiss, *On Exploring the "Dark Figure" of Crime*, 374 ANNALS 1 (1967); Biderman, *Surveys of Population Samples for Estimating Crime Incidence*, 374 ANNALS 16 '(1967). Dr. Biderman supervised a project for the District of Columbia and National Crime Commissions wherein the Bureau of Social Science Research surveyed unreported crime and public attitudes as to crime and law enforcement in the District of Columbia. BUREAU OF SOCIAL SCIENCE RESEARCH, FIELD STUDY I: REPORT ON A PILOT STUDY IN THE DISTRICT OF COLUMBIA ON VICTIMIZATION AND ATTITUDES TOWARD LAW ENFORCEMENT (1967).

siderably, and corruption is not a major problem in court and correctional systems. The degree of criminal activity in a society varies inversely with the strength of the threat of apprehension. More jobs and better schools will decrease crime rather than create new forms of criminality. The FBI crime index measures the most serious crimes rather than the ones about which information is most readily available.

Some of these assumptions were altered by the Commission; others were preserved pending further research and study. Lack of knowledge created a further gap in the Commission's work. For example, there is no accurate account of the amount and costs of criminality among the various classes of people who wield political, economic, and moral power in America.

The work of the staff proceeded simultaneously, by necessity, on both the general report and the individual task force reports. Consultant papers were completed at various times and integrated into the staff work. Several leading scholars worked full-time as part of the staff during the summer of 1966. With a few notable exceptions, the writing of the reports was accomplished by the staff utilizing the assembled data and many ideas from the consultant papers. Drafts were submitted to Commission members prior to their meetings. They met a total of seven times, two or three days per session. Changes and ideas offered by Commission members at full sessions, in individual communication, and in task force meetings were incorporated into the reports. The members probably received over two and one-half million words of material.

Naturally, most of the work was performed by staff and consultants; theirs was the job of educating and persuading Commission members as well as each other. But in the end, the general report was that of the members themselves. In it, they are saying as a body to the President and to the American people: this is the way we feel about the crime problem and this is what we think our nation ought to do about it. A consensus among nineteen prominent persons to whom all kinds of approaches have been presented balances the general and the specific, the radical and the conservative, the ideal and the practical, the long-term and the short-term considerations. The National Crime Commission clearly made this choice of consensus. An already polarized society would not receive a polarized report. The separate statements by Commission members on religion, police and court procedures, and narcotics bespeak little conflict with most of the broad sweep of the reports.[84]

Again, evaluation must be left to others. I do believe firmly, however, that if the American public and its government officials achieved the same level of knowledge and attitudinal response created in the Commission and its staff by

---

84 CRIME REPORT 302-08. Short of writing a book filled with specific examples, it is difficult to convey the bustling flavor that precedes the development of a consensus — the frustrations, the in-fighting, the evolution of a reconciliation of polarized views among both staff and commission members, the educational process that induces genuine changes in perception and beliefs. The only expressed major disagreement in the body of the report pertained to wiretapping and electronic surveillance. Although the Commission agreed upon a recommendation that federal law in this area should be clarified and that use of such devices should be outlawed, only a majority of the members agreed that an exception should be made for law enforcement officers' use of such surveillance under stringent, carefully-prescribed limitations. *Id.* at 203. It became clear during the course of the Commission's work that the Johnson Administration earnestly disagreed with the majority position.

two years of study, the nation would be launching significant, progressive steps on a wide basis in every field of crime prevention and criminal justice. If the reports can be said to reflect the bases for this belief, the goals that the Commission set for itself will have been accomplished. Criticism should be focused upon the validity of these goals in light of all the given factors surrounding the Commission and its work. It should be noted that criticism of this type would be particularly valuable to the establishment and work of future commissions studying any subject.

V. Implementation of the Commission's Proposals

Other sections of this symposium will explore individual proposals and directions set by the Commission. The theme of the general report is stated therein:

> The Commission finds, first, that America must translate its well-founded alarm about crime into social action that will prevent crime. It has no doubt whatever that the most significant action that can be taken against crime is action designed to eliminate slums and ghettos, to improve education, to provide jobs, to make sure that every American is given the opportunities and the freedoms that will enable him to assume his responsibilities. . . . To speak of controlling crime only in terms of the work of the police, the courts and the correctional apparatus, is to refuse to face the fact that widespread crime implies a widespread failure by society as a whole.

> The Commission finds, second, that America must translate its alarm about crime into action that will give the criminal justice system the wherewithal to do the job it is charged with doing. Every part of the system is undernourished. There is too little manpower and what there is is not well enough trained or well enough paid. Facilities and equipment are inadequate. Research programs that could lead to greater knowledge about crime and justice, and therefore to more effective operations, are almost non-existent. To lament the increase in crime and at the same time to starve the agencies of law enforcement and justice is to whistle in the wind.

> The Commission finds, third, that the officials of the criminal justice system itself must stop operating, as all too many do, by tradition or by rote. They must re-examine what they do. They must be honest about the system's shortcomings with the public and with themselves. They must be willing to take risks in order to make advances. They must be bold.

> Those three things are what this report is about.[85]

Inherent in these directions is a belief that the degree of crime in a society may not bear close relation to the effectiveness or ineffectiveness of the criminal justice system. The core concepts of crime prevention and reintegration of the offender into an acceptable social framework depend upon social and individual factors to which the criminal justice system merely contributes rather than

---

85 CRIME REPORT 15.

controls. Prevailing social conditions and society's failures to acknowledge and meet them form the most significant starting point in crime control. Thus, the Commission made clear their belief that crime would continue to rise during the next decade no matter what changes or reforms were instituted by police, courts, and correctional officials. There were no immediate solutions compatible with the competing values of our society.

Two basic themes pervaded a great majority of the Commission's recommendations as to the criminal justice system. First is the philosophy that the criminal label and the complete, formal criminal process should be reserved for offenders involved in the most serious crimes or in repeated criminal conduct. This orientation guided specific recommendations for the exercise of police discretion, diversion of arrested persons by the prosecutor out of the court system, development of alternative tracks for such persons to services in the community, diversion of juveniles at the intake stage away from the adjudicatory process, full use of community services at the disposition and correction stages. Such an approach led to specific needs in the agencies themselves: new career patterns and a greater variety of skills in police departments, improved information gathering and processing by the prosecutor and the court, and flexibility and community treatment in the corrections field. A more discriminating use of the full panoply of the criminal justice system would permit more effective processing of those offenders whose criminal conduct interferes most severely with public order and individual security.

The second basic theme revolves around the need to inject into the criminal justice system positive programs for juveniles, misdemeanants, and for offenders who have had the original charge against them reduced from a felony to a misdemeanor. Prosecutors, judges, and correction officers have been devoting most of their time, concern, resources, and procedural fairness to offenders processed in the felony courts; yet these are the offenders who probably have already developed criminal careers and for whom diversion away from future criminal activities is least hopeful. Increased emphasis upon the minor and first offenders led to many of the above recommendations and to others: the need for defense counsel, pre-sentence reports, and individualized discretion by the prosecutor in the lower courts; informed and consistent sentencing practices; massive infusion of resources into juvenile aftercare; the introduction of procedural fairness into the juvenile court process; the need for probation and parole supervision, with available community services and youth service bureaus, for those processed by the juvenile and lower courts; reorganization of court, prosecutive, and correctional structures; the need to remove drunkenness offenders from the criminal process. The Commission called for a development of individual justice, processing, and treatment in every agency to replace the mass justice of this and preceding eras. Throughout the reports one can detect a sense of futility in improvement of the police apprehension process without a concomitant, or perhaps preceding, reform in the court and correctional process.

The general report was released by the President in February of 1967 and the nine task force reports were released seriatim during April-June of that year. The consultant papers were published at the end of June.

VI. Implementation of Recommendations

Implementation had been a concern of the Commission and the staff from the very beginning. The initial thrust in this area was devoted to one of the principal purposes of the Commission, public education. A former magazine and TV news writer was hired for public information purposes and was named an assistant director of the staff. Members and staff spoke throughout the country about crime and the Commission's study. Numerous articles appeared in the mass media. An unprecedented ninety-minute presentation of the network television show, "Meet the Press," featured five Commission members and the executive director of the staff immediately after the release of the general report.[86] Newspaper, television, and magazine coverage of the Commission's reports was quite extensive from February through June of 1967.[87]

Of course, this was merely an ephemeral phase of the implementation task. Through the course of the Commission's work, many conferences were held in cooperation with other agencies and organizations not only to gather ideas but also to lay the groundwork for acceptance of the recommendations. A symposium on science and criminal justice was sponsored to acquaint industry with law enforcement needs.[88] A conference on legal manpower needs explored the implications for the Bar in extending the right to counsel to virtually every legal proceeding involving possible loss of freedom.[89] In March of 1966, the Attorney General invited each governor to establish a state criminal justice committee to cooperate with the National Commission and to implement Commission recommendations through statewide programs when the National Commission had completed its work. A resolution of the National Governors' Conference urged each governor to create such a committee.[90] In October of 1966, the President's Commission sponsored a conference for governors' representatives from each state; the work of the Commission and the directions thereof were discussed. A massive federal aid program for criminal justice reform was formulated by the Commission and its staff and became the basis for President Johnson's proposed Crime Control Act.[91] The involvement of so many practitioners in the Commission's study created a base of experts who understood and for the most part advocated the Commission's recommendations. In March of 1967, a two-day conference of seven hundred representatives from federal, state, local, and private

---

86 NATIONAL BROADCASTING COMPANY, MEET THE PRESS (1967).
87 Of the hundreds of editorials appearing in newspapers throughout the nation, the consensus as to the general report was favorable. Most newspapers and magazines termed the report a call for a needed massive infusion of resources.
88 See PROCEEDINGS OF THE NATIONAL SYMPOSIUM ON SCIENCE AND CRIMINAL JUSTICE (1966). The symposium was sponsored by the National Crime Commission, the President's Office of Science and Technology, and the Office of Law Enforcement Assistance, U.S. Dept. of Justice. The Illinois Institute of Technology plans to hold annual symposiums on the subject of law enforcement, science, and technology. The first was held in March of 1967. Papers presented thereto are reprinted in LAW ENFORCEMENT, SCIENCE AND TECHNOLOGY (A. Yefsky ed. 1967).
89 See Report of the Conference on Legal Manpower Needs of Criminal Law, 41 F.R.D. 389 (1967). The conference was sponsored by the National Crime Commission, the American Bar Association Project on Minimum Standards for the Administration of Criminal Justice, and the National Defender Project of the National Legal Aid and Defender Association.
90 39 STATE GOV. 204 (1966).
91 See S. 917 and H.R. 5037, 90th Cong., 1st Sess. (1967).

agencies, organizations, and institutions served in part to explain and discuss the Commission's findings and recommendations.[92]

At the conclusion of the two-year study, approximately one hundred thousand of the various reports were distributed at government expense, including forty thousand copies of the general report.[93] They were sent to persons in the criminal justice field; to scholars and educators; to mayors, city managers, and legislators at all levels; to governors, businessmen, and other community leaders. Copies of the reports are sold by the Government Printing Office at modest expense, and by December of 1967, over one hundred eighty thousand of the various reports had been purchased by individuals, organizations, and agencies. The general report was the subject of about one-third of these purchases. Each of the reports has been reprinted several times, and the demand continues.[94]

What of the future? Does all this motion lead to progress? Attorney General Ramsey Clark stated recently:

> Now we are engaged in a great renaissance in crime control. President Johnson's Crime Commission has just completed the most comprehensive study of crime, its cause and cures, ever undertaken. This is the easy part. Implementation, as always, is the major task.
>
> It is an appropriate time to recall an earlier study of crime only a generation ago; a time of comparative simplicity.
>
> In 1931 the Wickersham Commission . . . concluded, in these words, "that the present prison system is antiquated and inefficient. It does not reform the criminal. It fails to protect society." The Commission added that if the system as then comprised were unable to rehabilitate, then it should be "so reshaped as to insure a larger measure of success." America failed to accept the challenge and 36 years later . . . (i)t is not surprising that the challenge unheeded in 1931 is resurrected in 1967. Our reaction to the challenge will be crucial to the control of crime in America, to the quality of our lives and those of our children.[95]

The implementation failures following the Wickersham Commission are evident. The reasons therefore are manifold. Certainly two of the principal problems were its publication at the heart of the Great Depression and its loss of credibility and respectability in public and legislative eyes by reason of ambivalent and unpopular recommendations on the issue of prohibition.[96] A com-

---

92 *See* PROCEEDINGS, FIRST NATIONAL CONFERENCE ON CRIME CONTROL (1967).
93 This was part of the dissemination program of the Office of Law Enforcement Assistance, U.S. Dept. of Justice.
94 Letter from Rowland E. Darling, Deputy Supt. of Doc., U.S. Gov. Printing Office, to Henry S. Ruth, Jr., December 29, 1967. Of the nine task force reports, those relating to the police, organized crime, and the courts have been requested in greatest volume. The three volumes account for approximately fifty thousand of the one hundred ten thousand task force reports sold. *Id.*
95 *Report of the 97th Annual Congress of Correction,* 29 AM. J. OF CORR. 13, 17-18 (1967).
96 The judiciary and the Bar probably took greatest note of the Wickersham Commission's work. And, undoubtedly, reforms in police interrogation practices and criminal procedure did receive impetus from the Commission's reports. However, the public, legislators, and other public officials apparently disregarded the findings and recommendations for the most part. The following are merely illustrations of the reaction:
The public and the press, in their disappointment at the Commission's failure to

mission can serve only as a catalyst to national reform. Many other factors in society dominate the extent of that catalytic influence. It is doubtful if anyone can truly assess the effect of a commission's work in such a broad field as crime and crime control. No matter what the state of readiness for reform in the practitioners' world of criminal justice, they can move forward only if public opinion and elected officials permit them to do so.

There are discouraging factors: riots in over one hundred cities in the summer of 1967, an apparent hardening in police and public attitudes, the failure in the recent session of Congress to pass the President's crime control bill,[97] a presidential campaign in 1968 that promises to feature the simplistic "lawlessness" cries of 1928 and 1964.[98]

---

identity itself squarely with one side or the other of the prohibition controversy, have manifested a disposition to brush aside its work with a wave of the hand and a few disparaging remarks. *Foreword, Reports of the National Commission on Law Observance and Enforcement,* 30 MICH. L. REV. 1, 3 (1931).

"The Commission became a subject of contumely and contempt." Strout, *Mr. Wickersham's Platform,* 234 No. AM. REV. 196 (1932).

"In Congress, the report (as to prohibition) was received with a mixture of adverse criticism and ridicule." Wolf, *The United States,* 33 CUR. HIST. 911 (1931).

In McNamus, *Unhappy Warrior: A Portrait of George W. Wickersham,* 156 OUTLOOK 85, 116 (1930), the author stated that among Washington, D.C. correspondents there was a unanimous indifference to the Commission's work.

As to the prohibition report, an editorial in 133 CATH. WORLD 99 (1931) stated: "Seriously and solemnly they reported that conditions are very bad and recommended that nothing be done about it."

In the middle of the Commission's study, one periodical advised that the best possible course for the Commission members was to go home quietly and quickly. 155 OUTLOOK 374 (1930).

In 1934, the Attorney General of the United States called a conference of six hundred representatives of states, cities, and professional organizations to discuss all problems of crime and criminal justice and particularly to discuss the Department of Justice's role in helping state and local law enforcement. H. CUMMINGS AND C. McFARLAND, FEDERAL JUSTICE 476-85 (1937). At the conference, the Attorney General and President Roosevelt made no mention of the Wickersham Commission in their addresses to conference delegates. PROCEEDINGS OF THE ATTORNEY GENERAL'S CONFERENCE ON CRIME 3-8, 17-20, 456-61 (1935). The then president of the American Bar Association stated at the conference:

Consider the Wickersham Commission, which made one of the most thorough investigations of law observance and enforcement of our time. The thirteen (sic) volumes of that report are now gathering dust on the shelves of college libraries, and copies of most of them are no longer available. *Id.* at 198, 199-200.

The work of the Commission received very little mention during the course of the 1934 conference.

A full appraisal and description of the implementation of the Wickersham Commission reports will be published in the Spring of 1968 by the Institute of Criminal Law and Procedure of the Georgetown University Law Center. Unfortunately, that material is not available at the time of the writing of this article.

97 A version of this bill may have been passed in the second session of the Ninetieth Congress by the time this article appears. *See* S. 917 and H.R. 5037, 90th Cong., 1st Sess. (1967).

98 Richard Nixon wrote recently:

Far from being a great society, ours is becoming a lawless society. First, there is the permissiveness toward violation of the law and public order by those who agree with the cause in question. Second, there is the indulgence of crime because of sympathy for the past grievances of those who have become criminals. . . .

. . . . .

Our opinion-makers have gone too far in promoting the doctrine that when a law is broken, society, not the criminal, is to blame. Our teachers, preachers and politicians have gone too far in advocating the idea that each individual should determine what laws are good and what laws are bad, and that he then should obey the law he likes and disobey the law he dislikes.

Nixon, *What Has Happened to America?,* Reader's Digest, Oct. 1967, at 49. A recent New

On the other hand, there are encouraging factors as well. Many professional organizations have utilized the Commission's reports as an added impetus for recommended change. Governors' crime committees have adopted Commission recommendations for action within several states. Many police departments have implemented some key proposals of the Commission. Federal agencies, such as the Department of Housing and Urban Development and the Office of Economic Opportunity, have awarded grants to urban communities for experimental programs that adopt particular recommendations of the Commission.

Directions for the future hang in the balance. Other commissions have already commenced or are completing their work: The National Advisory Commission on Civil Disorders, The National Commission on Reform of Federal Criminal Laws, and a presidential commission on obscenity, pornography, and crime.[99] But anyone who appreciates the use of power by various branches of government realizes all too well that a commission is not a power device. The course of crime control lies with each public official's choice between expediency and responsibility in this time of great national crisis. Upon these factors also depend the epitaph that historians will place upon the National Crime Commission's reports.

York Times Editorial commenced this way
    One of the biggest applause-getters in this fading year has been the get-tough speech against crime in the streets. Public officials and prospective candidates on all levels have found it especially successful in areas where civil rights demonstrations have taken violent turns. . . .
    The contagion of crack-down tactics is spreading. N.Y. Times, Dec. 31, 1967 at 10E, col. 1.
 99 The report of the National Advisory Commission on Civil Disorders should have been published by the time this article appears. The National Commission on Reform of Federal Criminal Laws will submit its final report in November 1969. The obscenity commission report is due in January 1970.

THE EFFECT OF SOCIAL CHANGE ON CRIME AND LAW ENFORCEMENT

*Lloyd E. Ohlin**

I. Introduction

Americans have come to take for granted that constant changes in the social, economic, and cultural conditions of life are inevitable and on the whole desirable. Our major institutions are expected to increase steadily in productivity and effectiveness. Yet we regard with concern and accept with resignation a corresponding growth in the size of many of these institutions and the complexity of their interrelationships. Furthermore, only in recent years are we beginning to appreciate fully that the same social forces that fuel this growth also create major social problems equally large and difficult to understand. The central purpose of this symposium is to inquire how such problems arise and how they can be dealt with more successfully. Since the focus is on urban contemporary problems, there is implicit the assumption that the simple homespun solutions that guided economic, social, and moral decisions about these problems in a rural society may no longer be adequate.

It is becoming increasingly difficult to arrive at a balanced assessment of the crime problem — an assessment that takes adequate account of the many other costs and benefits of the profound social changes that have also made crime a prominent national problem. Public alarm about crime has been rising steadily. The President's Commission on Law Enforcement and Administration of Justice, commonly referred to as the National Crime Commission, reported last year that opinion polls in recent years have shown a steady increase in the percent of persons concerned about their personal safety against street crimes.[1] Furthermore, most people questioned thought the situation was getting worse.[2] Under such conditions pressures mount rapidly for quick and decisive solutions accompanied by a growing impatience with analyses or solutions that seek to take account of the intractability and complexity of the problem. It is all the more important, therefore, that symposiums such as this be employed for realistic and frank discussion of the actual dimensions of the problem of crime and law enforcement.

II. Explaining Crime Trends

Virtually everywhere throughout the country, in big cities, suburbs, towns, and rural areas, the crime statistics show a sharp increase in all types of crime since 1960. The number of violent crimes against persons including willful homicide, forcible rape, aggravated assault, and robbery that were reported

---

* Professor of Criminology, Harvard Law School.
1 THE CHALLENGE OF CRIME IN A FREE SOCIETY, A REPORT BY THE PRESIDENT'S COMMISSION ON LAW ENFORCEMENT AND ADMINISTRATION OF JUSTICE 50 (1967) [hereinafter cited as CRIME REPORT].
2 *Id.*

by police to the FBI in 1966 were 49 percent more than the number reported in 1960.[3] The crime rate for these offenses per hundred thousand persons in the population was 37 percent higher in 1966 as compared to 1960.[4] Crimes against property increased even more drastically. Reports of burglaries, larcenies over $50, and auto thefts were 64 percent more numerous in 1966, and the rate of these offenses per hundred thousand persons was up 50 percent.[5]

Furthermore, the most recent figures released by the Uniform Crime Reports Section of the FBI show an accelerating trend in crime reports. In the first nine months of 1967, as contrasted with the same period in 1966, the number of reports for all seven crimes listed above, which form the Crime Index used by the FBI, was up 16 percent.[6] The number of increased reports for some crimes are fantastic — willful homicide up 16 percent, forcible rape up 7 percent, aggravated assault up 9 percent, burglary up 16 percent, larceny up 15 percent, and auto theft up 17 percent.[7] The most striking change of all was an increase in reported robberies of 27 percent.[8]

Confronted with such figures, it is hardly surprising that public alarm about crime is increasingly more openly expressed. This is to be expected when each year quarterly reports, in addition to a very detailed annual report, which are backed by the authoritative prestige of the FBI, constantly reiterate the message. The Uniform Crime Reports Section is careful to break the figures down by individual crimes as well as providing totals for all crimes. However, the mass media are frequently less detailed in their reporting. Headlines will often simply quote the FBI report of a large percentage increase in "serious crimes," which is the phrase commonly used to describe those offenses included in the Crime Index. Since the average citizen is likely to regard physical assaults by strangers as the most serious type of crime, there is undoubtedly a natural inclination to assume that this is what the report is about. Actually, of course, the three property crimes, burglary, larceny over $50, and auto theft, make up over 87 percent of the crimes covered by the Index. Thus, not only the soaring figures but the way these figures are reported in the mass media will exert a strong influence on the public perception of the crime problem. Given this situation, persons who have never been victimized by crime could still justifiably manifest a growing concern. Since these figures on crime trends may have such an important effect on public attitudes about crime, it is worthwhile to inquire how reliable they may be and how they may be affected by other social changes occurring in our society at the same time.

A. Changes Affecting the Reporting of Crime

A great number of illustrations could be offered to demonstrate the way

---

3 FEDERAL BUREAU OF INVESTIGATION, DEP'T OF JUSTICE, UNIFORM CRIME REPORTS FOR THE UNITED STATES — 1966, at 3 (1967).
4 *Id.*
5 *Id.*
6 FEDERAL BUREAU OF INVESTIGATION, DEP'T OF JUSTICE, UNIFORM CRIME REPORTS — QUARTERLY REPORT — SEPTEMBER 1967, at 1 (1967).
7 *Id.*
8 *Id.*

changes in police reporting practices affect the figures on volume and trend of crime. Especially dramatic are the changes in the Chicago and New York crime reports brought about by the establishment of a central reporting unit through which all citizen complaints are routed. In the early fifties, during the first year of operation of the new central unit in New York, reported burglary offenses increased 1300 percent and robberies 400 percent.[9] Chicago had a similar experience following the installation of a central complaint and dispatching system in 1959.[10] The way crimes are handled and classified by the police can also make a great difference. For example, in recent years the professionalization of the police and an increased tendency to make formal records of complaints, particularly against juveniles, may have contributed to the sharp increases reported in juvenile crimes. There is also a large element of discretion in whether the forcible appropriation of a boy's bicycle by another youth should be classified as a misdemeanor, a petty or grand larceny, or a robbery. According to a recent report, the revised reporting system that was initiated in New York City in March, 1966 tends to upgrade the classification of such offenses to a more serious level.[11]

On the other hand, there are several reasons why one might expect the police to be reluctant to report as much crime as they find. Probably most important is that the effectiveness of their performance will ordinarily be judged by whether the crime rate goes up or down. In most other situations in our society, when we wish to reach a reliable evaluation of achievement on the part of a person or organization, we search for or construct objective measures not subject to the control of those being assessed. Yet our judgment of police effectiveness depends in large part on the crime statistics they are urged to supply voluntarily. I cannot imagine a situation with more pressures and opportunities for subterfuge and management control over the results reported. The history of crime statistics is replete with repeated exposures of fabrication of reports. In fact, given this control over reporting by the police, the pertinent question is why the reported volume and rates of crime have increased so greatly throughout the country in the last two years.

I believe we are now getting fuller and more accurate reporting by the police than we have ever had before. The pressures on the police not to report more crime have been substantially reduced and in many large jurisdictions reversed. One factor in this situation has been a series of Supreme Court decisions widely regarded by law enforcement officials and influential groups of citizens as constituting a severe handicap to effective crime control. I do not wish to get into the very complex questions involved in that debate. However, it should be noted that a "handcuffed" police force cannot be held as fully responsible for sharp increases in crime as one that is not.

A second factor is that increasing public concern about the safety of the streets has generated vigorous demands for more police protection and a growing public recognition of the limited capacity of many police agencies to mount

---

9   CRIME REPORT 26.
10   *Id.*
11   N.Y. Times, Feb. 4, 1968, at 58, col. 1.

an effective program of crime control and prevention. Crime seems to be getting out of hand, engulfing new neighborhoods and erupting in riotous assault, looting, and arson in the central slum areas of the big cities. A statistical report that did not show more crime under such conditions would seem puzzling indeed to the ordinary citizen. A cyclical pattern has been set in motion where the increasing public readiness to accept an accurate portrayal of the full dimensions of the crime problem meets an increased willingness to supply it. As the iceberg of crime rises to the surface of public visibility the need to bring new and more sophisticated resources to bear on the law enforcement task will become increasingly evident.

The evidence for these observations rests largely on attitude surveys and interviews with police and samples of citizens conducted under the auspices of the President's Commission on Law Enforcement and Administration of Justice and also on the continuing reports from the major opinion poll organizations. They are also supported by the impressions I have received in contacts with law enforcement officials. However, there is an additional factor that must be taken into account — the reservoir of crime not reported to the police. A national survey of 10,000 households was conducted for the President's Commission to discover the experiences of the general public as victims of crime.[12] This survey showed, for example, that "forcible rapes were more than 3½ times the reported rate, burglaries three times, aggravated assaults and larcenies of $50 and over more than double, and robbery 50 percent greater than the reported rate."[13] Other surveys in high crime rate districts of large cities revealed greater discrepancies. In Washington, D.C. the number of offenses reported to the survey proved to be three to ten times more, depending on the type of offense, than the number of police reports.[14] Among the most frequently mentioned reasons for not reporting were that the victim felt it was a private matter, he did not want to harm the offender, the police could not be effective, or he would not want to be bothered.

Though these surveys of individual citizens and households reveal a substantial amount of crimes not brought to police attention, they represent only a part of the reservoir of unreported crime. Commercial establishments, building industries, trucking firms, warehouses, business offices, and a number of other economic enterprises suffer robberies, burglaries, and thefts that are not reported. Similarly the thefts from and damages to schools, government installations, public utilities, and community service institutions often do not get recorded. There are of course many forms of fraud, embezzlement, tax evasion, and other white collar crimes that are not reported to the police and are not reflected in crime statistics. However, I am primarily concerned here with the common crimes that now arouse the public.

The main point is that there exists a large pool of unreported crime that can be tapped in a number of ways to swell the totals of reported crime. Sig-

12 NATIONAL OPINION RESEARCH CENTER, CRIMINAL VICTIMIZATION IN THE UNITED STATES: A REPORT OF A NATIONAL SURVEY, reprinted in FIELD SURVEYS II, THE PRESIDENT'S COMMISSION ON LAW ENFORCEMENT AND ADMINISTRATION OF JUSTICE (1967).
13 CRIME REPORT 21.
14 *Id.*

nificant increases in police manpower and efficiency will result in more crimes being discovered. Greater confidence by citizens in the possibility of effective police action would inspire more citizens to report to the police. But how is one to know whether an increase in reported crime represents merely a deeper drain on the reservoir of unreported crime or an actual increase in the volume and rate of criminal acts in the society? Our crime reporting system has no objective base line against which to measure the success of improvements in crime control and prevention.

The police are victimized by this situation as much as anybody. If they increase the efficiency and effectiveness of their operations, they will produce an increase in the rates of complaints, arrests, and convictions. However, as matters now stand these figures are also used to show that crime conditions are getting worse. Only if it could be shown that the rates of victimization of individuals, households, and organizations were going down at the same time would the police clearly get credit for doing a better job. They would also then have some objective means of testing the relative effectiveness of different crime control measures. Though there are still many limitations in the survey approach to the establishment of an objective rate of criminal victimization, concentrated work on such devices could take law enforcement out of the "numbers game" and provide some of the tools for a rational development of policies and programs of crime control.

B. Social Changes Affecting the Volume and Trends of Crime

It should not be inferred from these observations that recent increases in the volume and trend of reported crimes are wholly attributable to changes in reporting practices. Clearly such changes can have a significant impact, but there are very good reasons for expecting large increases even if reporting practices stayed the same. One of the most important grounds for such a prediction is in the changing age distribution. Most major crimes are committed by young men under the age of twenty-five.[15] The highest arrest rates are for the 15 to 17 year-old age group and the next highest for those age 18 to 20.[16] For example, teenagers from 11 to 17 years of age account for approximately half of the burglaries, motor vehicle thefts, and larcenies over $50, and offenders arrested for the crimes of forcible rape and robbery are concentrated most heavily in the 18 to 24 year-old group.[17] It should also be noted that since "1961 nearly 1 million more youths have reached the ages of maximum risk each year than did so in the prior year."[18] The sharp rise in property crimes already experienced will be followed by significant increases in crimes against persons as these youth become 18 to 24 years of age, which they are already doing in large numbers. Our jails as well as our colleges are bulging at the seams. The President's Commission concluded that 40 to 50 percent of the total increase in reported arrests between 1960 and 1965, assuming no change in the rate

15   *Id.* at 56.
16   *Id.*
17   *Id.*
18   *Id.* at 28.

of arrests in that period, "could have been expected as the result of increases in population and changes in the age composition of the population."[19]

Another important social trend is the massive migration of rural dwellers to the cities, which for many years have had much higher crime rates than the rural areas. The average rate for every Index crime except burglary is at least twice as great in cities over a million in population than in suburbs or rural areas.[20] Estimates prepared by the President's Commission concluded that the movement of population between metropolitan, small city, and rural areas accounted for about 7 to 8 percent of the increase in Index crimes between 1960 and 1965.[21] Clearly much more of the increase could be predicted if data were available to take account of the complex interactive effects of age composition, urbanization, sex, race, income levels, and the number of slum dwellers. However, the incompatibility between crime data and demographic data and the lack of detail prohibit such studies, regardless of how useful they might be in predicting the dimensions of the crime problem in future years.

There are other changes in our society that are probably having a significant effect on the number and rate of crimes, but they are hard to measure. Greatly increased material prosperity means there are more goods around to be stolen. Affluence may also breed careless attitudes toward the safeguarding of property. Cars with keys inside or unlocked ignitions account for more than 40 percent of the auto thefts.[22] Theft of accessories or goods from cars represents 40 percent of all reported larcenies.[23] We tolerate increasing rates of branch-bank robberies, shoplifting, and employee theft because the various types of cost associated with adequate protection may exceed the current losses from these crimes. We do not know to what extent the increasing sale of comprehensive homeowner insurance policies, including protection against crime losses, invites indifference about protecting goods and locking doors. Yet we do know that burglaries are increasing rapidly in the suburban areas. The FBI reported a 17 percent increase in suburban burglaries in the first nine months of 1967 as compared to a similar period in 1966.[24] Even more startling is the increase in robberies in the same period, for example, business houses — 38 percent, chain stores — 39 percent, and banks — 60 percent.[25] The failure to take adequate security precautions to reduce the attractiveness of these opportunities to increasingly mobile offenders may be part of the explanation.

In marked contrast to this rising affluence is the relative deprivation of the urban slum communities. Big cities have always offered such contrasts. The difference, today, appears to lie in the rising expectations of the poor for a share in this affluence. They are impatient to lay claim to this share and resent the limited opportunities to do so, especially when the barriers to these opportunities are reinforced by racial discrimination. The depth of this anger and frustration has been made abundantly clear in the ghetto riots and in the

19   *Id.*
20   *Id.*
21   *Id.*
22   *Id.* at 29.
23   *Id.* at 30.
24   Uniform Crime Reports, *supra* note 6, at 1.
25   *Id.*

violent encounters between police and residents of the ghetto areas. The riots
release people from the normal constraints of everyday life and create a Roman
holiday atmosphere where widespread involvement in looting gains crowd
support. I cannot help believing that these same social pressures also greatly
reduce the restraining influence of conventional morality or law for many individuals outside riot situations. The New York Police Department recently
reported that in 1963 there were 2621 assaults on police and in 1967 there were
4409.[26] In such a climate of hostility to law enforcement, it would seem reasonable to expect higher rates of individual as well as collective law violation.

The changes taking place in the relationships between police and residents
of slum neighborhoods, especially in Negro areas, are not solely toward greater
conflict. Changes are taking place in several directions at once. Surveys of
police-community relations in ghetto areas reveal conflicting attitudes about
police and law enforcement. On the one hand the residents of these communities are more critical of the police than are other citizens for what they regard
as improper, undignified, brutal, or discriminatory treatment. At the same time
they are more insistent than the residents of other areas concerning more and
better police protection and are willing to support the police in their demands
for more resources, better training, and more adequate salaries.[27] Yet this
apparent ambivalence is not hard to understand when it is recognized that the
residents of ghetto communities also bear the heaviest burden as victims of
crime.[28]

In the opinion of police experts, the residents of these areas are not only
demanding more protection but getting more than they used to. Prior to World
War II the police were called on to preserve order in the urban ghettoes, to
settle serious domestic disputes, to break up street fights or tavern brawls, and
to keep crimes of vice within the limits of community tolerance. Laws were
enforced only when the residents demanded it and were ready to appear as
complainants.

Now expectations have changed. Residents in the ghetto communities
demand their right to protection by the police and the law, equal to that accorded other areas of the city. They want active law enforcement in these
communities, not just maintenance of the peace, and they want it performed
with the same regard for the dignity and rights of citizens that would be shown
in other areas. Furthermore, police officials say that they are getting law enforcement comparable to that accorded other areas more than they ever have before.
In fact, studies of the most developed professional police departments show that
great care is taken to provide "color-blind" law enforcement.[29] It seems inevitable
that this change will produce higher rates of reported crimes where at one time
those same crimes were ignored by the official reports. In addition, if the police
show a greater willingness to take action in behalf of victims of crime, this will

---

26   N.Y. Times, Feb. 4, 1968, at 58, col. 3.
27   THE PRESIDENT'S COMMISSION ON LAW ENFORCEMENT AND ADMINISTRATION OF
JUSTICE, TASK FORCE REPORT: CRIME AND ITS IMPACT — AN ASSESSMENT 91-93 (1967)
[hereinafter cited as TFR ON CRIME ASSESSMENT].
28   Id. at 92.
29   Wilson, The Police and the Delinquent in Two Cities, in CONTROLLING DELINQUENTS
13-14 (S. Wheeler ed. 1968).

in turn produce a greater readiness to appeal to the police for help and to appear as complainants. Under such circumstances there may not be any more crimes committed in these neighborhoods than there were twenty years ago, but now they will be officially recorded and will boost the total amount and rate of reported crimes.

One further social change that undoubtedly exerts a powerful influence on the higher crime rates for individual cities should be noted. With the growth of the large metropolis, middle-income groups that once lived in the city now live in the suburbs. The pressures of urban redevelopment and the need of the ever growing mass of low-income urban migrants for housing has caused invasion and displacement of populations from areas that formerly housed upper and middle-income families. High crime rates have constantly been associated with high density and low-income areas of residence. As the low-income groups come to occupy a greater proportion of the available housing within the city boundaries, the amount and rate of crime for the city can be expected to increase. Thus, when we compare the crime rate of a city with the rate of crime it had 10, 20 or 30 years ago, it is much like comparing a high crime district with the city as a whole. The President's Commission compared the 1940 robbery rates in several cities to those in 1965 within the city and within the metropolitan area. Allowing for improvements in police reporting today, the rates of the cities in 1940 and the metropolitan areas in 1965 were roughly comparable, while city rates in 1965 varied from 70 percent to 400 percent higher than in 1940.[30]

C. Evaluation of Crime Trends

There is no doubt that there are more crimes committed today than there were 10 or 20 years ago. Simply on the basis of population increase, urbanization, and disproportionate growth of the youth population, one could safely make this statement. It is also undoubtedly true that many areas within the boundaries of large cities threaten much greater risk of victimization by serious crimes than they did in years past. However, no one can prove on the basis of the information we now have that people today have a greater propensity to commit crime than they did formerly. In fact it would be equally difficult to prove that the crime rate is really increasing as fast as the reported figures suggest. If proper allowance could be made for the effects of the various social changes described above, the increase might be very little or none at all. In other words, if we had better data we might conclude that crime rates were not of epidemic proportions but within predictable limits.

III. The Control of Crime

The foregoing discussion should not be taken to mean that we do not have a serious problem with crime today. Instead it highlights how much of the problem would have been predictable if we had had better data. In fact, the dis-

---

30   TFR on Crime Assessment, table 17, at 37.

cussion of unreported crime suggests that we are probably worse off than current figures show and have been for some time without realizing it. Public fear of crime is unquestionably widespread and increasing. Some of the possible reasons for this fear have already been mentioned, but two more reasons should be taken into account.

Repeatedly the complaint is heard that parks, passageways, and street corners in the city which once were safe are now dangerous. As I have already indicated this may at least partly be attributed to the fact that traditionally high crime producing, low-income groups are spreading throughout the city and increasing population density in formerly thinly populated areas. Thus it is undoubtedly true that serious crimes now occur in city areas where once they were rare.

The second point is that public fear of violent crime has undoubtedly been greatly aggravated by the ghetto riots of the last few summers. Fear of crime in the streets has to a considerable extent become merged with a pervasive fear of the often strident and violent demands of Negroes for greater equality of access to the economic, political, social, and cultural opportunities of the American way of life. Fear of crime serves as an easily justified camouflage for a more pervasive fear of racial integration, which is much harder to debate publicly. In fact, fear of crime is so often associated with fear of Negro violence and competition that it is impossible to tell where one leaves off and the other begins. It must also be admitted that these assertions are frankly speculative. The evidence on which they rest is more impressionistic and intuitive than factual. Nevertheless, I do believe that we would be able to do a far better job if we could clearly separate the race relations problem from the crime problem. The fact that Negroes form the vast majority of the new urban poor and appear in such disproportionate numbers in our police lockups, courts, and prisons makes this separation difficult to achieve, despite the fact that the urban poor have always been disproportionately represented in the criminal dockets whether they were of German, Irish, Polish, or Italian extraction.

Nevertheless, the public fear of crime is a fact that must be met by action. Where these fears are unrealistically inflated, there is a public obligation to provide accurate accounts of what the dangers really are so that people can judge for themselves what precautions they wish to take or what risks they will run. Where these fears are realistically grounded in the increasing threat of violent crime, effective crime control and prevention programs must be developed. It is not possible at this time to review all that might or ought to be done to achieve better control of the crime problem. The President's Commission presented 205 recommendations for action.[31] Many of them were designed to convert a creaking and outmoded system of criminal justice, better suited to a rural frontier society, into a system adapted to the problems of modern urban living. I should like instead to comment on several strategic problems and proposals.

31 CRIME REPORT 293-301.

A. Effectiveness of Aggressive Law Enforcement Practices.

One of the most commonly encountered proposals is that the police should get tougher and engage in more aggressive patrol and law enforcement in the urban Negro ghettoes and other high crime rate areas. Such proposals have a beguiling, logical simplicity. If criminals are running amuck, fight them with a vastly superior repressive force. However, the relative cost and effectiveness of such an approach in comparison to alternative or supplementary forms of crime prevention and control must be taken into account.

Police on patrol provide citizens with a sense of security. They observe crime and make arrests in great numbers to preserve the public order. However, forty-five percent of all arrests involve "crimes without victims," such as drunkenness, gambling, prostitution, vagrancy, disorderly conduct, and liquor law violations.[32] Police patrols are also available for radio dispatch when complaints are received at the control center. However, very few of the arrests for major felonies are a result of police discovering a crime in process and catching the criminal "red-handed." Virtually all major felony arrests occur as a result of citizen complaints and identifications of suspects. A study conducted by the President's Commission in Los Angeles found that a total of 1905 crimes studied from the records resulted in arrests or other clearances in 25 percent of the cases.[33] The patrol force made 90 percent of the arrests, over half of which occurred in the first eight hours.[34] But the most significant factor in arrest was whether or not a suspect was named by the victim or by others at the scene of the crime. The clearance rate in cases with named suspects was 88 percent and for cases with unnamed suspects 12 percent.[35] In addition, the speed of the police response to a complaint made a difference. The faster the response the more likely an arrest could be made.[36]

Most of the crimes of violence occur between relatives, friends, or acquaintances. According to several different studies, about 70 percent of the willful homicides, almost two-thirds of the aggravated assaults, and a sizeable majority of forcible rapes are committed by persons previously known to the victim.[37] Such offenses are virtually impossible to prevent by patrol since they occur mainly in bedrooms, kitchens, and bars. Also most crimes of burglary, larceny, and auto theft are crimes of stealth undertaken with a view to evading police observation or anyone else's for that matter.

In an effort to increase the deterrent effect of police patrols and the number of observations of crimes in process, police departments are employing saturation methods. This technique consists in putting an extra large number of policemen in high crime rate areas on a randomized schedule. Sometimes tactical patrols composed of selected, highly trained men are switched from one area to another to catch offenders off guard. Another aggressive patrol tactic is stopping, question-

---

32 *Id.* at 20.
33 *Id.* at 247-48.
34 *Id.* at 248.
35 *Id.*
36 *Id.*
37 *Id.* at 18.

ing and sometimes frisking persons in situations that appear in any way unusual. In New York City, rowdyism, robbery, and assault on the subways led to assignment of uniformed transit patrolmen to every train during the late night hours. This led to a 36 percent decline in the number of crimes committed in the subways.[38]

Police report that these tactics work in the areas they are used. There are unfortunately no studies to show whether or not crime stopped in one place pops out at another like the flow of air in a squeezed balloon. The use of aggressive patrol tactics may also soon raise constitutional questions relating to arrest, search and seizure, and questioning of suspected persons in field situations that have not yet confronted the Supreme Court in relation to the protection of individual rights. Such aggressive tactics are also viewed with great hostility by residents of ghetto areas in large cities and may cost more in unfavorable police-community relations than they are worth in arrests unassisted by complainants. Clearly these aggressive types of patrol practices have an impact on the crime problem, but it is still not clear what costs and benefits are derived from their use.

B. Science and Technology.

Many suggestions were offered by the President's Commission's Task Force on Science and Technology for improving the effectiveness of the criminal justice system. They included such proposals as the development of early warning systems by which citizens could mobilize the police, new types of police communications to increase police mobility, nonlethal weapons, devices to make autos and other objects more difficult to steal, computerized systems for information storage, retrieval and analysis, and more experimental programs of operational research.

Unquestionably these technological aids can be helpful in facilitating criminal justice procedures. However, as with aggressive law enforcement practices, their ultimate usefulness in crime control depends on the cooperation citizens are prepared to give in reducing the lure of criminal opportunities and in informing and assisting the police. The public wants police protection but good police-community relations are essential to secure the public's active cooperation.

C. The Criminal Repeater.

The hard core of the crime problem is the offender who develops crime into a way of life. Such offenders learn how to make crime pay despite occasional arrests and imprisonments. The costs are not only in the injuries they inflict or the property they steal, but in the example they offer to younger men of a set of attitudes toward life that leads inevitably to a criminal career. Most of these careers start early. The President's Commission concluded that

Studies made of the careers of adult offenders regularly show the

38 *Id.* at 95.

importance of juvenile delinquency as a forerunner of adult crime. They
support the conclusions that the earlier a juvenile is arrested or brought
to court for an offense, the more likely he is to carry on criminal activity
into adult life; that the more serious the first offense for which a juvenile
is arrested, the more likely he is to continue to commit serious crimes,
especially in the case of major crimes against property; and that the more
frequently and extensively a juvenile is processed by the police, court, and
correctional system the more likely he is to be arrested, charged, convicted,
and imprisoned as an adult. These studies also show that the most frequent
pattern among adult offenders is one that starts with petty stealing and
progresses to much more serious property offenses.[39]

The greatest failure of our system of crime control is our inability to induce
known offenders to undertake a law-abiding course of life. Considering the
way initial acts of delinquency escalate into careers of serious crime, it appears
undeniable that the most strategic focus of crime prevention and control would
be to devise effective means for terminating criminal careers at the earliest possible stage. If we were successful in this, a major share of the grave losses we
now suffer from serious crimes could be averted. A study of the probation records of 932 felons convicted during the years 1964 and 1965 in Washington,
D.C. showed that 80 percent had adult criminal records.[40] In addition, more
than half (52 percent) had six or more prior arrests, and 65 percent of them
had previously been confined in a juvenile or adult institution.[41]

To release offenders with such histories of crime is to run a high risk of
further offenses. Yet such men cannot be confined permanently. Neither law,
humanity nor economic cost would permit it. The only answer is the development of intensive processes for rehabilitation and reintegration of these men into
constructive and satisfying patterns of everyday living. This would require a
much higher correctional cost per man than we now are expending. It would
also require a greater readiness on the part of the law-abiding community to
provide to these men a measure of acceptance and opportunity that is not now
available. We must come to learn that to pay this kind of cost and take this
kind of risk is in the end much the easier and safer path. The idea that criminals
can be persuaded by ill treatment and stiff sentences to acquire a respect for
and obedience to the law is simply a middle-class delusion. If anything it works
precisely the opposite. The implementation of the law should be firm and just,
but the treatment it accords its convicted offenders should be designed to restore
them to a constructive role in society. This cannot be done for persons of low
status in this complex bureaucratic world by trying to instill fear of further
punishment. It can only be accomplished by helping the offender to find a
new, law-abiding place for himself and encouraging him until he settles into it.
I know of no better protection against crime than a truly effective system of
correctional treatment for convicted offenders. I also do not know of any
existing system today that is "truly effective." Research evaluation studies are
just now beginning to sort out the programs that work best. I am confident,

---

39   TFR on Crime Assessment 79-80.
40   *Id.* at 79.
41   *Id.*

however, that such a system can be developed if the financial resources, freedom to experiment, and community backing can be secured.

D. Crime Prevention.

The character of the crime problem would also change greatly if the broad programs to rebuild the cities, to erase the slums, to transform the patterns of race relations, and to raise the general level of economic, political and cultural achievement of our poorest people were ever able to get under way. The violent crimes have always occurred most frequently among the lowest socio-economic groups in our large urban centers. As these groups have moved up and become socialized to a middle-class way of life, their crimes have changed to the white-collar variety of economic crimes. The war on poverty may not change the total crime rate, but it may serve to make the crime burden more tolerable.

In the short run, strict law enforcement and strong crime suppression strategies may make an impression on the crime problem. In an emergency, such as a full-scale riot, no other alternative exists. But in the long run, the only hope for curtailing the various forms of individual and collective violence we are now experiencing is to develop a system of open opportunities that will give each citizen a chance to stake out a claim to a successful, satisfying, and law-abiding way of life.

THE PRESIDENT'S CRIME COMMISSION TASK FORCE REPORT ON NARCOTICS AND DRUG ABUSE: A CRITIQUE OF THE APOLOGIA

Irving Lang *

I. Introduction

In an obviously apologetic fashion, manifesting some discomfort, the Report of the Task Force on Narcotics and Drug Abuse began:

> This Commission has not and could not have undertaken to duplicate the comprehensive study and report on drug abuse so recently completed by another Presidential Commission. Yet any study of law enforcement and the administration of criminal justice must of necessity include some reference to drug abuse and its associated problems. In the course of the discussion in this chapter, recommendations are made where they seem clearly advisable. In many instances these recommendations parallel ones made by the 1963 Commission.[1]

The President's Commission properly assumed that "drug traffic and abuse were growing and critical national concerns."[2] It recognized that opiate addiction was widespread, especially in big city ghettos, and that depressant, stimulant, and hallucinogenic drugs were the subject of increased abuse, particularly by students. The Commission also mentioned the role of organized crime in narcotic traffic and attempted to discuss the relationship between drug abuse and other crimes.

Structurally, the Commission broke down its Report into the following categories: drugs and their regulation, enforcement, drug abuse and crime, marijuana, treatment, civil commitment, medical practice and addiction, and education. Four recommendations in the field of enforcement and three recommendations in the field of research and education were made. With regard to enforcement, the Commission recommended an increase in the staffs of the Bureau of Customs and the Federal Bureau of Narcotics, the adoption of state drug abuse control legislation, the amendment of federal drug abuse control laws with respect to record-keeping, and the revision of sentencing laws to provide more flexibility. In the area of research and education, the Commission recommended research with respect to the regulation of drugs, research by the National Institute of Mental Health on the use of marijuana, and the development of educational materials.

While it is difficult to quarrel with these recommendations, primary attention should focus on what the Commission did not do, the questions to which it did not address itself in any meaningful fashion, the lack of depth of the Report,

---

* Judge, Criminal Court of the City of New York; former Chief Counsel, New York State Narcotic Addiction Control Commission; B.A., Columbia University, 1949; L.L.B., Columbia Law School, 1952.

1 The President's Commission on Law Enforcement and Administration of Justice, Task Force Report: Narcotics and Drug Abuse 1 (1967) [hereinafter cited as TFR on Narcotics].

2 *Id.*

37

and, particularly in the enforcement area, the failure to discuss the peculiar problems of drug enforcement in relation to the major problems facing law enforcement in general. Drug abuse is more than a combination of police, medical, federal, and state matters. It is, in the deepest sense, a philosophical and societal problem which must be viewed not only in the light of its manifestations in the United States but in the rest of the world as well, and in its proper historical perspective.

II. Drugs — History, Liberty, and Society

Prohibitions against drug abuse are not found in the Ten Commandments, nor was the possession or sale of narcotic drugs a common law crime. We must therefore ask these questions: What are the dangers of narcotic and drug abuse to society and the individual? In light of those dangers, if any, does society have the right to regulate and control drug use and drug traffic to the point of imposing penal sanctions for failure to comply with such regulations? Does society have the right to treat narcotic addicts by means of compulsory commitment and treatment procedures in the absence of any evidence of specific violations of law?

In his essay, *On Liberty*, John Stuart Mill wrote:

> the sole end for which mankind are warranted, individually or collectively, in interfering with the liberty of action of any of their number, is self-protection. That the only purpose for which power can be rightfully exercised over any member of a civilized community, against his will, is to prevent harm to others. His own good, either physical or moral, is not a sufficient warrant. He cannot rightfully be compelled to do or forebear because it will be better for him to do so, because it will make him happier, because in the opinions of others, to do so would be wise, or even right. These are good reasons for remonstrating with him, or reasoning with him, or persuading him, or entreating him, but not for compelling him or visiting him with any evil in case he do otherwise. To justify that, the conduct from which it is desired to deter him, must be calculated to produce evil to someone else. The only part of the conduct of anyone, for which he is amenable to society, is that which concerns others. In the part which merely concerns himself, his independence is, of right, absolute. Over himself, over his own body and mind, the individual is sovereign.[3]

At first glance, it would seem that Mill's strictures would give solace to those who maintain that if narcotic addicts choose to destroy themselves by using drugs, it is a right to which they, as members of a free society, are entitled. But the nature of narcotic addiction and its history prove otherwise. Physiologically and emotionally the drug process and the drug life create a situation opposed to the exercise of free will, a dependency and enslavement which nullify the ability to choose. As was pointed out by Dr. William Park in a study of drug addiction in China in 1899,

---

3 J. S. MILL, *On Liberty* in ON LIBERTY, REPRESENTATIVE GOVERNMENT, THE SUBJECTION OF WOMEN 15 (Cumberlege ed. 1912).

[o]pium is no respecter of persons. It enslaves everyone who comes under its influence, be he an Englishman or a Chinese, black or white, young or old, rich or poor, bond or free, whether he swallows it or smokes it, or injects it hypodermically, and an overdose of it will kill the prince or the pauper.[4]

And as Mill himself said:

But by selling himself for a slave he abdicates his liberty; he . . . therefore defeats, in his own case, the very purpose which is the justification of allowing him to dispose of himself. . . . The principle of freedom cannot require that he should be free not to be free.[5]

Secondly, and this is more important in Mill's terms, is the fact that narcotic addiction does have ramifications beyond the self-destruction of the addict. Narcotic addiction is a threat not merely to the addict himself but to the fabric of society in general. It is primarily for this reason that society must be concerned with drug addiction, and it is for this reason that society does have the right to institute measures such as compulsory civil commitment to protect itself.

As Mr. Richard H. Blum points out in his consultant paper to the Task Force Report,[6] it is immaterial that there are conflicting studies about whether or not addicts are involved in violations of the law before or after their addiction.[7] Narcotic addiction is a contagion that poses a grave societal hazard whether or not addicts commit crimes to support their habit. The lesson of history in this regard is clear and uncontradicted. In 1767, the East India Company, a predecessor to the Mafia in drug trafficking, began exporting opium from India to China as a revenue-raising device for Her Majesty's government. The use of opium became so widespread in China, and its devastating effects on the population became so apparent, that in 1820 the Chinese authorities banned its importation. This led to the tragic Opium Wars of the 1840's and the subsequent English victory opening Chinese boundaries to narcotic traffic.

In the early 1800's, a pharmacist's assistant separated a substance from opium and aptly named it "Morphium" after Morpheus, the god of dreams. During the Civil War, army doctors used this substance so frequently that many soldiers became addicted. So marked was the increase in morphine addiction in the United States after the War that it soon became known as the "army disease." Then the ready availability of opium in patent medicines without prescription, the development of the hypodermic needle, and the growth of opium smoking in the West, spread by Chinese who were brought in to help build railroads, combined to create a situation of epidemic proportions by 1900.

---

4 W. PARK, OPINIONS OF OVER ONE HUNDRED PHYSICIANS ON THE USE OF OPIUM IN CHINA 88 (1899).
5 MILL, *supra* note 3, at 126.
6 *See* TFR ON NARCOTICS 40.
7 *Id.* at 55-57. Actually, there is no conflict at all. The studies are from the 1930's, when there was one pattern of opiate addiction in the United States, and the post-World War II period, when there was a new and distinct pattern of addiction in the United States.

This problem, however, was confined mainly to the South and primarily involved whites, a high percentage of whom were women.[8] The development of heroin (originally proposed as a cure for morphine addiction) greatly increased the problem, and by the turn of the century it was estimated that there were more than 200,000 narcotic addicts in the United States. The spread of this contagion ultimately led to federal legislation: the Food and Drug Act of 1906[9] and the Harrison Act of 1914.[10] Possibly as a result of this legislation, between 1914 and World War II there was a marked decline in addiction despite a rapid population growth. During this period, morphine was the most popular drug. It was only after World War II that heroin addiction started to become prevalent in our urban areas.

Thus, as was pointed out by Dr. John Ball,[11] we have two quite distinct patterns of narcotic addiction in the United States. One addiction pattern, the one of gravest concern, is manifested by young heroin users who come predominantly from large metropolitan centers and often engage in unlawful activities which are related to their addiction. The other pattern is typified by the middle-aged southern white who uses morphine and paregoric, often obtaining his drugs through quasi-legal means. This second pattern preceded the passage of the Harrison Act in 1914 and has decreased materially since that time. The point to be emphasized, however, is that the pre-World War II non-criminal, morphine pattern and the post World War II criminal, heroin pattern were both legitimate objects of societal concern and action.

The basic premise that drug addiction is a proper matter for general concern is supported by racial statistics also. There are many who feel that narcotic addiction, in view of its prevalence in urban ghetto areas, is primarily a Negro problem. According to the Federal Bureau of Narcotics, however, at the end of 1966 Negroes constituted 50 percent of all addicts in the United States. Forty-nine percent were white.[12] Significantly, there has been a steady decline in newly reported cases of Negro addiction since 1955 and a concomitant rise in cases of addiction among whites. This is most dramatically illustrated by the racial composition of the addict group with which we are very concerned today — the group composed of those under 21 years of age. In December of 1966, according to the Federal Bureau of Narcotics, only 25.2 percent of the active narcotic addicts under 21 years of age were Negro; 74.6 percent were white.[13] While it is recognized that these statistics are in no way complete (and, indeed, one of the major endeavors in the area of drug abuse must be the obtaining of greater accuracy in statistical reporting), the very fact that law enforcement efforts are, of necessity, centered in the minority group, high crime rate

8   Eugene O'Neill's play, *Long Day's Journey into Night,* graphically and dramatically portrays the effect of addiction on a family.
9   34 Stat. 768 (1906).
10   38 Stat. 785 (1914).
11   Ball, *Two Patterns of Narcotic Drug Addiction in the United States,* J. CRIM. L.C. & P.S. 203 (1965).
12   TRAFFIC IN OPIUM AND OTHER DANGEROUS DRUGS, TREASURY REPORT BUREAU OF NARCOTICS 51 (1967).
13   *Id.* at 53.

areas indicates that teenage white addiction may be even greater than these figures show.[14]

The conclusion to be drawn with respect to this plethora of racial statistics is that addiction does not respect racial origin. We delude ourselves if we gear our educational treatment and enforcement efforts along racial lines alone.

III. Penal Law and Civil Commitment

Accepting the premise that society has the right and, indeed, the obligation to curb narcotic abuse, the question to be answered is: What forms of intervention are most effective and humane? Clearly, penal sanctions for the possession and sale of narcotic drugs are within the purview of the police power of the state. As the Supreme Court of the United States pointed out in *Robinson v. California:* "Such regulation, it can be assumed, could take a variety of valid forms. A State might impose criminal sanctions, for example, against the unauthorized manufacture, prescription, sale, purchase, or possession of narcotics within its borders."[15] The use of penal sanctions has been the primary method of regulation by both the federal government and the states. However, most persons who are apprehended in connection with violation of narcotic laws are either users or small-scale sellers. This leads to either the "revolving door" problem: *i.e.*, a short-term period of incarceration, return to the community, re-arrest, and return to prison for another short term, or inordinately long jail terms for users who are relatively low on the scale of culpability in narcotic traffic.

A new type of intervention that is currently emerging adopts a plan of compulsory commitment for meaningful treatment instead of meaningless incarceration. The compulsory treatment approach is geared not only to the offender convicted of a crime but is also directed at the narcotic addict who is not the subject of criminal charges. This utilization of treatment procedures for convicted offenders and for those arrested addicts who volunteer for such assistance has received general approbation, with Professor Aronowitz's caveat that no treatment period should be longer than that allowed for a conviction of the crime itself.[16]

The problem of involuntary civil commitment where no criminal charges are pending is an area of primary concern to those who seek to protect civil liberties. The Task Force did address itself to the pros and cons of civil commitment and concluded:

> [T]he Commission believes that involuntary civil commitment offers sufficient promise to warrant a fair test. But it must not become the civil

---

14 For example, in the Borough of Queens in New York City, whites constitute most of the addicts.

15 370 U.S. 660 (1962).

16 This outlook reflects a "time syndrome," *i.e.*, any amount of societal control or management of the life of an individual constitutes "doing time," whether it be straight jail time or a rehabilitative process.

equivalent of imprisonment. The programs must offer the best possible treatment, including new techniques as they become available, and the duration of the commitment, either within or outside an institution, must be no longer than is reasonably necessary.[17]

This makes good sense. Even if, in Mill's terms, it has been established that narcotic addiction is a threat not only to the addict but to others, a just and fair society cannot sanction this extreme remedy unless civil commitment programs are entirely geared to the rehabilitative process. In the *Robinson* case, the majority of the Supreme Court declared: "In the interest of discouraging the violation of such laws, or in the interest of the general health or welfare of its inhabitants, a State might establish a program of compulsory treatment for those addicted to narcotics." (Footnote omitted.)[18] Mr. Justice Douglas, concurring, said: "The addict is a sick person. He may, of course, be confined for treatment or for the protection of society." (Footnote omitted.)[19]

I submit that both Mr. Justice Stewart and Mr. Justice Douglas should have insisted that the protection of society and the treatment of the addict are both essential ingredients of a constitutionally feasible treatment program rather than alternative justifications. Such a view obviously entails the use of flexible treatment programs geared to the determination of which types of programs benefit which type of addict. It also involves a constant awareness on the part of the courts and the administrators of such programs of the nature and quality of the treatment.

IV. Other Dangerous Drugs — Hard and Soft

Comments made about opiates and society's responses to their abuse are not necessarily valid when made about other dangerous drugs plaguing America today. Cultivation of opium has been reported as far back as seven centuries before Christ. Despite many unknowns in this area, there is indeed a large body of knowledge and historical perspective about opiate abuse. Widespread abuse of amphetamines, hallucinogens, barbiturates, and tranquilizers, however, is relatively new and poses fresh problems of understanding, regulation, and control. It may be said that while opiates are drugs of retreat, hallucinogens and stimulants are drugs of rebellion. We need, as the Commission has pointed out,[20] much more data to determine if a similar degree of criminality attends the use of "soft drugs" as attends heroin abuse. I suspect not. Unlike the case of heroin, millions of legitimate medical prescriptions are issued every year for stimulants, depressants, and tranquilizers. Unlike the situation with respect to heroin, there is evidence to indicate that many people can function on a socially acceptable level despite use of these drugs. Finally, unlike the opiate situation, it appears that soft drug abuse is often a phase rather than a long term involvement.

---

17   TFR on Narcotics 17.
18   370 U.S. 660, 664-65 (1962).
19   *Id.* at 676.
20   TFR on Narcotics 14.

V. A Statutory Guideline

From the empirical data available, it must be concluded that "soft drugs" are proper subjects of government regulation and control. It is important, however, that legislation in this area, particularly penal legislation, be selective, sophisticated, and structured in an intelligent manner. While the Commission, in discussing this problem, urged "further development of a sound and effective framework of regulatory and criminal laws with respect to dangerous drugs,"[21] they did not pose specific suggestions. I submit that New York's newly revised Penal Law[22] provides a proper framework for an effective statutory structure. Article 220 of this law, entitled "Dangerous Drug Offenses," divides dangerous drugs into four basic categories: narcotic drugs, depressants, stimulants, and hallucinogenic drugs. It provides varying degrees of penalties for both possession and sale of these dangerous drugs, but, in general, narcotic drug violations carry very high penalties, and other dangerous drug violations carry more moderate penalties. Unfortunately, the definition of narcotic drug in the Penal Law makes a cross-reference to the definition of narcotic drug in the Public Health Law,[23] which, as in many other states, includes marijuana within its purview. This creates many problems, one of which is that, as concern with heroin abuse rises and penalties are increased, penalties for the use of marijuana are increased concomitantly, which results in what I call "legislative overkill." Such a result is unfortunate since judges, district attorneys, and, indeed, law enforcement officials in general recognize that marijuana violations do not contain the same measure of societal threat as heroin violations.[24] It would be appropriate, therefore, in devising a regulatory scheme, to place marijuana in the same category as LSD and other hallucinogens. This also seems logical in view of the frequent cases of multi-habituation with respect to marijuana and dangerous drugs. Marijuana, for example, is often used in conjunction with amphetamines, LSD, or peyote. An arrest will often result in the seizure of marijuana and LSD or marijuana and pep pills. Less frequently, however, is there an arrest where both marijuana and heroin are seized.

Cocaine is also defined in federal[25] and state[26] law as a narcotic drug. As the Commission points out, however, cocaine is a stimulant.[27] While it is undoubtedly more dangerous than marijuana, I believe that it should be categorized as a stimulant rather than as a narcotic. This would not necessarily mean that one would have to modify the penalties for cocaine violations; it simply means that a legislative body could provide special penalties for its illegal use while recognizing that it is a stimulant.

By utilizing this type of structure, penal law provisions dealing with the abuse of dangerous drugs would have both consistency and reasonableness —

21 *Id.* at 6.
22 N.Y. Pen. Law § 220 (1967).
23 N.Y. Public Health Law § 3301 (1967).
24 This recognition is reflected in the high incidence of "bargain pleas" and suspended sentences.
25 Int. Rev. Code of 1954, § 4731 (a).
26 Uniform Narcotic Drug Act § 14 (11).
27 *Id.* at 3.

factors often lacking when legislators view such emotionally charged matters.

Finally, it cannot be denied that sentencing for penal law violations is obviously a basic function of legislative bodies. However, few can quarrel with the Commission's recommendations that courts be given enough discretion to enable them to deal flexibly with violators of drug laws rather than being forced to impose mandatory terms of confinement.[28]

VI. Marijuana

The Commission made a point of commenting specially on marijuana. The selection of marijuana for special comment is amply justified by the current furor over its use on college campuses. Marijuana is fast becoming a focal point for student rebellion and protest against authority. It has created situations whereby college administrators are torn between their obligation to help students and their duty to cooperate with law enforcement officials; it has led to cries for legalization and liberalization and to cries for expulsion and the imposition of more stringent penal sanctions. The Commission's informative and unbiased analysis of the situation and its recommendation for more research are welcome, but again salient considerations are omitted.

The protagonists of marijuana have two basic contentions. First, marijuana, unlike heroin, does not produce physical dependence nor withdrawal, nor does it build up tolerance. The Commission recognizes this as true.[29] Secondly, the protagonists maintain that not only is marijuana not comparable to heroin but, even more important, it is less dangerous than alcohol which is a far greater threat to society. Often, those who oppose legalization of marijuana in any form fall into the trap of attempting to prove that marijuana is, indeed, a far greater menace than alcohol.

In view of the Commission's discussion on alcohol[30] and its enormous detrimental impact on the nation, this counter-argument is quite hollow. A more meaningful response would be to point out that merely because over a long period of time a tradition has been established whereby consumption of a toxic substance has been sanctioned in varying degrees on a mass level does not logically lead to the conclusion that society should release another toxic substance for mass consumption.

Then too, alcohol is, in fact, one of the most regulated drugs. There are laws dealing with the licensing of manufacturers, laws dealing with the age at which purchase is permissible, penal laws prohibiting public intoxication, and laws creating both penal and administrative penalties for driving under the influence of alcohol. The latter, of course, is a matter of extreme importance and an important factor in the death and injury tolls on our highways.

A person driving under the influence of marijuana is as dangerous as a

---

28   TFR on Narcotics 12.
29   See *id*. at 13.
30   The President's Commission on Law Enforcement and Administration of Justice; Task Force Report on Drunkenness (1967).

person driving under the influence of alcohol.[31] How can society deter driving under the influence of marijuana? We can, of course, impose the same form of deterrent as we did with alcohol, that is, making it a criminal offense to drive under its influence. Theoretically, however, the law does not do vain and foolish things. Unenforceable statutes should not be passed. With respect to alcohol, it is relatively easy to prove that a person was driving under its influence. Smelling of alcohol on the breath, visual observation, blood alcohol tests or breath tests, make successful prosecutions possible. The same cannot be said for marijuana. Proof of driving while under the influence of marijuana would be a virtual impossibility. Accordingly it may properly be argued that a measured response is possible in connection with alcohol but if such a limited response is not possible with respect to marijuana at the present time, society has the right to ban its possession for all purposes.

VII. Law Enforcement

If there is one section of the report where it can be positively asserted that the Commission failed to come to grips in any meaningful fashion with a significant area, it is in the section on enforcement. If there is any one area of criminal law in which the recent court decisions relating to search and seizure, informers, wiretapping, eavesdropping and confessions[32] have particular importance, it is enforcement of narcotic and dangerous drug laws. Such vital areas as the problem of the proliferation of agencies which deal with this issue, the cooperation or lack of it among these agencies, the rivalries between and among these agencies, the need for coordination of criminal intelligence and problems of proof either were not mentioned at all or tangentially discussed. It is also a source of concern that the Report of the Arthur D. Little Company which surveyed the field of law enforcement was not included in the consultants' papers. This seems to me a grave omission. If one is to discuss law enforcement and the administration of justice and the area of narcotic and drug abuse, these issues cannot be avoided. They are not, obviously, easy of resolution. But problems do not disappear by refusing to acknowledge them. The failure to pose the questions and suggest alternatives casts a pall over the Commission's Report.

---

31   In this connection it is relevant to point out that there is, generally, no quarrel with the proposition that the physiological effects of marijuana include altered consciousness and disturbance of time and space perception. See GOODMAN & GILMAN, THE PHARMACOLOGICAL BASIS OF THERAPEUTICS 300 (1965).

32   See, e.g., Katz v. United States, 389 U.S. 347 (1967) (wiretapping and eavesdropping); Berger v. New York, 388 U.S. 41 (1967) (eavesdropping); Miranda v. Arizona, 384 U.S. 436 (1966) (interrogation of accused); Beek v. Ohio, 379 U.S. 89, (1964) (informers); Rugendorf v. United States, 376 U.S. 528 (1964) (informers); Ker v. California, 374 U.S. 23 (1963) (probable cause); Wong Sun v. United States, 371 U.S. 471 (1963) (search and seizure—interplay of 4th and 5th amendments); Mapp v. Ohio, 367 U.S. 643 (1961) (applicability of 4th amendment to states); Ross v. United States, 349 F.2d 210 (D.C. Cir. 1965) (police practice in narcotic sale cases); People v. Rivera, 14 N.Y.2d 441, 201 N.E.2d 32, 252 N.Y.S.2d 458 (1964) (stop and frisk).

VIII. Conclusion

The Presidential Commission's agonizing appraisal of the drug problem was based upon two fundamental assumptions. The first assumption was that there is a great deal of misinformation and emotionalism involved in the ideas of the average citizen about drug abuse. The second assumption was that new approaches have to be made in society's handling of the problem. With respect to the second assumption, the Commission was obviously unwilling or unable to analyze the drug problem in sufficient depth or to deal with its underlying philosophical issues.

PERSPECTIVES ON THE REPORT OF THE PRESIDENT'S CRIME COMMISSION — THE PROBLEM OF DRUNKENNESS

*Peter Barton Hutt**

The United States Crime Commission's recommendations concerning drunkenness offenses can be stated very simply. First, it recommended the repeal of those laws that handle simple public drunkenness, as distinguished from disorderly intoxication, as a crime. Second, the Commission recommended that a comprehensive treatment and rehabilitation program be instituted for inebriates' and alcoholics under public health and welfare auspices to replace antiquated solutions provided by the present system of criminal law enforcement.[1] In retrospect, these recommendations may seem obvious. When the Commission began its work, however, they were far from that, and indeed were regarded by many with grave suspicion. This article will examine some of the factors that led to the Commission's action on drunkenness offenses and will consider the impact that the Commission's work may have upon the future of law enforcement in this country.

The Commission concluded that the drunkenness statutes mentioned above should be repealed for three basic reasons: (1) such statutes are ineffective; (2) they burden the police and courts; and (3) they degrade the criminal process.[2] In the year since the Commission issued its Report, no one has seriously challenged either this conclusion or the findings on which it rested. Indeed, the recommendation that these drunkenness statutes be repealed has been widely supported.[3] Thus, there is no need to re-examine here the validity of the Commission's criticisms of public intoxication laws.

But these criticisms are applicable not only to the public intoxication laws. They apply with equal force to statutes declaring criminal such offenses as abortion, adultery, consensual homosexual relations, the use of marijuana, and prostitution. Such statutes define a public morality rather than protect the public from harm and violence. The utter futility and harm of proscribing these other forms of behavior through criminal statutes is even more readily demonstrable than in the case of public intoxication statutes. What caused the Commission to concentrate so heavily on the drunkenness laws and virtually ignore these other statutes? Why were the drunkenness statutes the only criminal statutes, of all the federal and state statutes presently in force, that the Commission recommended be repealed? Appreciation of some of the factors

---

* Former Consultant to President's Crime Commission on Drunkenness; member, District of Columbia Bar, New York Bar; B.A., Yale, 1956; LL.B., Harvard Law School, 1959; LL.M., New York University, 1960; associate, *Covington & Burling*, Washington, D.C.
1 THE CHALLENGE OF CRIME IN A FREE SOCIETY, A REPORT BY THE PRESIDENT'S COMMISSION ON LAW ENFORCEMENT AND ADMINISTRATION OF JUSTICE 236-37 (1967) [hereinafter cited as CRIME REPORT]
2 *Id.* at 235-37.
3 Brief for American Civil Liberties Union, American Medical Association, Correctional Association of New York, Methodist Board of Christian Social Concerns, North American Association of Alcoholism Programs, North American Judges Association, North Conway Institute, Texas Commission on Alcoholism, and Washington D.C. Area Council on Alcoholism as Amici Curiae, pp. 2-3, Powell v. Texas, *appeal docketed*, No. 405, U.S., 1967 Term.

that led to the Commission's recommendation will, I believe, afford a better perspective for viewing all of the Commission's work.

Undoubtedly the most important factor leading to the Commission's recommendation for the repeal of public drunkenness statutes was the existence of two decisions by United States Courts of Appeals holding that chronic alcoholics may not be punished for public intoxication — *Easter v. District of Columbia*[4] and *Driver v. Hinnant.*[5] In 1964, a year before the Commission was appointed, litigation of these test cases was begun for the purpose of challenging the constitutionality of handling chronic alcoholics as criminals under public intoxication statutes. It has long been recognized that the vast majority of the inebriates arrested under drunkenness statutes are chronic alcoholics.[6] Indeed, experience in the District of Columbia since *Easter* shows that perhaps 90 to 95 percent of the drunkenness offenders who appear in court are suffering from this illness.[7] If the courts were to rule that an alcoholic could not be convicted of public intoxication, a radical change in the entire approach to public intoxication would be required throughout the country.

Judgments for the defendants in both *Easter* and *Driver* were handed down in early 1966, when the United States Crime Commission was about halfway through its deliberations. These two cases could not be ignored. Neither the Fourth Circuit nor Judge Bryan, who wrote that court's opinion in *Driver,* could be shrugged off as unreasoning radicals. Nor could the unanimous *en banc* decision of the District of Columbia Circuit Court in *Easter* be dismissed as an unimportant judicial aberration. It was obvious that these decisions were of major importance to the country and that the Commission's Report had to deal with the problems that they created.

In contrast, there were no comparable decisions relating to the other behavioral offenses mentioned above. No one had successfully challenged the constitutionality of the adultery or homosexual conduct laws. Thus, there was no significant pressure from the courts for the Commission to examine statutes dealing with those offenses. The Commission therefore relegated consideration of those offenses to a rather brief discussion, concluding that it was not in a position to resolve the issues involved and suggesting that state legislatures weigh carefully the kinds of behavior that should be defined as criminal.[8]

It would be naive, of course, to suggest that the mere existence of *Easter* and *Driver* required the Commission to confront the problem of public drunkenness statutes. As it did with respect to other offenses, the Commission could simply have recommended that each state resolve this question in its own legislature. Because the Commission's staff, and particularly Mr. Gerald Stern, forcefully pressed the Commission to make a substantive resolution of the issue, this simple recommendation was not made. Strong advocacy from Mr. Stern and other members of the staff was eventually reflected in the final Commission

---

4 361 F.2d 50 (D.C. Cir. 1966) (*en banc*).
5 356 F.2d 761 (4th Cir. 1966).
6 Brief, *supra* note 3, at appendix G.
7 THE PRESIDENT'S COMMISSION ON LAW ENFORCEMENT AND ADMINISTRATION OF JUSTICE, TASK FORCE REPORT: DRUNKENNESS 111, n. 29 (1967).
8 CRIME REPORT 126-27.

recommendations.[9] Yet it must also be remembered that equally strong advocacy for a substantive resolution of analogous problems — notably the use of marijuana and homosexual conduct — did not prevail upon the Commission.

One reason for this seemingly inconsistent result was the extent of law enforcement resources committed to the treatment of the drunkenness problem. The Commission discovered that in 1965 two million arrests — one of every three arrests in the United States — were for the simple offense of public drunkenness.[10] An additional large number of arrests for drunkenness were made under disorderly conduct, vagrancy, loitering, and other related misdemeanor statutes.[11] The cost of these arrests in terms of police, court, and correctional resources was incalculable. It was estimated that, in some areas, 90 percent of the inmates of short-term correctional institutions at any given time had been convicted of intoxication.[12] Police spent millions of hours simply picking up incapacitated citizens again and again and waiting in crowded criminal courts to testify only that an unfortunate derelict was, indeed, drunk on the occasion specified.

None of the other morality offenses previously mentioned commands an even remotely comparable expenditure of law enforcement resources. However much the infamous peep-hole vice squads may degrade the entire criminal process, they represent a relatively small expenditure of time and money. Indeed, some of the morality offenses, such as adultery, are dead letters and therefore entail no waste of law enforcement resources.

It must be remembered that the Commission viewed its mandate from the President to consider only recommendations with regard to the enforcement and administration of justice, not the revision of substantive law. It was therefore natural that, unless a given problem of substantive law directly and substantially impinged upon the functioning of the law enforcement process, the Commission was disinclined to deal with it. Only with respect to drunkenness, out of all the morality offenses, could this substantial impact be readily demonstrated.

There was no substantial element of American society that stood out in solid opposition to repeal of the drunkenness statutes. Under early English common law, drunkenness without disorderly conduct was not a crime. Simple public intoxication was first made a criminal offense in England by a statute enacted in 1606, entitled "An Act for Repressing the Odious and Loathsome Sin of Drunkenness."[13] The drunkenness statutes have a very clear origin in biblical disapproval of intoxication, culminating in the experiment with Prohibition in this country. But since the repeal of Prohibition with the twenty-first amendment, the moral issue has subsided. Even the Methodist Church, which led the movement for the eighteenth amendment, now agrees that drunkenness should no longer be considered a criminal offense.[14] Many judges, doctors, correctional officials, and law enforcement personnel have,

---

9 See Id. at 235-37.
10 Id. at 233.
11 TASK FORCE REPORT: DRUNKENNESS, supra note 7, at 2.
12 Id. at 4, n.39 and accompanying text.
13 4 Jac. 1, C. 5.
14 Brief, supra note 3, at 3-4.

over the years, voiced unusually strong views that the drunkenness laws make no sense.[15] This virtual unanimity of informed public opinion permitted the Commission to deal with the drunkenness problem with far greater confidence than if it had been a more controversial issue.

There is, in contrast, no consensus on the proper handling of abortion, adultery, the use of marijuana, or other similar questions of morality. The myths created by the Bureau of Narcotics — that marijuana causes crime and leads to heroin addiction — will undoubtedly be exposed to public ridicule at some time in the future, paving the way for needed reform in this area also.[16] But the issue is still too charged with emotion and irrationality for a presidential commission to deal with it comfortably today. Indeed, even the issue of private consensual relationships between adult homosexuals could not be confronted because of such an atmosphere, despite the fact that the Wolfenden Committee in England[17] and the American Law Institute[18] have resolved it sensibly. Perhaps the failure to obtain implementation of the recommendations of these two groups in either England or the United States convinced the Commission that it should not delve into these potentially controversial areas. It must also be recognized that any discussion by the Commission of these explosive moral issues might well have diverted public attention from its more important findings and recommendations.

In the case of drunkenness, moreover, the Commission could also rely upon the well-established medical view that alcoholism is a disease. In 1956, the American Medical Association officially recognized alcoholism as a disease that is properly within the purview of medical practice.[19] It has reiterated this position on numerous occasions since then and has advocated repeal of public intoxication statutes. Thus, the Commission had a clear statement from medical authorities that, even though our public health resources may be strained to the breaking point, they nevertheless recognized that the handling of drunkenness was properly a function of the medical profession rather than a function of the criminal system.

The Commission's handling of drunkenness offenses was also undoubtedly buttressed by the recommendations of the President's Commission on Crime in the District of Columbia. The D.C. Crime Commission Report, which was completed several months before the United States Crime Commission Report, recommended repeal of the District of Columbia's public intoxication law.[20] And like the United States Crime Commission, the D.C. Crime Commission had felt that it should deal only with problems of the administration of justice and leave substantive law reform to a later law revision commission. Thus, of the morality offenses, the D.C. Crime Commission dealt only with the problem of public drunkenness. Although this did not compel the United States Crime

15   *Id.* at 30-35 and appendix G.
16   THE PRESIDENT'S COMMISSION ON LAW ENFORCEMENT AND THE ADMINISTRATION OF JUSTICE, TASK FORCE REPORT: NARCOTICS AND DRUG ABUSE, 12-14 (1967).
17   Report of the Committee on Homosexual Offenses and Prostitution (1957).
18   MODEL PENAL CODE § 213.2 (Proposed official draft, May 4, 1962).
19   Brief, *supra* note 3, at 1a-2a.
20   REPORT OF THE PRESIDENT'S COMMISSION ON CRIME IN THE DISTRICT OF COLUMBIA 490-91 (1966).

Commission's approach, it certainly encouraged it. Had the Commission ignored the drunkenness problem, or not resolved it, it might have looked somewhat unusual after the very strong and detailed report made by the D.C. Crime Commission.

Finally, one must take into consideration the Crime Commission's members themselves. I have not conducted any research into their personal habits or private lives, and I would not suggest that I or anyone else do so. Nevertheless, a few generalizations can properly be made. First, it is likely that almost every member of the Commission consumes alcoholic beverages. It is virtually certain that they have friends and relatives who have drinking problems and may even be alcoholics. Not only have they seen friends and relatives drunk in public, in violation of criminal statutes, but at some time in their lives they may well have violated these same criminal statutes themselves. In fact, I doubt that there are many Americans today who have not, at one time or other, violated a public drunkenness statute. It must be remembered that one need not be unconscious or offensive to violate the law. It is sufficient simply to be intoxicated. All that is required in most jurisdictions is the word of a policeman that he smelled liquor on your breath and that you were not walking in an absolutely straight line.

The Commission members undoubtedly found it relatively easy to recommend the repeal of a type of criminal statute that sweeps under its broad terms the everyday conduct of many friends and relatives, and perhaps even their own past activity. They live in a society that condones drinking and tolerates even excessive drinking. Current social mores therefore preconditioned them to acceptance of the position that drunkenness should be handled as a public health problem rather than as a criminal problem.

In contrast, I think it fair to assume that something less than a majority of the Commission members smoke marijuana or have performed an abortion or have engaged in prostitution. Nor do they live in a society in which these activities are regularly exposed to public view without condemnation. Thus, the Commission members were undoubtedly predisposed by prevailing social mores to avoid these particular issues.

Social mores do, of course, change with succeeding generations. They are obviously changing today. It neither denigrates the Commission nor condemns today's younger generation to point out that if the President had appointed nineteen representative college students instead of the people he did appoint, the Commission would have been more inclined to recommend the repeal of marijuana laws than to recommend the repeal of drunkenness statutes. And from what I know of both problems, at least as strong a case can be made for repealing the marijuana laws. In any event, although this problem of the generation gap certainly is not the sole explanation for the Commission's actions, failure to recognize it as an important factor would be naive indeed.

It is equally important to recognize a factor that was not involved in the Commission's deliberations. It is quite clear that the recommendations on drunkenness were entirely *ad hoc* conclusions rather than an attempt to formulate general jurisprudential principles governing the proper function of the criminal law in preserving the moral values of society. The Commission did not undertake to resolve the great debate between John Stuart Mill and H.L.A. Hart on the one hand, and Lord Devlin and Professor James Fitzjames Stephen on the other.[21] I doubt that many Commission members are even familiar with that debate. The Commission acted upon very practical considerations in this area, not on philosophical doctrines.

The Commission has recently been criticized for failing to enunciate in its Report any underlying doctrine of the criminal law.[22] In the first place it is doubtful that any nineteen persons of diverse backgrounds could possibly agree on such an abstract principle. For practical reasons I am rather happy that the attempt was not made. I doubt that any Presidential Commission could sufficiently divorce itself from purely political considerations to give adequate dispassionate consideration to such a task. Even if uncontrovertible evidence showed the utter foolishness of retaining private moral standards as criminal prescriptions, respected public figures might not wish to put themselves in the position of seeming to advocate the abandonment of widely-accepted moral principles. If an attempt had been made to develop some all-encompassing principle governing the criminal law, I fear that the recommendations made with respect to drunkenness would have been sacrificed in the process.

Thus, I am content with the approach that evolved. And I would certainly hope that, in the future, new commissions will be established that can again recommend piecemeal *ad hoc* reforms in the criminal law comparable to the recommendations on drunkenness made by this Commission. Eventually, the criminal statutes embodying private moral standards will be abolished, and we will look back on them as rather ludicrous examples of paternalistic oppression. I personally look forward to that day.

I shall now consider what the future holds for the Commission's recommendations about drunkenness. Ironically, it appears that they may be the first of the Commission's recommendations to be implemented throughout the country. And if this happens, it may well lead to reform in other areas of the criminal law.

In the District of Columbia, the *Easter* decision has led to revolutionary changes in the handling of public inebriates. Some 5,000 individuals, most of them homeless derelicts or indigents, have now been adjudicated chronic alcoholics. Under *Easter*, they can no longer be jailed for their public intoxication. This has, in turn, forced the development of substantial treatment facilities for alcoholics in the District. Not all of the D.C. Crime Commission's recommendations have yet been put into effect, but definite progress has been made.

Shortly after the D.C. Crime Commission Report was released to the public, legislation was introduced in Congress to repeal the District's public intoxication statute and to enact public health, welfare and rehabilitation procedures for the handling of inebriates and alcoholics. The House of Represen-

---

21 *See* H. Hart, *Law, Liberty and Morality* (1963); Devlin, *The Enforcement of Morals* (1959); J. Stephen, *Liberty, Equality, Fraternity* (1873); J. Mill, *On Liberty* (1859).
22 *See* Packer, *Copping Out*, The New York Review of Books, Oct. 12, 1967.

tatives has now passed that bill, and it appears likely that it will be enacted into law within the next few months.[23]

The same thing is about to happen on a national scale as a result of *Powell v. Texas*,[24] which raises the same issue as the *Easter* and *Driver* cases. A brief filed for nine *amici curiae* points out to the Court that the only real chance of obtaining widespread implementation of the United States Crime Commission's recommendations is through judicial action. The *amici* urge that, in effect, *Powell* will determine whether public intoxication is handled as a public health problem or is continued as a criminal offense. The identity of the *amici* who urge that the Court's decision in *Powell* follow *Easter* and *Driver* is important. They include the American Civil Liberties Union, the American Medical Association, the Correctional Association of New York, the Methodist Board of Christian Social Concerns, the North American Association of Alcoholism Programs, the North American Judges Association, the North Conway Institute, the Texas Commission on Alcoholism, and the Washington D.C. Area Council on Alcoholism.

If the Supreme Court were to uphold the State of Texas in *Powell* and rule that alcoholism is not a defense to public intoxication, I would be very pessimistic about the possibility of convincing any state legislature to repeal its drunkenness statute. Derelict alcoholics wield no political power. And repeal of the intoxication statute can too easily be misunderstood by an unsophisticated public as an immoral invitation to debauchery and licentiousness. Thus, the possibility of a legislator championing criminal reform in this area, absent a court decision forcing the issue, is very small indeed. I am convinced, however, that the Supreme Court will not uphold the lower court decision in *Powell*. I believe that the Court will follow *Easter* and *Driver* and that the issue will be forced throughout the country. When that happens, the recommendations of the Crime Commission will prove extremely important.

The Commission's recommendations concerning the type of procedures that should replace the criminal handling of inebriates are rather brief, but nonetheless explicit. Like the D.C. Crime Commission, the United States Crime Commission recommended essentially three stages of treatment. An incapacitated inebriate must first be detoxified, or sobered up. The Commission recommended that this be done in a medical center, preferably a hospital, rather than in a police precinct. It must be remembered that delirium tremens, the withdrawal symptoms of alcoholism, are more dangerous to human life than the withdrawal symptoms from a hard narcotic like morphine.[25] The second stage should consist of intensive in-patient treatment to dry out the patient and formulation of detailed treatment program for the future. Hopefully, this stage will be held to a bare minimum amount of time. Incarceration in a health facility for a substantial period of time, like incarceration in jail, is likely to cripple any

---

23 H.R. 14330. See also *Hearings on H.R. 6143 Before Subcomm. No. 3 of the House Comm. on the District of Columbia*, 90th Cong., 1st Sess. (1967).
24 36 U.S.L.W. 3142 (U.S. Oct. 10, 1967); oral argument reported, 36 U.S.L.W. 3353 (U.S. March 12, 1968).
25 World Health Organization Expert Committee on Alcohol and Alcoholism, *Report*, Tech. Rep. Ser. No. 94, at 6-7, 11 (June, 1955).

chances of rehabilitation by developing dependence upon the institution itself. The third, and by far the most important stage, is outpatient treatment. It is evident that outpatient treatment must become the primary focus for any substantial attack upon alcoholism and intoxication. Related to this, the Crime Commission found that the homeless, derelict alcoholics who comprise the vast majority of those arrested for drunkenness in our cities cannot be treated without supportive residential housing that can be used as a base from which to reintegrate them into society.

Both the United States and D.C. Crime Commissions flatly recommended voluntary treatment for alcoholics.[26] They recognized that involuntary civil commitment procedures are as inappropriate and as punitive as criminal incarceration. State legislatures, which are accustomed to thinking in terms of involuntary civil commitment for mental illness, may be somewhat disinclined to accept this recommendation. Thus, substantial time and effort must be expended by the medical and legal professions if voluntary treatment is to be accepted and if future litigation concerning civil commitment procedures is to be avoided.

There are, I believe, important stakes riding on the success of the attempt to take drunkenness out of the criminal system. This attempt represents a major effort to reform our criminal law. Ironically, in a certain sense the Commission picked the most difficult area of all in which to test the feasibility of criminal law reform. The problem of drunkenness will not vanish with repeal of the public intoxication statutes. And society undoubtedly will not permit the streets to be littered with unconscious inebriates. Repeal of the drunkenness laws therefore requires establishment of a new system for handling the problem in a more humane and more effective way. In contrast, such private behavior as adultery, the use of marijuana, and homosexual conduct need no alternative handling. They are "public problems" only because the criminal law defines them as such. If the statutes were repealed, this conduct would no longer be a public problem.

The massive difficulties involved in a nationwide changeover from handling public drunkenness under the criminal law to the use of new public health procedures can, of course, be alleviated by the support and leadership of the federal government. Recently, the President sent to Congress a proposed Alcoholism Rehabilitation Act to accomplish this purpose.[27] This proposed legislation, which is intended to anticipate the Supreme Court's decision in *Powell,* should provide a major impetus for implementation of the United States Crime Commission's recommendations. It will be many years before the success of these recommendations can be gauged. I firmly believe, however, that they will prove to be of great importance to law enforcement in this country.

---

26 CRIME REPORT 236-37; REPORT OF THE PRESIDENT'S COMMISSION ON CRIME IN THE DISTRICT OF COLUMBIA, *supra* note 20, at 490-91.
27 S. 2989, 90th Cong., 2d Sess. (1968); H.R. 15281, 90th Cong., 2d Sess. (1968); H.R. 15758, 90th Cong., 2d Sess. (1968).

THE LIMITS AND POSSIBILITIES OF THE CRIMINAL LAW

*Frank J. Remington**

I. Introduction

This article discusses the application, or misapplication, of the criminal process to certain socio-legal problems. I will start with a fairly basic assertion about what the criminal law is today and then explore briefly what I think are some of the implications of this. An important reason for raising the question of the "limits and possibilities of the criminal law" is to enable us to respond in some consistent and hopefully intelligent way to questions that arise quite often in the administration of the judicial system. The principal question usually is whether the scope of the criminal law should, in the future, be drastically limited.

II. The Criminal Process Today

The criminal law today is, and it historically has been, relied upon when other less drastic methods of social control either fail or are too expensive. The drunk is a responsibility of the police and, to a lesser extent, prosecutors, courts, and correctional agencies, not because these agencies want the business, but rather because no other agency at the municipal, state, or federal level is willing or has demonstrated an ability to take the drunk and deal with him in an effective way. The prostitute is a responsibility of the criminal law, not because law enforcement could not get along well without having to deal with the prostitute, but rather because there has been no other agency that has demonstrated either a willingness or an ability to take the prostitute and to deal with her in a way more effective than she is now dealt with by the criminal process. The husband and wife fight, which occupies as much as fifty percent of the calls of the patrol officer in a high crime area, is a responsibility of the police rather than the social worker, not because the police want this responsibility or feel that they have discharged it with the kind of effectiveness one might desire, but rather because most social agencies are open only for limited times during limited days of the week, and most husband-wife quarrels occur at a time when social agencies are closed. By default the police are left with this responsibility of major importance. The responsibility is large whether it is measured by the danger to the parties or to the police officer or by the impact of the police response to these calls for service on the community's attitude toward the legal process.

The prosecutor and court do a lot of things for the same reason. Non-support is given a great deal of attention by the prosecutor solely because it is the community's feeling that husbands ought to support their families and should be threatened with a severe sanction if they do not do so. If put to the test, the community is required to either do something effective or allow the evil to exist. The usual response is reliance on the criminal law, an unhappy alternative,

---

* Professor of Law, University of Wisconsin Law School.

but the only one that exists. In the bad check case, reliance on the prosecutor is not a result of a philosophical decision that it is desirable to subject to criminal liability the person who writes a bad check. Rather, it is because the ability of most of us to cash a check with ease is dependent upon a workable system of enforcement against those who write checks and have insufficient funds in their accounts. To date the alternative to the criminal process is a different credit system, a price we have been unwilling to pay.

So when we talk about the limits or the philosophy of the criminal law, it is sort of like talking about the philosophy of a wastebasket. It is the place where all things go that are not wanted. To analyze its content is difficult because it is filled with all kinds of stuff that has been rejected by other less drastic methods of social control whether governmental, family, or religious.

III. Reasons for Limiting the Scope of the Criminal Law

We increasingly hear expressions of discontent about the broad scope of the criminal law and suggestions, like that of the President's Commission on Law Enforcement and Administration of Justice, that conduct such as drunkenness be removed from the criminal process.[1] There are several reasons given in support of such changes. The first is that the criminal law does an ineffective job in dealing with the drunk, the prostitute, the husband-wife dispute, the nonsupporting husband, and the writer of bad checks. The criminal process is said to be a poor way of rendering a social service to a person such as the drunk or of insuring the integrity of commercial transactions. This is a fair comment. The difficulty, however, is not so much with finding fault with the effectiveness of the criminal process but rather in finding more effective alternatives. It is much easier to point out the weaknesses of the criminal processes than to point to an alternative that will work better. In the Report of the President's Commission, more emphasis is put on the disadvantages of the criminal process dealing with the drunk than upon the advantages of a detoxication center or other alternative.[2] In asserting this, I would not want to be understood as saying we ought not to use better alternatives to the criminal process if they can be devised or that I think the handling of these problems by the criminal process should not be improved. There is an obvious and urgent need to do all we can to improve the handling of social problems that exist in our communities. But it is not an effective argument against reliance on the criminal law to point out that it is not a happy solution, when the conduct is left to the criminal process in the first place precisely because of our lack of ability or desire to devise a better alternative.

A second reason for drastically limiting the scope of the criminal law is that the drunk, the prostitute, and the domestic disturbance clog the criminal justice system and thus consume far too much time of the police, prosecutors,

---

1 THE CHALLENGE OF CRIME IN A FREE SOCIETY, A REPORT BY THE PRESIDENT'S COMMISSION ON LAW ENFORCEMENT AND ADMINISTRATION OF JUSTICE 4 (1967).
2 *Id.* at 3.

courts, and, to a lesser extent, correctional agencies. There is no question that police spend a great deal more time dealing with drunks, prostitutes, and fighting husbands and wives than they do with murderers, armed robbers, and burglars. But again the real need is to produce a better alternative. Even in proposals to deal with the drunk in the detoxication center, police will still have the responsibility to pick up the down-and-out drunk. From the point of view of the police, detoxication is a great advantage only when it means a cure, since only then will the down-and-out drunk not have to be picked up again. It has yet to be demonstrated that this is an objective that can be achieved. Mental health experts have doubts, I understand, about the desirability of detoxication centers because they say that this is to treat the symptom rather than the causes and is likely to drain resources from more productive approaches to community mental health problems. Certainly we ought to try to develop better alternatives to the criminal process. But the basic problem of public order and safety and sensibility will be left in the hands of police, and it is misleading to urge that behavior like drunkenness be taken out of criminal law so that the police will no longer have to deal with the problem. I don't think any of us will see the day when the police do not have major responsibility for dealing with the wide variety of deviant behavior that occurs twenty-four hours a day, seven days a week.

A third reason for narrowing the scope of the criminal law is that the use of the criminal process for the drunk, the prostitute, and the domestic disturbance degrades the process. I understand what this means, although I do not think murderers are uncomfortable being in the same category as drunks. Probably it reflects a feeling that judges lack effective ways of dealing with drunks, and as a consequence they tend to handle the cases very quickly and this adds to the crowding, the confusion, and the degrading atmosphere of the lower criminal court. If removing the drunk and the prostitute would improve the lower criminal court, this would be a great gain, but the ills of the lower trial court are so great that most will look just about as bad as they do now even though the drunks were gone.

A final reason for limiting reliance upon the criminal process is that an overly broad criminal law gives too much power to police. This is often what is meant when people decry the fact that adultery is a crime, that gambling is as broadly defined as it is, and that the possession of marijuana or consensual homosexuality is criminal. The average legislative response to the suggestion that these ought to be repealed goes something like this: "What's the problem with having these statutes on the books? We have always had them and from the legislative point of view they seem to do no harm even though they may not do a great deal of good." One response has been that having overly broad criminal proscriptions that are not going to be fully enforced creates an undue risk of public corruption or private blackmail. The assumption seems to be that if conduct, like homosexual behavior, were not criminal, the homosexual would be less likely to be a victim of blackmail. Yet, this seems questionable. So long as the conduct remains socially disapproved, there is risk that the corrupt individual or public officer can victimize the person who desires to keep his conduct from public view. The idea that the corrupt public officer can be eliminated by repeal of some criminal statutes seems naive.

The issue of how much discretion ought to be left to police is, in its own right, one of the most important, and very debatable, issues that presently confronts the criminal system of justice. So complex is the issue that it cannot be dealt with adequately in this article except to assert that there probably must be a balance between an inflexible rule and unlimited discretion. Where the optimum point is on the continuum between rule and discretion is properly subject to debate. But it certainly does not seem realistic to conclude that the discretion of police or prosecutors can be significantly reduced by repealing some criminal statutes. If the drunk is to be taken to a detoxication unit rather than a jail, the police officer still must make the choice and what he decides will still be important to the individual involved and to the community. We have learned that changing the name from criminal to juvenile, the objective from punishment to "the best interests of the child," does not make the exercise of discretionary power any less important or lessen the need for subjecting discretion to adequate control.[3] Concern about the way public officials exercise discretionary power in dealing with social problems is vitally important today and will remain so whether the conduct is or is not criminal.

IV. Solutions

It has always been popular to urge that the scope of the criminal law be narrowed so that the police, prosecutor, judge, and correctional agency will only have to worry about the "real criminal." The famous Wickersham Commission Report had an article by August Volmer, the great early police leader, who said that police should not be burdened with the responsibility for dealing with vice.[4] His reason was an obvious one: If police could deal only with criminal conduct like armed robbery and burglary, no one would have any difficulty in identifying the good from the bad. Police would have total community support in their fight against serious crime and they would not have to face the very complexing problems that law enforcement agencies have to confront in dealing with borderline criminal behavior. Today we have that kind of police unit in the detective division of most police departments. Volmer's proposal would make detectives of all police and presumably leave to some other governmental agency the responsibility for dealing with much of the work, like mediating the husband-wife fight, now performed by the patrolman. The difficulty is that, to date at least, there have been singularly few volunteers for that kind of duty. The logical candidate is the social worker. If someone other than police is going to deal with drunks, prostitutes, and embattled husbands and wives, it ought to be the social worker. The social workers would have to go on a twenty-four hour basis seven days a week and be located in places where they could respond promptly to calls for service. Because they probably would be concerned about

---

3   *E.g., In re* Gault, 387 U.S. 1 (1967).
4   NATIONAL COMMISSION ON LAW OBSERVANCE AND ENFORCEMENT, REPORT ON POLICE 22-33 (1931).

the personal danger involved, they might have to be armed and before long social workers might well become very much like the good patrolmen ought to be today.

If it is neither desirable nor realistic just to repeal a lot of criminal statutes, then what ought to be done? A few solutions can be briefly discussed. First, it is important to recognize the complexity of the task presently confronting the criminal system of justice. Once this is accomplished, society must take the steps that are necessary to equip it to do the best possible job. Second, it is important that the police themselves scrutinize very carefully the quality of their responses to calls for service. A large amount of the patrolman's time is spent in responding to calls for help; police have more contact, particularly with members of the ghetto community, than any other governmental agency. Hence, they have the maximum opportunity either to aggravate the situation, if their response to calls for service is poor, or to make a significant contribution to improvement if their response to calls for services is of high quality. By high quality I mean the same kind of response they would make in a more affluent neighborhood. This would include treating people with respect, attempting to effectively mediate the husband-wife dispute, making referrals to other social agencies if they are available and willing to accept referrals, and taking a leadership role in calling the attention of the community to the need for the development of new social services where they are currently inadequate.

Third, there is a need to re-evaluate the traditional process of criminal justice. For example, correctional agencies have not made as effective a contribution as they might. Too often correctional services are thought of as something that is not needed until after conviction. Yet it seems apparent that there are many social problems existing today to which the entire process of arrest, prosecution, and conviction is unnecessary. The President's Commission on Law Enforcement and Administration of Justice recommends a maximum use of alternatives to prosecution and conviction.[5] If this is to be achieved, it will require a basic rethinking of the correctional role. What is needed is a closer working relationship between correctional agencies and the police in the early stages of the criminal process so that some social problems can be dealt with without having to go through the process of prosecution and conviction.

The last point, a very major point, is that we ought to recognize that law enforcement agencies in this country have a great deal of discretionary power and that they will continue to have a great deal of power, responsibility, and discretion even if we repeal criminal laws dealing with adultery, marijuana, gambling, prostitution, and other related problems. It is important that we do not merely object to this fact and then simply wait for the day when the criminal law can somehow be so narrowly drafted that it can be mechanically applied by the policeman without ability, without training, and without education. It is much better to recognize our system as one that puts a very heavy responsibility on the police officer and then to take an active role in making the changes that are necessary to equip the police officer with the training and education necessary

---

5 THE CHALLENGE OF CRIME IN A FREE SOCIETY, A REPORT BY THE PRESIDENT'S COMMISSION ON LAW ENFORCEMENT AND ADMINISTRATION OF JUSTICE 18-20 (1967).

to deal with the major social problems that he confronts. It is in this frame of reference that we ought to discuss the need for improved education, training, pay, organization, and other matters concerning the police profession.

V. Conclusion

I want to conclude by repeating what I said at the outset. The criminal law has had, and will continue to have, the job of dealing with a wide variety of antisocial conduct which cannot be, at least has not been, dealt with effectively by other less drastic means. Thus it is not productive, in my view, to merely urge the removal of conduct, like drunkenness, from the criminal process and stop there. The need is to develop better alternatives and, in the meantime, to make very substantial improvements in the administration of criminal justice. It is necessary to equip the police, prosecutors, courts, and correctional agencies with the tools necessary to deal effectively not only with traditional crime, but also with a wide range of social problems that are increasingly important, particularly in our urban communities.

Even with the best efforts of all of us, the day is far off when we will have developed a really effective way of dealing with the very perplexing behavioral problems that are manifested by the drunk, the prostitute, and the husband and wife who cannot get along. But this is no excuse for inhumane or otherwise offensive treatment of persons who have those problems. It is possible to have a system of criminal justice that is sensitive to these kinds of behavioral problems and deals with them much more fairly and effectively than we do today. And, in the process of rendering more adequate service, we may narrow the gulf between the police and the community, particularly the ghetto community. There is reason to believe that today the poor and disadvantaged can gain a great deal if only the police and the entire criminal system will view the major objective to be a more adequate, effective, and respectful response to the many calls for service that come from the part of the community where the socially deprived live. The criminal justice system may not be the ideal way to respond to these behavioral problems, but it is the only system we now have and it can be greatly improved while waiting for better alternatives to be devised.

FEDERAL AID TO STATE AND LOCAL LAW ENFORCEMENT — IMPLICATIONS OF A NEW FEDERAL GRANT PROGRAM

*Norman Abrams**

I. Introduction

In its recently published Report, the President's Commission on Law Enforcement and Administration of Justice briefly summarized the diverse forms of the federal government's "contribution to the national effort against crime":

> The Federal Government carries much of the load of financing and administering the great social programs that the America's best hope of preventing crime and delinquency . . . .

> The Federal Government has the direct responsibility for enforcing major criminal statutes against, among other things, kidnapping, bank robbery, racketeering, smuggling, counterfeiting, drug abuse and tax evasion. It has a number of law enforcement agencies, a system of criminal courts and a large correctional establishment. . . .

> The Federal Government has for many years provided information, advice and training to State and local law enforcement agencies. . . . In many towns and counties, for example, the Federal Bureau of Investigation's on-site training programs for police officers and sheriffs are the only systematic training programs available. The Department of Justice, under the Law Enforcement Assistance Act of 1965, has begun to give State and city agencies financial grants for research, for planning, and for demonstration projects.[1]

The Commission then proceeded "not only to endorse warmly federal participation in the effort to reduce delinquency and crime, but to urge that it be intensified and accelerated."[2]

Until recently, the most significant form of federal participation in the nation's law enforcement and criminal justice[3] efforts has been what the Commission described as the federal government's direct responsibility for enforcing major criminal statutes. Direct financial aid such as that provided under the

---

* Professor of Law, Bar-Ilan University, Ramat-Gan, Israel; former Professor-in-Residence, Criminal Division, U.S. Dept. of Justice, Washington, D.C., 1966-67.

1 THE CHALLENGE OF CRIME IN A FREE SOCIETY, A REPORT BY THE PRESIDENT'S COMMISSION ON LAW ENFORCEMENT AND ADMINISTRATION OF JUSTICE 283 (1967) [hereinafter cited as CRIME REPORT].

2 *Id.*

3 This phrase or the words "law enforcement" are used interchangeably in the text. These words are used in the same sense as defined in H.R. 5037 as originally introduced into the 90th Congress. See section 501(a):

> "Law enforcement and criminal justice" means all activities pertaining to crime prevention or the enforcement and administration of the criminal law, including, but not limited to, activities involving police, prosecution or defense of criminal cases, courts, probation, corrections and parole.

As passed by the House in August, 1967, the words "or defense" were not included in section 501(a). The deletion may not result in a different scope for the legislation. If it does, however, it is unfortunate, for any program in this area should be comprehensive. As the Commission put it: "The relationships among the parts of the criminal justice system . . . are so intimate and intricate that a change anywhere may be felt everywhere." CRIME REPORT 280.

Law Enforcement Assistance Act[4] has been relatively limited and is of recent vintage. Federal financing of social programs designed to reduce crime and delinquency is of larger dimensions, but its impact upon law enforcement has been indirect and difficult to measure. If the Commission's principal recommendations regarding the federal role in law enforcement are adopted, the major emphasis on the federal level in this area may shift from direct law enforcement to direct financial aid to state and local governments. For the Commission recommended a large-scale program of federal spending to improve the quality of state and local law enforcement and administration of justice.

> The Federal program the Commission visualizes is a large one. During the past fiscal year the Federal Government spent a total of about $20 million on research into crime and delinquency, and another $7 million, under the Law Enforcement Assistance Act, on research and demonstration projects by local agencies of justice. The Commission is not in a position to weigh against each other all the demands for funds that are made upon the Federal Government. And so it cannot recommend the expenditure of a specific number of dollars a year on the program it proposes. *However, it does see the program as one on which several hundred million dollars annually could be profitably spent over the next decade.* (Emphasis added.)[5]

The Commission justified such a large federal financial support program on three grounds: crime is a national phenomenon that does not respect geographical boundaries; there are important needs that individual jurisdictions cannot meet alone; federal funds can be used to encourage changes that will make criminal administration more effective and more fair. But at the same time, the Commission felt it necessary to remind the reader that:

> [T]he Commission is mindful of the special importance of avoiding any invasion of state and local responsibility for law enforcement and criminal justice, and its recommendation is based on its judgment that Federal support and collaboration of the sort outlined below are consistent with scrupulous respect for — and indeed strengthening of — that responsibility.[6]

The Commission's reminder is not unusual. Almost every public statement by a public official about an expanded federal role in law enforcement and criminal justice carries with it a similar caveat. Thus, in his 1967 message to Congress on crime in America, the President stated: "The Federal Government must not and will not try to dominate the system. It could not if it tried. Our system of law enforcement is essentially local: based upon local initiative, generated by local energies and controlled by local officials."[7]

This same theme has been repeated by the Attorney General:

> But law enforcement is a local responsibility. As a nation we have preached local law enforcement. As a nation we have practiced it. There are more of New York's finest, the police of New York City, than there are Fed-

---

4 The Law Enforcement Assistance Act of 1965, 79 Stat. 828.
5 CRIME REPORT 284.
6 *Id.* at 285.
7 White House Press Release, Feb. 6, 1967, p. 6. The President struck a similar note in his most recent State of the Union Address on Jan. 17, 1968.

eral law enforcement officers for the Nation. Los Angeles County has six times more deputy sheriffs than there are deputy U.S. marshals for the whole United States, and the Los Angeles Police Department is larger than the sheriff's office.

A single county has twice as many probation service officers as the entire Federal Probation Service. The Federal Bureau of Prisons has less than 5 percent of the prison population of the Nation. The Federal judiciary is but a tiny fraction of the judiciary of the States, smaller than the judiciary of even a single State.

We would have it no other way. Our safety and our liberty depend on the excellence of local and State law enforcement.[8]

A financial aid program as large as that envisaged by the Commission inevitably raises important questions about the proper relationship among federal, state and local governments in the law enforcement and criminal justice field. The question of federal versus state or local responsibility for a particular governmental function is, of course, a pervasive one in our system, but it takes on a special dimension in the law enforcement and criminal justice context. The possibility that a federal financial support program might be used to lay the foundation for the creation of a national police force or to permit the federal government to control local law enforcement is often raised as a spectre, albeit sometimes for partisan purposes.[9] The related issue of the role to be played by state government in implementing such a financial aid program is also a subject of some controversy. These issues, currently before the Congress in connection with proposed legislation designed to implement the Commission's recommendations, merit detailed examination.

II. A National Police Force

Any discussion of the possibility of federal control of local law enforcement must begin with the most extreme horrible thrown up by those who debate the issue — the bugaboo of a national police force. There is an odd universality in the abhorrence of the idea of a national police force in this country. Conservatives and liberals alike seem opposed to the notion. Strangely enough, one of the most forceful spokesmen on the subject has been the head of the federal law enforcement agency that undoubtedly would become the cornerstone of any national police operation, were that ever to come to pass. J. Edgar Hoover has said:

The danger of a national police force is that it centralizes into one place and into the hands of one man too much authority. The Federal

---

8 Statement of Ramsey Clark, *Hearings on H.R. 5037, 5038 Before Subcomm. No. 5 of the House Comm. on the Judiciary,* 90th Cong., 1st Sess. 29 (1967) [hereinafter cited as *House Hearings*].

9 For example, see the statement of General Minority Views accompanying the House Judiciary Committee Report on H.R. 5037:
> As we have seen with the 458 existing Federal categorical grant-in-aid programs, he who pays the piper must necessarily call the tune. Do Americans want law enforcement in all 50 states to be declared by a non-elected Federal officeholder in Washington? H.R. REP. No. 488, 90th Cong., 1st Sess. 28 (1967) [hereinafter cited as HOUSE COMM. REP.].

Government, of course, has no cure-all for the crime problems existing in any community. The need is for effective local action, and this should begin with the wholehearted support of honest, efficient, local law enforcement.[10]

Undoubtedly for some people rejection of the idea of a national police force merely involves a specific application of a particular political philosophy. According to this philosophy any federal operation of a governmental function is presumptively bad; state or local governmental control, or even absence of any governmental involvement at all, is almost always preferable. But the idea of a national police force also conjures up images inconsistent with our democratic ideal and touches sensitive nerves deeply-rooted in our traditions. Many who are not opposed to substantial extensions of federal power in other areas would be violently opposed to this type of extension. People do not just reject the idea, they find it abhorrent.[11] It almost seems to qualify as a kind of taboo. To test this notion, I recently conducted a quick, informal and unscientific "free association" poll among some of my colleagues. Reactions varied to the question, "What image do the words 'national police force' conjure up for you?" But the dominant pattern of responses revolved around words like "Gestapo," "Nazism," "stormtroopers," "government by tyranny," and "foreign or European systems where police snoop about."

What accounts for this seemingly strange pattern of responses?[12] It may, of course, be foolish to attempt to account in rational terms for what are, after all, free-association-type reactions. It is suggested, however, that underlying these reactions is the image of a very large police force saturating the country, being used for political purposes and subject to the control of one man. Such a force smacks of dictatorship and tyranny. No doubt, the experience in Europe in the 1930's has markedly conditioned our attitudes. Control over such a force has in many countries been the instrument for assuming dictatorial power. And the potential for power inherent in a federal police complement of between six and seven thousand men (taking into account only the FBI)[13] and a nationally-controlled force of between three and four hundred thousand men (the present number of police on the local and state levels) is readily apparent. One could argue, of course, that the potential for power is already present. The armed

10 *Interview with J. Edgar Hoover,* U.S. NEWS AND WORLD REPORT, Dec. 21, 1964, p. 38. For his most recent statement on the subject in the same vein, see *Message from the Director,* FBI LAW ENF. BULL., Feb. 1, 1968, at 1.
11 Interview with J. Edgar Hoover, *supra* note 10.
12 One colleague has suggested that the test was not a fair one — that the words "federal police force" should have been used. He theorized that the word "national" carries with it association with national socialism and that this accounts for the pattern of reactions. Though possible, I am skeptical. Also, it is suggested that this proposed phrase does not carry with it the connotation of as complete a taking-over of the law enforcement function as the words "national police force." The FBI, for example, might legitimately be identified as federal police. Moreover, I am doubtful that the use of the word "national" so frequently used in our vocabulary conjures up national socialism just because it is juxtaposed to the words police force.
One might suppose that the reaction is to the word "police" with all the connotations that word has. But here is a marked difference in the image created by the words "local police" and "national police."
13 The President in his recent State of the Union Message asked for an increase in FBI complement by 100 men.

services are subject to the will of the commander-in-chief. This, however, has not resulted in dictatorship. Perhaps the fear is that men performing police functions might lend themselves to more abuse than the armed services which, fortunately, up to the present have not been used to serve political ends.

The unusual reaction to the notion of a national police force may have other bases too. Many people think of such force simply as involving an expansion of the FBI. Thus, reactions to Mr. Hoover, his long tenure and attitudes toward the Bureau, in general may lie behind this response. Indeed, it may be — this is very speculative — that the very efficiency and effectiveness of the FBI are a principal cause of concern. Perhaps expanding such a force to perform the entire law enforcement function of the nation is more than we are willing to accept. Perhaps we prefer that our police not be "too good" at their job. In each of us there is a little bit of the lawbreaker. Perhaps our attitudes toward the national police force idea reflect this fact.

Rejection of a national police force can, of course, be explained in the more traditional terms that are used in other areas such as education. In the law enforcement context the argument takes the following familiar form: It is undesirable to have the law enforcement function controlled by men in Washington. They are too far away and do not have a feeling for, or understanding of, local concerns and problems. This argument undoubtedly has some merit. A partial answer to such a point is that central control does not necessarily mean distant control. If one really wanted a national police operation, regional and even local offices subject to a central authority could be set up to cope with local concerns. Such a structure would no doubt resemble our present system, with one significant change. The local offices would be subject to the ultimate control of officials in Washington.

I do not propose the establishment of a national police force. Although such a force would have some law enforcement advantages, e.g., in coordinating law enforcement efforts and promoting improved communications on a nation-wide basis, there are too many persuasive reasons, reflected in the concerns described above, for rejecting the notion. Moreover, most of the advantages of a national force may be obtained within our traditional allocation of law enforcement authority.

Though few seriously advocate a national police force, it remains an important issue. For discussion about it arises most frequently in debates over the possibility of the development of outside control over local law enforcement through a large-scale federal financial support program. Not only do opponents of such a program hold up the bugaboo of a national police force, but all of us, it is submitted, are influenced in our thinking in this area by our reactions to this notion. It behooves us, therefore, to be aware of and understand what we mean by and what we fear in the concept of a national police force.

A national police force might also evolve in this country through the extension of federal criminal law jurisdiction and an expansion of the powers and numbers of the FBI to enforce that jurisdiction. The Commission made few recommendations relating to the substantive federal criminal laws although it did refer approvingly to the federal commission currently charged with responsibility for reform of the federal penal law, *i.e.*, the National Commission on Reform of Federal Criminal Laws. That commission is thus faced with issues relating to this subject.

III. Federal Control of Local Law Enforcement

Although the national police force idea is often mentioned in debate, few would allow that there is imminent danger that such a force will be established — at least in the present state of national affairs. It is, however, viewed by some as the possible end result of a growing federal role in local law enforcement. The more immediate concern for many is that through the development of new federal programs, the federal government will begin to exercise *control* over local law enforcement.

The problem is posed most sharply by legislation currently under consideration in the Congress. As a direct outgrowth of the Commission's recommendations, one year ago the Administration introduced the Safe Streets and Crime Control Bill.[14] This proposal, amended and renamed the Law Enforcement and Criminal Justice Assistance Act, was passed by the House in August, 1967,[15] and is currently under consideration by the Senate Judiciary Committee. Although there are numerous and substantial differences among the Administration's original bill, the bill reported out by the House Judiciary Committee, the bill passed by the House, and the bill under consideration in the Senate, all versions contemplating large-scale financial aid to state and local law enforcement. The issue is whether such a program is likely to lead to federal control.

The power over the purse strings undoubtedly includes the power to exercise control over those who are dependent on that purse. Our initial inquiry, therefore, must determine how great that dependency is likely to become. The extent of potential federal authority over local law enforcement will depend greatly on how significant a part of the local law enforcement budget the federal dollar is likely to become. That, in turn, may be determined by the amounts of money involved, the purposes for which the money may be used, and the extent to which there is discretion in the grant-making agency to withhold funds unless the applying local law enforcement agency meets certain conditions.

The Commission saw the federal support program as one on which several hundred million dollars could be spent annually over the next decade.[16] The Administration's bill, as originally submitted to Congress, called for fifty million dollars the first year, and the Attorney General testified that three hundred million would be requested the second year. He saw the program as possibly involving the annual expenditure of a billion dollars within the next five years.[17] The bill passed by the House called for seventy-five million dollars,[18] and in his recent State of the Union Message the President asked for one hundred million

---

14   H.R. 5037, 90th Cong., 1st Sess. (1967).
15   *Id.*
16   CRIME REPORT 284.
17   *House Hearings* 30.
18   H.R. 5037, *supra* note 14.

dollars for fiscal 1969.[19] Expenditures for law enforcement and criminal justice purposes, as estimated by the Commission, presently amount to four billion dollars a year.[20] The bulk of this goes to the police, and "85-90 percent of all police costs are for salaries and wages."[21]

Even assuming a substantial increase (apart from the increase represented by federal money) in local law enforcement expenditures during the next five years and taking into account other appropriate qualifications,[22] if the Attorney General's rather liberal estimate is accurate, federal money could in a short time constitute a significant proportion of local law enforcement budgets. And even assuming the somewhat more conservative estimate made by the Commission, federal financial aid would soon become an important part of the nation's total law enforcement expenditure. Whatever the uses to which such federal money might be put, such an extensive support program undoubtedly would tend to make local governments dependent on the federal government for part of their budgets.

There will be an even greater potential for control if the federal funds are used for regularly-recurring costs such as salaries, where additional costs, once undertaken, are almost impossible to abandon. In addition, of course, the use of federal money for salaries poses a large problem simply because the salary item looms so large in law enforcement budgets. In this connection, it is interesting to compare the Administration's proposal concerning the salary issue with the version of the bill reported out by the House Judiciary Committee and the one finally passed by the House.

The original proposal took a fairly restrictive approach on the salary issue and provided that:

> [N]ot more than one-third of any grant . . . shall be expended for the compensation of personnel, except that this limitation shall not apply to the compensation of personnel for time engaged in conducting or under-going training programs and specialized personnel performing innovative functions.[23]

The House Judiciary Committee reported out a bill that went even further and completely barred the use of grants for compensation of personnel, with the same two exceptions provided for in the original bill.[24] The bill passed by the House, however, contained neither provision and would appear to authorize federal grants to be used for salary purposes without limitation.[25] If it is true, as suggested, that the use of a grant for such a continuing expense — particularly one that is such a major portion of the law enforcement budget — gives a larger potential for control to the grant-making authority, the bill passed by the House

---

19 N.Y. Times, Jan. 18, 1968, at/16, col. 5.
20 CRIME REPORT 35.
21 *Id.*
22 For example, the fact that a substantial amount of federal money will not go into direct support of law enforcement but rather into research by universities, research institutes and the like.
23 H.R. 5037, § 202(a)(2), *supra* note 14.
24 Law Enforcement and Criminal Justice Assistance Act § 202(b), HOUSE COMM. REP. 18.
25 H.R. 5037, *supra* note 14.

goes further in this direction than any of the earlier versions. Interestingly enough, as developed later in this paper, that potential under the House bill seems to be vested in the states and not the federal government.

Another element that may affect the potential of a large grant program for federal control is the amount of discretion in the grant-making authority to impose conditions on the recipient of a grant. All three versions of the proposed legislation give to the grant-making authority a certain amount of discretion through the requirement that an approved plan must be submitted if a grant is to be obtained.[26] The power to approve the plan[27] carries the discretion with it. The bills themselves describe the expected content of the plan in general terms; presumably, further details will be spelled out in regulations. Inevitably, though, some discretion will remain in the grant-making authority to determine whether there has been compliance with the standards contained in the statute and regulations. In view of this, it seems fair to say that the type of program contemplated carries with it a potential for the exercise of some control by the grant-making authority over local law enforcement. The question remains whether that leverage is likely to be exercised, and if so, how.

At the outset, it is worthwhile pointing out that no one can predict with certainty the course of development of a governmental program of the type described. At best, one can engage in reasonable speculation based upon those elements presently perceived. There are, of course, many analogies that could be relied upon — such as federal aid to education and the poverty program. Although such analogies are not irrelevant, it must be remembered that each federal grant program has its own special characteristics. The risk that the federal government will use the potential for control inherent in a grant program of this sort to begin to "take over" the operation of local police agencies is minimal, despite the dire predictions of opponents of the program.[28] This conclusion is not based on an altruistic view of the world or on the notion that officials of the federal government are any the less corruptible by power than the average man. Rather, the exercise of detailed control over local operations by a central authority — even given the leverage that a large-scale grant program would provide — is just not feasible. The number of local police jurisdictions in this country is enormous, by one count over forty thousand.[29] Any attempt to regulate the details of so many police operations would require the creation of a huge federal establishment. At the very least, a large number of regional and local offices would be required, and a large staff of federal inspectors to police the police would be necessary. There is no indication that anything like that is contemplated. Such an establishment could not be created without congressional awareness and objection. Surely Congress would not stand still for it, and ultimate power over this and any other government grant program remains in the hands of Congress through the device of the annual appropriation. Indeed, the

---

26   *See, e.g., id.* § 204.
27   *Id.* § 202. The administration's bill, as originally introduced in the House of Representatives on Feb. 8, 1967, contained a fairly detailed formula, abandoned in later versions, application of which would affect the amount of the grant but not the extent of discretion possessed by the Attorney General.
28   HOUSE COMM. REP. 40-41 (separate views of Hon. Edward Hutchinson).
29   *House Hearings* 29.

executive may control the drawstring of the purse, giving him some power over local agencies, but Congress, in the last analysis, controls the size of that purse.

There remains to consider the argument that this program of federal grants is just the opening wedge — that:

> [G]eneral acceptance of the scheme of this bill will result in making State and local law enforcement agencies so financially dependent upon Federal support that they will be unable to give it up. And in order to keep receiving Federal aid they will more and more, a little at a time, give up their local and State control over police, until finally they are persuaded that law enforcement is a national problem and no longer a local or State responsibility.[30]

One may as well argue that the establishment of the FBI was the first step down the primrose path toward a national police force. It will be time enough to worry about such dangers when they loom larger and more realistically on the horizon.

To conclude that comprehensive federal control over the details of police operations will not come about as a result of this type of grant program does not entirely dispose of the federal control issue. A persuasive argument can be made that a financial aid program might cause "selective" control over local law enforcement. By selective control the grant-making authority may require a particular applying local jurisdiction to meet certain conditions, to do or not do something, or to modify its practices in a specified manner. Because of the limitations of manpower and the number of jurisdictions involved, this would necessarily occur only on a selective basis. It would not involve a comprehensive takeover of the local police operation, nor would it constitute the first step toward such a takeover or toward a national police force. Nevertheless, it would involve "those fellows" in Washington (or in a state capital) telling a local authority how to run some aspects of its affairs. This would clearly constitute a departure, though limited in scope, from the long-standing tradition of complete independence of the local government in the police area. The question is whether or not this is objectionable.

The answer has to be that it depends on how wisely and judiciously this newfound power is exercised by the grant-making authority. The mere expenditure of additional sums of money will not automatically improve our systems of law enforcement and criminal justice. Simply adding to the number of police will not solve our problems. There must be improvements of all types in the functioning of the system. The entire thrust of the Commission's Report was to this effect. There was a large emphasis on specific types of improvements such as more training, pooling of resources, services and information, and the use of innovative methods generally.[31] On one level, it might be said that the grant-

---

30 HOUSE COMM. REP. 40-41.
31 The program of Federal support recommended by the Commission would be directed to eight major needs:
    (1) State and local planning.
    (2) Education and training of criminal justice personnel.
    (3) Surveys and advisory services concerning the organization and operation of police departments, courts, prosecuting offices, and corrections agencies.

making authority has a responsibility to see that the new funds are used responsibly in a way that will best contribute to the improvement of the system. No one believes that the Department of Justice as a grant maker will have extraordinary wisdom in these matters. But it will have the advantage of its position as a central coordinating agency.[32] If it does its job well, it will quickly accumulate a wealth of experience and knowledge. In administering the program it will, for example, be able to apply the experience in the use of new techniques that will be fed into it from all over the country. Undoubtedly local officials will always have a better sense of their own problems, but there is no reason in principle why the grant maker should not use his leverage to encourage improvements in local practice. No doubt, if used excessively, such exertion of authority will result in friction between grantor and grantee. The local jurisdictions should generally welcome a certain amount of guidance of this sort, provided that it is sensible and does not concern itself too much with the matters of detail.[33] There are some who will find *any* such selective influence on local law enforcement objectionable. Others will only object if the type of influence exercised interferes with local interests deemed particularly important.

There are familiar areas where the exercise of this type of leverage will be objected to by the local governments. For example, when the federal grant-making authority attempts, as it must, to invoke the provisions of Title VI of the Civil Rights Act of 1964[34] against a Southern county that discriminates in its hiring of police officers, there will undoubtedly be a large outcry. That issue will be a sensitive one whether the federal program involved education, urban redevelopment, poverty, or law enforcement. While most persons have no difficulty justifying this type of string on the use of federal funds, it is conceded that one's reaction to such an exercise of control may be determined by one's attitude toward the merits of the matter. It should be emphasized, however, that the congressional policy judgment has previously been made in Title VI of the Civil Rights Act and that the problem is not peculiar to this particular grant program. Members of the Senate sub-committee hearing testimony on this

---

(4) Development of a coordinated national information system for operational and research purposes.
(5) Funding of limited numbers of demonstration programs in agencies of justice.
(6) Scientific and technological research and development.
(7) Development of national and regional research centers.
(8) Grants-in-aid for operational innovations. CRIME REPORT xi.
  32 The Commission's final conclusion about a Federal anticrime program is that the major responsibility for administering it should lie with the Department of Justice:
  . . . In the Department of Justice alone among Federal agencies there is a large existing pool of practical knowledge about the police, the courts and the correctional system. . . . The Department of Justice has a Criminal Division, one of whose most important sections is concerned with organized crime and racketeering. It has the recently established Office of Criminal Justice, which has concentrated on criminal reform. Many of the research and demonstration portions of the Commission's program are already authorized under the Law Enforcement Assistance Act, which is administered by the Department of Justice. If it is given the money and the men it will need, the Department of Justice can take the lead in the Nation's efforts against crime. CRIME REPORT 284-85.
  33 *See, e.g.,* testimony on behalf of the National League of Cities, *House Hearings* 381-86.
  34 The pertinent statutory language is to be found in 42 U.S.C. § 2000(d) which provides: "No person . . . shall . . . be excluded from participation in, be denied the benefits of, or be subjected to discrimination under any program or activity receiving Federal financial assistance."

matter raised the related problem of whether factors such as racial imbalance might be taken into account in determining whether to make a grant even where there was no evidence of discrimination constituting a violation of Title VI.[35] The issue is a difficult one. If racial imbalance were likely to introduce malfunctioning into the operation of the system — for example, in connection with the operation of a police community relations program — then it could plausibly be taken into account in determining whether to make the grant. Such factors, absent evidence of discrimination, generally would not be central elements in the grant-making process, and it would be regrettable if congressional concern about them were to affect the basic structure of the program.

Thus far, this article has focused on the potential for control of local law enforcement inherent in a large financial aid program. Before leaving this subject, however, it is important to call attention to the potential for control involved in other activities of the federal government related to local law enforcement. For it would seem likely that those who will not be reassured on the subject of federal control in connection with a grant program would also be concerned about other forms of increased federal activity. Consider, for example, the recommendations of the Commission for dealing with the problems of communications and obtaining information in a locally-oriented law enforcement system:

> An integrated national information system is needed to serve the combined needs at the National, State, regional and metropolitan or county levels of the police, courts, and correction agencies, and of the public and the research community. Each of these agencies has information needed by others; an information system provides a means for collecting it, analyzing it, and disseminating it to those who need it. Each can be kept in close communication with the others, and information transferred by voice, by teletype, or computer to computer.
>
> Since law enforcement is primarily a local and State function, the overall program must be geared to the circumstances and requirements of local and State agencies; and, wherever practical, the files should be located at these levels.[36]

In a similar vein, the Commission said:

> A national inquiry file (the National Crime Information Center — NCIC) is now being established by the FBI. This file will contain records of all cars reported stolen for more than 24 hours, all persons wanted for extraditable offenses, stolen guns, and all stolen identifiable property valued at over $1,000. This file will be maintained on a computer, with terminals initially connected to 15 police agencies, and with plans to include all States eventually . . . . The utility of a fully interconnected national inquiry file depends on the need for interstate and interregional communications and on the need to provide an inquiry capability for those States that do not establish their own files. . . . It is important that the States, in assessing their own needs and developing their own computer facilities, and the FBI in operating the NCIC, seek to develop information that will

---

35 *Id.*
36 CRIME REPORT 267.

provide a basis for a sound decision on the needs for and the form of a national inquiry system.[37]

It is worth noting that the Commission was extremely cautious in both of these recommendations and emphasized developments at the local level, for such inquiry and information systems also have a potential for growth into instruments of control. Indeed, dependence of local police operations on an outside authority might more easily come about through control over an information system upon which day-to-day operations are dependent than through a grant program where grants are made only annually.

Consider also the provisions of the bill passed by the House that provided for the establishment within the Department of Justice of a National Institute of Law Enforcement and Criminal Justice.[38] That Institute is "to establish and operate regional institutes for the training of State and local law enforcement personnel,"[39] "to make continuing studies and undertake programs of research,"[40] and "to carry out a program of behavioral research."[41] The Institute is also to "establish such laboratories and research facilities as may be necessary to carry out the program described."[42] The director may determine the "conditions" under which payments are to be made to individual trainees.[43] These, of course, are the type of activities described in the Commission Report that have been carried on for many years by the federal government. But the establishment and operation of regional training institutes would seem to involve a marked expansion of this type of direct activity by the federal government. Indeed, it is somewhat ironic that the House bill which in a sense attempted to limit the power of the federal government over financial aid to local law enforcement, actually expanded the direct involvement of the government in training and related activities. Again, the potential for influence and control over local law enforcement through mass training of its officers probably poses as great (or as small) a risk as that offered through a large-scale grant program.

These examples are cited not to oppose such developments in training and information systems. The fact, however, that they, too, do raise the control issue should be explicitly faced. It is not an evil for the federal government judiciously and on a selective basis to use the leverage it obtains through these various programs to effect improvements in local law enforcement and criminal justice systems. In many jurisdictions, it may be the only way to accomplish such changes.

IV. State Control

The question of whether, in a large-scale program of financial aid for state

---

37 *Id.* at 268. In this connection, attention should be called to an amendment incorporated into section 412 of the version of H.R. 5037 passed by the House that required annual reports describing data storage and retrieval systems employed for the storage of criminal intelligence data by the Department of Justice and by any recipient of funds under the act who uses such funds for such systems.
38 H.R. 5037, Title IV, *supra* note 14.
39 *Id.* § 301, as passed by the House, Aug. 8, 1967.
40 *Id.* § 303(2).
41 *Id.* § 303(3).
43 *Id.* § 307(b).
42 *Id.* § 304.

and local law enforcement, state governments should be involved other than as direct recipients of grants poses issues closely related to those previously discussed. If, for example — to consider the matter in its most extreme form — the federal government were simply to make large bloc grants to each state, perhaps according to a specified formula, and the state were then to make the specific grants to the various local law enforcement agencies within its borders, the issue of federal control would largely evaporate. Proposals for state involvement of this type raise other problems that have also come up in connection with other federal grant programs, e.g., aid to education, and involve problems of taxation and economics that transcend the scope of this paper. Those problems, however, that particularly relate to a financial aid program in the law enforcement field are the subject of this section.

The House action last August on H.R. 5037 provided for federal grants to state planning agencies which would then administer the money for the entire state.[44] Both earlier versions of the bill, the one introduced by the Administration[45] and the one reported out by the House Judiciary Committee,[46] had provided for the making of grants by the federal government directly to local governments. The issues here are, of course, central to the basic structuring of the entire grant program. Since the full Senate Judiciary Committee recently reported out a version of the bill that on this issue follows the pattern of the administration bill, as of the date of this writing, the issue is still an open one that may, if the Senate adopts its committee's bill, have to be resolved in conference between the two houses.

The bill passed by the House places primary authority over the distribution of funds and over guidelines for their expenditure in the state governments. The question thus becomes whether such an approach is preferable to one which gives the federal government that responsibility. Putting aside ideology, considerations of the general relationship between the functions of the state and federal governments, and the revenue and economic factors previously mentioned, the issue turns on which approach is best designed to improve the overall quality of law enforcement and criminal justice.

The case to be made for the House approach is not unpersuasive. The Commission, for example, recognized that "much of the planning for action against crime will have to be done at the State level"[47] and recommended that "[a] State or local government that undertakes to improve its criminal administration should begin by constructing . . . formal machinery for planning."[48] The Commission did not, however, go so far as to recommend that this state planning machinery should be used as a conduit for the federal funds to be distributed to local governments (although it did recommend that federal grants should be made to the states to support and encourage such planning).[49] There is in fact no dispute about the value of such planning and coordination activities on the

---

44 *Id.* §§ 201-03.
45 *Id.* § 201 (introduced in the House of Representatives by Congressman Emanuel Cellar, Feb. 8, 1967).
46 House Comm. Rep. 17-18.
47 Crime Report 280.
48 *Id.* at 279.
49 *Id.* at 285.

state level. Thus, for example, in response to a call from the President in October, 1966, the first meeting of the State Criminal Justice Planning Committee was held. And the bill introduced by the Administration provided for federal planning grants to both state and local governments.[50] On the same subject, the Attorney General testified:

> We think it is awfully important to get the States started where they are not, because their plan can affect the other jurisdictions. So we would hope to have all of the States really working toward a fully comprehensive plan for the State.[51]

The issue, then, is not whether states should be encouraged to engage in planning and coordination activities but whether they should be given a large or controlling voice in the distribution of money to local governments.

It can be argued that by channeling funds through the states, they will thereby be given the "muscle" to ensure that comprehensive planning and coordination on a statewide basis are carried out. Congressman William Cahill stated this argument in his Additional Views to the Report of the House Judiciary Committee:

> Under the planning mechanism provided by the present bill, pressure by local citizens and officials will force each individual local government to make hurried and separate applications for Federal assistance. In this nationwide competition for funding, there will be little time for the careful thought necessary to formulate "innovative" or "comprehensive" programs. Moreover, in the absence of *effective* State planning agencies there is little stimulus for increased coordination and cooperation among local law enforcement and judicial authorities; while the bill permits the chief executives of the several States to comment to the U.S. Attorney General on applications by local authorities, there is no *assurance* that such recommendations will be followed nor that final approval of the application will be in accordance with overall State objectives.
>
> .   .   .   .   .
>
> The administration's principal objection to statewide planning is that Governors have limited responsibility for and experience in law enforcement and are primarily concerned with the State police and their involvement in traffic control. (Emphasis added.)[52]

With respect to the Congressman's last point, it is worth repeating that no one objects to statewide planning. The question is how can that goal be best accomplished.

The discourse on this issue has tended to focus on the extent of state activities in the law enforcement and criminal justice field. The Attorney General has argued in this regard: "When you look at the state governments and look at their involvement in local law enforcement, you will see that it is almost nil."[53] Congressman Cahill has replied that "many Governors have sig-

---

50   H.R. 5037, § 102, 90th Cong., 1st Sess. (1967).
51   *House Hearings* 56.
52   HOUSE COMM. REP. 31.
53   *House Hearings* 65.

nificant roles in law enforcement and criminal justice."[54] With the exception of the operation of the courts and correctional systems, the Attorney General has much the better argument. But it has not been made clear why the nature and extent of present state involvement in law enforcement are relevant. The fact that state governments are or are not heavily engaged in law enforcement activities certainly directly affects the need of such governments for financial aid. It relates to the structuring of the grant program, however, only in a more indirect fashion.

In the first place, the extent of present state involvement in this area may affect the willingness of local governments to accept direction from the states. If, as the Attorney General suggests, state governments have not previously been very active in law enforcement, the problem of outside control of local law enforcement may be just as serious where the state government is attempting to provide direction as where the federal government uses the power of the purse for that purpose. For example, a local police chief might find it just as objectionable to be instructed by the state attorney general as by the U.S. Attorney General. Indeed, from the point of view of local government, the problem of control from outside may be more serious where the state government distributes the funds. By the very nature of things, state officials are likely to attempt to exercise tighter control than would federal officers, for they are closer to the scene. Whether this proximity is sufficient to justify greater intervention in local affairs, however, is debatable. Also, state officials have responsibility for a much smaller area and population than does the federal government. Such a factor, on the one hand, permits closer attention to what needs to be done; on the other, it makes probable much greater interference with essentially local control. The possibilities for a takeover of the details of local law enforcement operations, as distinguished from the type of selective control previously described, will be much greater where the effective grantor is the state rather than the federal government. This is particularly true where there are already aspects of the system traditionally operated by the states — courts and corrections. Thus, the possibility of the growth of true state police forces throughout the country under such an approach is not an unreal one. There are many who would consider such a development almost as bad as the idea of a national police force.

There is also the problem of existing friction between state and local government. It is, of course, present in some parts of the country and absent in others. This may reflect inter-party tensions — some of our larger cities are run by administrations of one party while the state houses are in the hands of the other party — or simply result from the fact that state and local governments continually come into contact and often conflict on many issues — for example, division of state tax revenues. The fact of closer contact, however, may also cut the other way. The balance of state politics may permit a local government to influence the administration of the grant program more easily where it is operated by the state.

Friction, of course, can also exist on the federal level, but historically there

54 HOUSE COMM. REP. 31.

have been fewer contacts between local government and Washington and therefore fewer conflicts. This pattern has been changing under recent federal grant
programs, and it may be that the problem on the federal level will grow worse.
Oddly, the fact that the basic decision making occurs in Washington may, at least
from the point of view of the Congress, ease the problem. For, if such friction develops, Congress can have a large impact in resolving the conflict. Giving the
primary responsibility to the states, however, may, in a sense, dilute or at least
adversely affect potential congressional influence over the tone of the program.

The nature and extent of existing state involvement in law enforcement
activities may be thought to affect the capability of the states to handle the
grant-making function. That involvement, limited in most states, has nowhere
involved state-wide planning or coordination of police activities. Nor, more
importantly, has it had anything at all to do with the discretionary distribution
of financial aid to local law enforcement. The states would thus come to this
activity with no significant background in grant making. To implement the
House bill they would be required to "tool up" quickly, to establish an office,
and to hire specialized personnel. Major legislative as well as executive decisions
would be necessary. A considerable effort would thus be required. For each
individual state, though, the task would not be insuperable. The planning committees initiated at the President's call in 1966 might provide the nucleus of the
operation, and some states have already taken legislative action to authorize such
an office. The California legislature, for example, recently established the California Council on Criminal Justice[55] to, *inter alia*, "develop plans to fulfill the
requirements of any federal act providing for the adoption of comprehensive plans
to facilitate the receipt and allocation of federal funds . . . ."[56]

Looking to the larger picture, however, it is too much to expect each of
the fifty states to tool up an adequate operation in the near future. The task
of staffing fifty such offices in a relatively short period of time seems an impossible
one. Indeed, one of the large, pervasive problems currently being faced in attempts to implement the Commission's recommendations is that of finding qualified personnel adequately trained in the problems of police, courts, and corrections. All of this is not to say that it will not be possible eventually to develop
and staff such an operation. To condition the entire program on the existence
of comprehensive state plans and to rely on the states to engage in the actual
distribution of the federal money, however, would cause intolerable delays in
implementing the grant program.

The House bill contains a provision that is apparently designed to meet
this problem;[57] if so, it fails miserably. It gives a state three months after the
effective date of the act to establish a state planning agency and six months after
the establishment of the state planning agency to file a comprehensive plan.
If these deadlines are not met, the Attorney General is authorized to make grants
directly to local governments. The deadlines, however, are unrealistic, although
the likelihood is that they will be met. Thus, this approach puts a premium

---

55 CAL. PENAL CODE § 13800 (1967).
56 *Id.* § 13806.
57 H.R. 5037, § 305, *supra* note 50.

on haste and sloppiness. Moreover, it is not just that the deadlines are wrong. Any time period will impose an unrealistic limitation on what ought to be a continuing planning process.

The objection may be made that the federal government also lacks experience in this field and will have to "tool up." But there are significant differences. The federal government has for almost three years been making grants to local law enforcement agencies and others under the Law Enforcement Assistance Act of 1965. During this period the Office of Law Enforcement Assistance has distributed approximately seven million dollars annually for research and a variety of experimental and demonstration projects to improve law enforcement and criminal justice operations.[58] It has a staff of more than twenty-five persons who have already built up a wealth of experience and expertise in this new field of grant making. Not only is the federal government more advanced in its preparations to undertake a large-scale grant-making program, but it is undoubtedly more feasible to quickly staff and organize a single, central office than it is to build up fifty such operations. Finally, there are some particular practical disadvantages in using the states as conduits for the funds. The money involved in such a program would necessarily pass through more hands. And more opportunities for bureaucratic mistake, mishandling, corruption, or delay would thereby be created.

Although a case can be made for enlarging the state's role in the grant program — in order to encourage statewide planning and coordination, to build diversity into the program, and to beef up operations on the state level — it is submitted that an approach that gives state governments the primary responsibility for distributing funds to local governments is bound to fragment and complicate the implementation of the program and hinder the progress of its development. It is suggested, however, that one can foresee how, at some future date, a state office might reach a level of operation where it could perform the distribution function as well as a federal office. Perhaps the answer then is to establish initially a federally-controlled program but to build into it a feature whereby, after a period of time, the federal office would hand over certain authority to a state operation that met specified criteria.[59]

V. Conclusion

One must be enough of a political realist to recognize that no matter how persuasive the arguments concerning the proper functioning of the program, there are other factors that weigh heavily in the legislative balance scale. And

---

58 *House Hearings* 33.
59 This approach might be viewed as the reverse of the provision of the House act that gave the federal government a power of reverter where the state failed to file a comprehensive plan. It is not clear under that provision whether, once a state fails to meet the deadline, the power of the federal government continues throughout the existence of the program or whether a late-applying state can re-obtain the power of distribution.
There are other possible compromises on the state control issue. The bill reported out by the House committee provided for submission of all applications to the chief executive of the state. Other grant legislation contains a governor's veto provision, *e.g.*, the Economic Opportunity Act. That legislation was amended in 1965 to give the Director of the OEO authority to override a veto by a governor.

what are those other factors? To cite just a few, political ideology no doubt plays a role for some. For others, the issue may be viewed as a simple question of raw political power. Where is it best to locate the power that will accompany the distribution of the funds that will be involved in this program? For still others, the matter may somehow be tied to civil rights issues. Based upon a civil rights criterion, is a federal or a state-oriented program preferable? Finally, there will be some for whom the state-federal control issue is itself not a matter of great importance. Rather, the question will present the opportunity to score political points or to trade off on other matters of legislative importance. An illustration in point is the fact that the full Senate Judiciary Committee recently reported out the Safe Streets measure with a new Title II containing provisions attempting, among other things, to overrule Supreme Court decisions in *Miranda v. Arizona*,[60] *United States v. Wade*,[61] and *Mallory v. United States*.[62]

Perhaps it is too much to ask that such considerations be ignored. For the legislative process is, after all, a process of compromise and adjustment in which the circle of relevance may be deemed very wide indeed. We can only hope that, whatever the reasoning, the resulting legislation will quickly be enacted in a form that will create a program well structured to "increase the effectiveness, fairness, and coordination of law enforcement and criminal justice systems at all levels of government."[63]

---

60   384 U.S. 436 (1966).
61   388 U.S. 218 (1967).
62   354 U.S. 449 (1957).
63   H.R. 5037, preamble, *supra* note 50.

STATE AND LOCAL GOVERNMENT CRIME CONTROL

Eliot H. Lumbard*

I. Introduction

(Control of crime is a difficult, complicated task, requiring deep commitment and day-to-day involvement by government.) For reasons rooted in their past, states generally have not assumed that full role. For reasons rushing at them, states must assume that role in the future since only they can blend the necessary twentieth century crime control mix: legal power, intimate local knowledge and involvement, financial resources, geographic spread, and political leadership.

Blending that proper "mix" is one of the most important matters in this country. For crime control in America is in trouble, however its performance is measured. Statistics, public opinion, political leadership, official agencies — our antennae — all tell us that. Strengthened state action, including new state agency structures and stronger leadership of local efforts, represents the most promising direction for major improvement of crime control in America. Federal and local government action can offer no similar prospects.

II. The States

Most state capitols are lovely old buildings with a smell of history and located squarely in the middle of a large tree-shaded block. Governors and state legislatures are quartered there, but to resist influence, the state's highest court usually meets elsewhere. Indeed, governors and legislatures are in the middle — caught between today's mushrooming crime problems and their primary responsibility for the system of administering criminal justice. Until the mid-sixties they did not overly concern themselves with the system other than to make state laws defining criminal conduct or delineating system procedures. Today's challenges lie on other ground. If there is to be significant change in crime control, there must be significant change in the understanding, attitudes, and involvement of governors and legislatures regarding the entire criminal justice system in their states. System strength or weakness starts with their motivation and commitment. Some have assumed that role. Their desks properly have become the command posts of crime control in their states.

The primary reason for the importance of the states' involvement in fighting crime is their legal power, which is reflected by the United States Constitution, and which is basic to our federal form of government. Each state is the central repository of all legal power within its borders. The national central government has only those powers specifically delegated to it by the states; to put it another way, those powers not granted in the Constitution are reserved to the states by the tenth amendment.[1] Local police powers or control of criminal justice in the states

---

* New York, New York. Former special counsel on law enforcement to Governor Nelson Rockefeller of New York.
1 U.S. CONST. amend. X.

was never delegated. While generations of court decisions and a greatly expanded concept of federal action have resulted in some confusion about this concept, it remains firm nonetheless. Thus, the *federal* government is confined to acting only as it is specifically *empowered* to act by federal constitutional provision or court interpretation; *states* are free to act except as specifically *prohibited* by the federal and their own constitutions or court interpretation; and *local* governments are confined to acting only as they are specifically *authorized* by their state or court interpretations. The middle of that legal sandwich is the state.

The states in turn have traditionally delegated almost all criminal justice system responsibilities to their subordinate local governments, including villages, towns, cities, or counties. Complex networks of legal authority, varying in detail between states, have established this delegation. Largely they reflect an outmoded system that grew out of rural eighteenth century America. Two centuries ago, locally operated crime control made good sense when crimes were elementary, involved only family or well-known neighbors harming each other, and travel was both a great burden and an unknown luxury. People spent their lives within a locus of a few miles.

More recently, however, a strong trend coinciding with urbanization has seen the states gradually take back many of the powers they earlier had delegated to local governments. It has been a troublesome course all the way. Starting first with corrections, where the sheer impracticality of small local governments trying to incarcerate a handful of long-term prisoners was apparent, a steady and increasing state responsibility has been assumed for criminal justice system functions. That part of the system concerned with convicted offenders is primarily under state control today. Now, with mounting tempo, the trend toward state centralization of crime control functions is embracing district attorneys, the criminal courts and, increasingly, local police (commencing with training and personnel standards).

Although, to be sure, wide variances exist between states in their criminal justice systems, the trend of strengthened state action is everywhere obvious. Moreover, we have only started to understand immense potential benefits to be gained from interstate compacts or other forms of interstate and regional agreement or cooperation. Interstate compacts now exist for supervision of parolees and probationers (including out-of-state confinement arrangements) and juvenile problems. There are formal agreements for clearing detainers lodged against prisoners and for fresh pursuit across government lines. Uniform state acts exist for extradition and for obtaining out-of-state witnesses.[2]

But another major step is necessarily ahead. The reason is simple: in today's America, local governments cannot do the job. Awareness of this regrettable fact is beginning to sink down to the marrow. Eighty-three percent of reported

---

2 *See* COUNCIL OF STATE GOVERNMENTS, HANDBOOK ON INTERSTATE CRIME CONTROL (1966). One example of interstate cooperation is the New England State Police Compact, initiated on December 14, 1967, when the attorneys general of five New England states signed an agreement of cooperation to combat organized crime. More than words appear to be involved for a central staff is established, and they will jointly collect and share information.

crime is in the 212 Standard Metropolitan Statistical Areas,[3] but their crime control abilities under present circumstances are shrinking.

III.   Local Governments

Why crime control is slipping away from the effective grasp of urban and suburban local governments is not complicated. First, the sheer complexity of current tasks overwhelms their abilities, along with a quickening pace of change through court decisions[4] and the momentum of general urban drift. The complexity is not lessened when well-meaning but ill-informed critics shower the overburdened few who administer the systems with a cascade of suggestions. Rural areas are under far less pressure in this regard.

Second, since local governments are dependent primarily on a local realty tax, they do not have a sufficiently broad tax base, as do the state and federal governments, to support necessary efforts at crime control. Police, incidentally, apparently now receive a smaller proportion of local budgets than sixty years ago. There is little hope for change in this area, since few officials will risk political suicide by expanding local tax powers.

Third, local governments are chronically plagued with questions of jurisdiction over local policing with consequent fragmentation of action and accountability.[5] Tiny police agencies of two, ten, twenty men attempt rather poorly to communicate and cooperate on an operational level. They are usually so weak that modern police service is beyond their capabilities. Information is not shared routinely; services often overlap.[6] While their web is complicated, it is also full of holes.[7]

---

3   THE CHALLENGE OF CRIME IN A FREE SOCIETY, A REPORT BY THE PRESIDENT'S COMMISSION ON LAW ENFORCEMENT AND ADMINISTRATION OF JUSTICE 119 (1967) [hereinafter cited as CRIME REPORT].

4   *E.g.,* Katz v. United States, 389 U.S. 347 (1967); Berger v. New York, 388 U.S. 41 (1967); Miranda v. Arizona, 384 U.S. 436 (1967).

5   The machinery of law enforcement in this country is fragmented, complicated and frequently overlapping. America is essentially a nation of small police forces, each operating independently within the limits of its jurisdiction. The boundaries that define and limit police operations do not hinder the movement of criminals, of course. They can and do take advantage of ancient political and geographic boundaries, which often give them sanctuary from effective police activity. CRIME REPORT 119.

6   The President's Commission demonstrates just how widespread this particular problem is: in 1960, almost 117 million people, about 70 percent of our population, resided in America's 18,000 cities. Of these, almost 113 million persons, 63 percent of our population, resided in the 212 areas designated by the Bureau of the Census as Standard Metropolitan Statistical Areas. According to FBI reports, approximately 83 percent of Part I crimes committed in the United States in 1965 were committed in these SMSA's. These 212 sprawling, metropolitan areas comprise 313 counties and 4,144 cities, each of which has its own police force. The majority of these departments are small and have only limited facilities services. Thus, the responsibility for dealing with most of the serious crime in this country is diffused among the multitude of independent agencies that have little contact with neighboring forces. *Id.*

7   An enormous structure proves Parkinson's Law once again.
        There are at least five strata of police services in America: (1) police agencies of the federal government; (2) state police forces and criminal investigation agencies; (3) sheriffs and their deputies in over 3,000 counties; plus a few county police forces which either duplicate the sheriff's jurisdiction or displace it; (4) police departments of a thousand cities and over 20,000 townships or New England towns; (5) the police of 15,000 villages, boroughs and incorporated towns. . . . This means that at the present time there are over 40,000 separate law enforcement agencies in the United States with a total personnel of about 420,000. Peterson, *Local and State Law Enforcement Today,* in CURRENT HISTORY, July, 1967, at 8.

Fourth, "people pressures" are increasing. Our population is exploding and forcing new kinds of volume problems on the system. Regrettably new jails follow new schools as a matter of statistical inevitability. Moreover, our population has gained extraordinary mobility. As it moves, so do criminal offenders. While "breakfast in New York and dinner in San Francisco" is an attractive cliché, interstate and large-scale, "white-collar" crimes are not fiction. Mobility on wheels is commonplace; when automobiles whip through many police jurisdictions on limited-access highways at the rate of one every two or three minutes, enforcement efforts cannot react adequately. Only in rural areas is relative stability of population characteristic.

Fifth, personnel in crime control agencies have not been strengthened in number or quality as the agencies' challenges have grown increasingly complex. Current recruiting is very difficult. All too often top brass and middle management — the most important roles — are unable to provide a high order of consistent leadership. They reflect a generation of only haphazard attention to personnel and the fact that tightening civil service strictures, in effect, confine future leadership almost exclusively to those drawn in as recruits. Local political realities straightjacket local governments so as to almost foreclose change.

Thus, our primarily local system of administering criminal justice is coming apart in heavy population areas. The system theory is still idealistic — even romantic — and grand. The old system practice is often so disastrous as to raise a real question of whether it can survive the pressures of enormous volume and loss of individual identity amidst mass system bureaucracy. And what local governments need by way of crime control machinery and finances, they must obtain through state action. Adaptation of our original rural system to present urban challenges, therefore, can only come from governors and legislatures.

IV. The Need for Change and the Resistance Thereto

These forces necessitating change in the crime control system are inexorable and swelling. Even though there is deep concern about the crime problem, these forces are still not now part of the American consciousness. In frustration the public is inclined to seek massive federal involvement or confine their thoughts about remedies to local government agencies. Most do not realize the constitutional limitations to federal action in this area or the threat to their liberty that would be posed by a massive, unified federal crime control apparatus.

By comparison, public education issues are widely understood. This understanding is the foundation of significant and wholehearted public acceptance of strong state direction to local education. Almost universally, the American public education formula consists of (1) state standard-setting, (2) state inspection to insure compliance with those standards, (3) some form of substantial financial aid from the state, while leaving (4) control and (5) administration in local hands sensitive to local conditions. That should be the formula for modern crime control. It evolved in the system of education for much the same reasons that crime control systems need revamping. Several generations ago, the public struggled to the decision that purely local educational efforts simply could not consistently develop the quality education it deeply desired. Crime control has arrived at the same troubled threshold some eighty years later. It now needs structural overhaul.

Change in the crime control system, however, is resisted for several reasons. Largely, those working in the system resist change under the misguided assumption that they need to protect themselves — and that means protecting the status quo. They say the system has served well in the past, and it has if one looks way back. They say change for change's sake is useless, and of course they are right. They say change is disruptive and raises problems in and of itself, and here too they are right in the abstract. Those working in the criminal justice system rationalize in all manner of means their insecurity, vested interest, or fear of change, although it is obvious that any increased effort will require their services.[8] Their opposition inordinately influences legislators and other government officials to resist change.

These fears of the government employees directly involved lay a dead hand on reform, especially since criminal justice agencies have no tradition of welcoming new ideas and risking new actions.[9] These agencies are security minded by nature and made more conservative by the essence of their daily activities to enforce law. Few believe way down that there can be any big new changes in the system; they accept what is. Yet, as illustrated by a recent example, reform is not impossible. Several recent, and entirely different, developments in New York State were first greeted with astonishment by a sizeable segment of the system. But now they are embraced in the Narcotics Addiction Control Council[10] (which includes a program for up to three-year mandatory civil commitment, among others[11]), and in the State Identification and Intelligence System[12] (a large computer-based information sharing system for all criminal justice agencies, as well as a sizeable research and innovative effort). Studies for these new state agencies showed that today's crime control problems do not fit yesterday's patterns. Only surgery, not band-aids, will do.

Many citizens also object to any state ("outsider") involvement in local government as an interference with "home rule," although their wives could not care less about philosophy if change may result in better protection from crime. Nevertheless, persons in public life do not underestimate the political sock of home rule appeals.

Deep down, the general public may have another and more fundamental uneasiness about changing any aspect of their crime control system. There is a general need, especially in rapidly moving and troubled times, to look on crime control as an essential element of stability in our society. Indeed some feel the whole system apparatus of police, courts and law is government's main stabilizing influence amidst an increasingly secular and turbulent population. Thus, that apparatus must itself be stable; and because it must be stable it should be un-

---

8   *See, e.g.*, N.Y. Exec. Law § 483 (b)-(d) (McKinney Supp. 1967).
9   Crime Report 291.
10   This commission was created pursuant to N.Y. Mental Hygiene Law § 203 (McKinney Supp. 1967).
11   *Id.* § 206(5)(b).
12   This system was created pursuant to N.Y. Exec. Law § 602 (McKinney Supp. 1967).

changing. Therefore, crime control innovation meets deep emotional resistance. The premise, however, is wrong: while maintenance of stability in society certainly is a prime objective of law and any crime control system, neither the law, the system, nor its agencies have ever been static in and of themselves. What human endeavors are static? Or could be? Recent momentous legal changes should not obscure understanding that system elements also are in flux. This is worthy of exploration.

Even grand juries provide an example of variation and controversy. In some states, including New York, they are thought to be the essence of stability. But only in some fifty percent of American states are grand juries now used to charge defendants with crime. The remainder of the world, including Mother England, functions entirely without them. Ironically, in some localities where grand juries are supported for their superior investigative possibilities, organized crime has become most deeply entrenched. In some cities, corrupt use of grand juries in tandem with corrupt prosecutors provides the most enslaving governmental instrument know in this country.

No better illustration of variety in crime control agencies exists than the unceasing adjustment to different conditions of what we now call "the police function." A brief recollection of the history of criminal law enforcement in the United States also refutes the premise that stability precludes change. Vigilantes and posses have almost disappeared; the importance of sheriffs has decreased substantially in the cities. In short, there is no set way in which criminal justice has been administered.

Consider as well enormous shifts in the very objectives of law as a social control tool. Criminal law before the Revolution was to enforce the morals and religion of the people.[13] Society became more secular, and legal emphasis shifted to protecting its "peace and safety."[14] Government's role thus veered from neutral arbiter of contests between private citizens[15] to active advocate of public order.[16] But the public is almost totally unaware of the rate and nature of change engulfing efforts to maintain law and order. They believe — and they want to believe — that crime control is a stable foundation of government, which it is, and solidly unchanging, which it is not.

V. The States

At all times the only central control point for American police development has been the state capitol. Permission for local police to develop, change, and withdraw was granted, rejected, or taken back in that building. All other criminal justice system elements were similarly controlled.[17] The federal government, due to constitutional limitations, has no power to affect these events in any consequential way.

---

13   Nelson, *Emerging Notions of Modern Criminal Law in the Revolutionary Era: An Historical Perspective*, 42 N.Y.U.L. REV. 450, 451 (1967).
14   *Id.* at 462.
15   *Id.* at 468.
16   *Id.* at 470-81.
17   *See* LEWIS, FROM NEWGATE TO DANNEMORA: THE RISE OF THE PENITENTIARY IN NEW YORK, 1796-1848 (1965).

By and large, state governments minimized their crime control responsibilities until the past five years or so. Somewhat earlier, in 1959, the key turn was made without realizing its future significance. Under Governor Nelson Rocke-feller's urging, New York became the first state to order local police training standards. That law was passed to end the practice of giving new policemen guns and arrest powers, without an hour's instruction about how to use those drastic weapons of force. Actually the law was a breakthrough, for thereafter states throughout the nation began establishing standards for local police and other criminal justice agencies.

Nowhere has the turn been so dramatic as in Florida. While New York State has a tradition of strong government and action to match its deep concern with criminal justice, Florida is an unfortunate example of the opposite tradition. It had the same constitutional provision as New York, mandating that "the Governor shall take care that the laws be faithfully executed,"[18] but Florida's conception of that duty could hardly have been more different. Florida has been in the grip of two forces: total unbroken domination by one party for 100 years; and such fear of power in a strong Florida state government which might *do* something that almost no power has been given the state government to do much of anything. For no function was this more true than criminal justice. Basic, reliable statistical information simply is not available; criminal justice system costs, workload, manpower, or effectiveness, for example, cannot be analyzed.

Executive leadership is split among seven officials, elected state-wide, con-stituting a "Cabinet" whose meetings appear on live television every week. These officials compete politically. Florida has no civil service of any consequence and no informative or program budget process. There is a trained and equipped highway patrol, but until recently it was confined to traffic offenses on Florida's highways. Outside investigators could enter a county only upon specific invita-tion from the local sheriff. The governor had no investigative personnel available to him for general criminal investigatory purposes, not even to inquire into corruption charges so he could take care that the laws be faithfully executed. Florida also had enormous fragmentation, including 67 separate county sheriffs and 438 separate police departments, ranging from two to two thousand men.

Between 1950 and 1960 Florida was catapulted into the twentieth century, ready or not. Many retired Northerners moved in. Now Florida has the nation's fastest growing population, ranking eighth. Industry moved in also. Cape Kennedy brought the space age. Tourism numbers some 19,000,000 annually. Urban areas grew. And crime followed suit, with Florida ranking fourth in the nation during 1966 for its rate of serious crimes per 100,000 population (behind only California, New York, and Nevada).

In 1966 Claude R. Kirk Jr., a Republican, was elected Governor. Shock resulted. His anti-crime campaign had brought him an avalanche of citizen requests for action about inefficiency, suspected local officials, and organized crime. But how were these piles of citizen complaints to be investigated? Florida's government provided no answer. So with funds contributed by his

18 FLORIDA CONST. art. IV, § 6.

supporters to a trust fund, Governor Kirk hired the Wackenhut Corporation, a private Miami guard and investigative service, to investigate the complaints. Troubled voices instantly were raised at mixing public police functions and private contractors.[19]

When the legislature convened in 1967, Kirk asked for a strong state organization of broad scope — a Florida Department of Criminal Justice — that would enable him to take necessary action within government channels and obviate the need for private expedients. Democrats controlled the legislature and they simply balked at any strong state role for criminal justice administration. They did not want Florida governors with strong executive powers or, particularly, investigative powers regarding local government improprieties or criminal justice officials themselves; nor did the sheriffs, who led opposition to any change they could not control.

After maneuver and struggle, the legislature passed a bill with far less impact than the one Kirk requested. Several days after the legislative session ended Kirk vetoed the bill, precipitating a crisis over the issue, and called a special session with a charge that included action about crime control. Public pressure increased. It was clear some action had to be taken. What emerged was a legislative chameleon establishing a Bureau of Law Enforcement. Nevertheless, the bill definitely was much better than nothing. The new state law enforcement agency now has rudimentary legal tools, jurisdiction to rove the state, and is charged with strengthening and coordinating crime control throughout Florida. Other laws established many related programs, including a police standards council and turning the highway patrol into a state police. A course has been set toward stronger state action. Muscles, money, and know-how are gathering.

What happened in Florida during 1967 is significant of several national trends: mushrooming political pressures to strengthen crime control generated by enormous public concern about crime; the inability — even groping — of most local governments to organize meaningful action; and serious strengthening of state-level concern, authority and efforts. The crime control focus finally has turned to the state capitol.

VI. The Federal Government

But why, many ask, is not creation of an all-powerful federal monolith a more efficient and simpler course to follow? A logical question with a logical answer: the federal government, for various reasons, cannot do what needs to be done.

First, and most directly, federal legal power is so limited as to foreclose any serious proposals for federal supervision or control of state and local criminal justice systems.

Second, there is absolutely no reason to believe the very large bureaucracy

---

19   Even the President's Crime Commission criticized this. *See* PRESIDENT'S COMMISSION ON LAW ENFORCEMENT AND ADMINISTRATION OF JUSTICE, TASK FORCE REPORT: THE POLICE 215 (1967).

necessary for such purposes would be efficient — or simple. Every lesson from Washington is to the contrary.

Third, almost no one wants to experience the Orwellian "1984" problems sure to arise with the monolith. Other than the military, no units of government represent a greater potential threat to individual liberty than law enforcement agencies. Step one in avoiding such troubles is to keep the nation's powers diffused according to present constitutional divisions.[20]

Fourth, federal agencies are minute by comparison with the overall task. Already burdened with their present duties, they could not begin to assume broad supervision without tremendous expansion.[21]

A fifth reason is that federal agencies offer no glittering potential for aid outside their present limited assignments. Some states do not now have adequate planning expertise, true, yet neither does the federal government except in a few narrow specialty areas within its jurisdiction (especially organized and white-collar crime). Able as those people are, that is the extent of it. No one in Washington is known for competence, for example, to advise San Francisco on prostitution policy problems arising from tides of servicemen flowing out to war in Vietnam and returning with a big binge in mind. Washington, D.C., as a federal jurisdiction, has enormous policing, court, and correctional problems and currently is no one's guide to crime control success. To administer the small although valuable Federal Law Enforcement Assistance Act grant program, it was necessary for the Department of Justice to set up a new office with new procedures and recruit outsiders to process applications. There are no superior crime control planners in Washington that can best order the affairs of state and local governments. Building from scratch can be done equally well by state and local officials, perhaps better.

Sixth, crime control is most creative today, far and away, on state and the larger local government levels. No wellspring of federal innovation is observable. Conservatism, caution, fear of change, fear to risk failures in research and experimentation — endemic to this field — are more characteristic of federal agencies.

Seventh, the federal government has yet to organize itself adequately. The twenty-six different federal investigative agencies have no communal home,

---

20   The Federal Government must never assume the role of the Nation's policeman. True the Federal Government has certain direct law enforcement responsibilities. But these are carefully limited to such matters as treason, espionage, counterfeiting, tax evasion and certain interstate crimes.
        Crime is essentially a local matter. Police operations—if they are to be effective and responsible—must likewise remain basically local. This is the fundamental premise of our constitutional structure of our heritage of liberty. THE CHALLENGE OF CRIME TO OUR SOCIETY, H.R. Doc. No. 250, 90th Cong., 2d Sess. 4 (1968) (remarks of President Johnson).
21   For example, nationally, crime control agencies cost taxpayers some $7 billion by my estimate; yet all federal efforts now only total something over $400 million, less than New York's police department. Federal investigative agents apparently do not number over 20,000 (some 6,500 FBI special agents include many assigned to investigate duties other than law enforcement: internal security, anti-trust, and civil cases such as under the Federal Tort Claims Act). In 1966 there were only 29,729 federal criminal cases filed in all United States District Courts, while New York County District Attorney Frank Hogan's office alone files some 60,000 cases yearly. Of the 425,000 Americans in custody every day, only some 19,500 are under supervision of the Federal Bureau of Prisons. CRIME REPORT 172.

are not known for brotherly love or any kind of sharing, and do not even assemble at the dinner table to carve the budget (or indeed assemble in any room at any time). Their example provides no leadership for necessary local police consolidation or pooling. But there is hope for improvement in the organization of these agencies. In his 1968 Special Message on Crime Control, President Johnson announced that he had issued an executive order authorizing the Attorney General to "coordinate" federal efforts at crime control.[22] This is only a half-step, however, in the right direction of administrative unity, since it will apply only to narcotics enforcement. In other areas serious agency fragmentation will apparently continue. These problems of coordination and cooperation among the federal agencies are not confined to crime control. Frustration with federal funding approaches is widespread, arising from the status quo mentality (peculiarly applicable to the federal law enforcement establishment), administrative structure, political mires, the impossibility today of obtaining congressional attention to anything other than major national emergencies, and problems in moving the bureaucracy.

Vintage New Deal liberals have added their support to the deep-seated forces around the nation that are now working to strengthen state governments. Their reasons are many; some are outlined above, others are variations.[23]

Practical manageability of federal affairs is central to everyone's concern. Size alone becomes a special bureaucratic problem. A widely supported view holds that states are as close to the people as it is feasible to have major government entities in a population of 200 million and still maintain necessary political strength to negotiate meaningfully with the federal government. Recent experience with actual field results and administrative snarls in all manner of programs, including housing, welfare, poverty, and education, has convinced many that Washington cannot successfully administer or supervise what are the traditional local government services; immediate decisions (distinct from broadest policy making) are too far removed from people and problems, neither of whom can seem to participate in or shape federal decisions often enough. And several thousand local governments cannot inform or be informed by, or successfully grapple with, the mammoth federal disbursing agencies. The average county or city is lost in the federal shuffle and often loses out to lobbying efforts of large cities, whereas states are manageable intermediaries with political power understood and felt in Washington.

Given this context, however, what can the federal government do to improve everyday safety on American streets? Money is the answer.[24] Broad-based

---

22   H.R. Doc. No. 250, 90th Cong., 2d Sess. 8 (1968).
23   An outstanding study was recently published by North Carolina's former governor, Terry Sanford. SANFORD, STORM OVER THE STATES (1967).
24   They [the American people] recognize that the frontline headquarters against crime is in the home, in the church, in the City Hall, and county courthouse and State house—not in the far-removed National Capital of Washington.
        But the people also recognize that the national government can and the national government should help the cities and the States in their war on crime to the full extent of its resources and its constitutional authority. And this we shall do. PRESIDENT JOHNSON, THE STATE OF THE UNION, H.R. Doc. No. 211, 90th Cong., 2d Sess. 7 (1968).

federal tax income can provide desperately needed financial assistance to state and local performance of their tasks.

VII. Federal Funding of State and Local Crime Control

Essential to future understanding of the federal funding approach will be the current history of President Johnson's proposed Safe Streets and Crime Control Act of 1967[25] and Juvenile Delinquency Prevention Act of 1967.[26] Great issues were raised by these proposals, although not widely recognized as such.

The President's plan was to vastly expand the federal government's role in areas of traditional local police power, tenth amendment or not. New federal funding programs ($50,000,000 and $25,000,000, respectively) for *both* state and local crime control were to be the mechanical devices. Recommendations by the President's Commission on Law Enforcement and Administration of Justice were to be used as the rationale. The President wanted to give the Attorney General tremendous power to control the money flow and thereby demand compliance by state and local officials with his edicts.[27] It was no secret, for example, that federal funds were to be used as incentives for consolidating police departments.

Significantly, the President's Commission had *not* said *how* the grants should be made.[28] Nor had it analyzed the political forces and governmental structure absolutely necessary for reforming, supporting, and directing crime control efforts, as the Commission itself stated.[29] These foundations are far more important to improving public protection than sprouting dozens of programs without a seed bed or fertilizer for crime control results only from government action. This omission ranks as the Commission's greatest failure, along with conveying almost no sense of priorities amidst its mass of over 200 recommendations.

Moreover, no language of the Commission supported the novel federal control aspects in the President's bill.[30] No similar proposal by a major public body or figure comes to mind. Here, an historic change in local police powers and federalism was proposed by surprise and without political preparation or proof that such a turn would either be effective to fight crime in local communities or be so administered as to allay fears of bureaucracy or intrusion. The federal government was coming with more than money.

Specifically, the President's Commission carefully confined its recommendations: " . . . the Federal Government can make a dramatic new contribution . . .

---

25   H.R. 5037, 90th Cong., 1st Sess. (1967).
26   H.R. 12120, 90th Cong., 1st Sess. (1967).
27   Attorney General Ramsey Clark described that power as "federal guidance" to the National Association of Attorneys General. Clark, *For the Advance of Criminal Justice*, in COUNCIL OF STATE GOVERNMENTS, STATE GOVERNMENT NEWS, 1967, at 138.
28   CRIME REPORT 283-88.
29   *Id.* at 279.
30   Indeed, the Crime Report states:
    In proposing a major Federal program against crime, the Commission is mindful of the special importance of avoiding any invasion of State and local responsibility for law enforcement and criminal justice, and its recommendation is based on its judgment that Federal support and collaboration of the sort outlined below are consistent with scrupulous respect for—and indeed strengthening of—that responsibility. *Id.* at 285.

by greatly expanding its support of the agencies of justice in the States and in the cities."[31] In so concluding, the Commission said it " . . . is mindful of the special importance of avoiding any invasion of State and local responsibility . . . . "[32] By establishing this impetus for federal crime control funding, the Commission realized a great success. It ranks equally with the Commission's acceptance of the criminal justice system concept, its description of the organized crime iceberg (which made it politically possible to break a generation-old impasse on electronic eavesdropping), and its ordering of a basic mass of valuable material for common reference.[33]

Rebellion broke out in state capitols immediately after the President's contrary recommendation in the form of the Safe Streets bill was filed. Under state and local impetus, the rebellion spread to Congress. For reasons never disclosed, the states had not been consulted by the Administration during bill drafting of a funding program affecting them. Since there is no tradition of federal funding in this area, lack of drafting participation in the first effort of consequence was keenly felt. Anger was stirred among both political parties by the Administration's attitude regarding the bill's preparation, presentation, and subsequent "take-it-or-leave-it" rejection of all inquiries.

Moreover, the bill, as a funding device, had two other fatal defects to states: (1) While direct federal-local relationships would be encouraged according to the recent pattern of federal funding programs, they would create chaos in the special instance of crime control due to strong state legal responsibility. Responsibility, and the money to satisfy it, cannot be separated. (2) Both state and local *long-term* commitments would be encouraged under the bill for planning, new programs and agency expansion.

In 1967, however, the states were living the financial crisis of the President's new Medicaid program. Following his inducement formula of matching contributions, New York, for example, extended itself so as to obtain full benefits. Then rumbles grew that the President would retreat from his promises. That disaster indeed occurred by 1968, leaving states overly committed to local agencies. States were extremely wary of building another such edifice, especially under the name of crime control "planning." In the House Judiciary Committee and on the House floor, a coalition of Republicans and Southern Democrats were in command when the Safe Streets bill was debated during the 90th Congress, first session.[34] Their amendments radically changed the President's bill. The resulting Law Enforcement Assistance and Criminal Justice Assistance Act instead would fund states through direct *block grants* for crime control purposes,

31 *Id.*
32 *Id.* at 285.
33 For an outstanding, although sharply critical analysis, see Wilson, *The Crime Commission Reports*, in THE PUBLIC INTEREST, Fall, 1967, at 64.
34 The House Judiciary Committee attached about twenty-five amendments to the Safe Streets bill. 113 CONG. REC. 9794 (daily ed. Aug. 2, 1967) (remarks of Representative Poff). Even with these changes, however, the bill was still sharply criticized throughout the first session of the 90th Congress because of the control given to the Attorney General. *E.g.*, 113 CONG. REC. 9795 (daily ed. Aug. 2, 1967) (remarks of Representative Poff); *id.* at 9796 (remarks of Representative MacGregor); *id.* at 9797 (remarks of Representative Cahill); *id.* at 9802 (remarks of Representative Railsback); 113 CONG. REC. 9889 (daily ed. Aug. 3, 1967) (remarks of Representative Hutchinson); *id.* at 9896-97 (remarks of Representative Biester); 113 CONG. REC. 10069 (daily ed. Aug. 8, 1967) (remarks of Representative Cramer).

with funds roughly apportioned to population, and states allocating local grants.[35] To a chorus of "amens" the Attorney General was shunted to the side with a relatively mechanical role — and definitely without the control features.

Emphasis changed from federal-local to federal-state-local with minimum federal involvement. Most important, all program funds within each state would be channeled through the governor, who would be responsible for developing a state-wide plan for *all* state and local government criminal justice system considerations. Money would force a useful self-examination and cohesion at state levels. The general system approach for criminal justice agencies (a major thrust of the President's Commission) would be fostered to a far greater extent than federal-local relationships would allow. Local agency consolidations, if any, would not be ordered by federal officials.[36]

President Johnson's Safe Streets bill[37] had an even more torturous course in the Senate Judiciary Committee. Assigned to a subcommittee headed by Senator McClellan, the President's proposed bill immediately became the vehicle for struggles over many deep-seated emotional criminal justice reforms or retreats, depending on the participant. Among those subjects discussed were electronic surveillance, confessions, speed of arraignment, concern with ghetto riots, and federal court jurisdiction over state criminal convictions.[38] A so-called "Christmas tree" bill emerged from committee in December, 1967, with goodies for all committee members.[39] In the Senate, then, the bill really became a safety valve for pressures on Congress "to do something" about crime. A similar fate apparently awaits the President's companion proposal, the Juvenile Delinquency Control Act of 1967, which has passed the House with amendments providing direct block grants for states.[40]

Now that the second session of the 90th Congress has opened, it seems certain that some kind of federal-state block grant funding bill will pass, and whatever bill passes will be signed by the President. For he called again in his State of the Union[41] and 1968 Special Crime Message[42] for passage of his Safe Streets (with funding up to $100 million) and Juvenile Delinquency (with funding up to $25 million) bills. Congressional critics were certain they would pass their own versions, with or without Christmas tree ornaments. As amended, this funding program bears promise of truly historic events.

---

35 This version is contained in 113 CONG. REC. H10105-06 (daily ed. Aug. 8, 1967).
36 Oregon's Governor Thomas McCall is a former President of the Oregon Prison Association and especially sensitive and knowledgeable about the state crime control "mix." Last June he expressed the views of the states when he told the National Council on Crime and Delinquency, at its annual meeting in Anaheim, California:

> As Governor of Oregon, I heartily endorse both of these pieces of legislation [Safe Streets and Juvenile Control]. But this legislation must give strong and undeniable emphasis to the role of state government in the disbursement and allocation of federal funds. We have sufficient experience with federal programs at this point to realize that the state must have a much more direct role in undertaking the comprehensive planning and implementation for either [of the drafts then pending]. 13 CRIME AND DELINQUENCY 29 (1967).

37 S. 917, 90th Cong., 1st Sess. (1967).
38 113 CONG. REC. 17284-85 (daily ed. Nov. 28, 1967) (remarks of Senator McClellan).
39 113 CONG. REC. 17284 (daily ed. Nov. 28, 1967) (remarks of Senator McClellan).
40 113 CONG. REC. H12485-89 (daily ed. Sept. 26, 1967).
41 H.R. DOC. No. 211, 90th Cong., 2d Sess. 7-8 (1968).
42 H.R. DOC. No. 250, 90th Cong., 2d Sess. 5-6 (1968).

Demands for adequate crime control plans, and a flow of federal funds that must be allocated, will accelerate growing criminal justice awareness and competence in state capitals. Systems thinking will be accepted. As of today, however, more people, planning agencies, technicians, and know-how must be developed. Perhaps a dozen states have strong capabilities today; twenty-five have some form of planning agency. Force fed through their own government planning efforts, and other federal programs such as the Department of Housing and Urban Development's state planning impetus, capabilities for state-level planning are mushrooming. Overall they now surpass average large-city competence. Governors and their high priests in budget offices necessarily will become personally involved in new ways to strengthen crime control. They will ask the same kind of questions they now ask about education, health, transportation, and other functions; since answers will be few at first, they will demand the ability to generate answers for policy making. Thus the nexus will grow. Action will follow — *if there is meaningful funding*.

But meaningful funding is the present problem. Spread nationwide, $125 million budgeted to fund the crime control program is wholly insignificant to force these events or to make the slightest difference in a national strategy for a war on crime. National priorities are badly garbled when the President's proposed budget for fiscal 1969, on the other hand, would allot $4.4 billion for space exploration,[43] $5.6 billion for aid to farmers,[44] $2.5 billion for atomic energy development,[45] and $574 million for continuing research and development of a model supersonic transport plane (the "SST" project).[46] Moreover, the President's "program budget" lists ten individual analyses by function,[47] and another for interest on government debt;[48] symbolically, though, there is no major program category for crime, which is tucked away in a last catchall titled "General Government."[49] Thus, with proposed funding at $125 million the Administration's crime control program is but a gesture — a cruel illusion of protection and safety.[50] There is no serious relationship between that sum, what is actually needed, and the rhetoric from Washington about solemn commitments to *do* something meaningful about crime.[51]

VIII. Some Notes on Federal Funding

Radical change of the Safe Streets bill was a significant event in federal-state

43 THE BUDGET OF THE UNITED STATES GOVERNMENT: FISCAL YEAR 1969 at 99 (1968).
44 *Id.* at 102.
45 *Id.* at 90.
46 *Id.* at 119.
47 *Id.* at 80-167.
48 *Id.* at 168.
49 *Id.* at 169.
50 For example, the Safe Streets bill has been called "too little, too late, and too bad." 113 CONG. REC. 9796 (daily ed. Aug. 2, 1967) (remarks of Representative Cahill).
51 The Report of the President's Commission addresses this point:
     Every part of the system is undernourished. There is too little manpower and what there is is not well enough trained or well enough paid. Facilities and equipment are inadequate. Research programs that could lead to greater knowledge about crime and justice, and therefore to more effective operations, are almost nonexistent. To lament the increase in crime and at the same time to starve the agencies of law enforcement and justice is to whistle in the wind. CRIME REPORT 15.

relationships. But federal funding of any program must be employed wisely and carefully. In the 1960's a pattern had developed of direct federal grants to local governments. Changing attitudes toward state governments have led to changing attitudes toward inter-governmental financing techniques. There is much at stake: a fantastic variety of federal grant-in-aid programs has almost doubled from 1964 to today. A serious threat to federalism is presented by funds in this order of magnitude. Their pattern and control are of the greatest moment. For decision-making over funds means power over both money and grant regulations, and thus control.

Several months ago the prestigious Advisory Commission on Intergovernmental Relations reported its views on "Fiscal Balance in the American Federal System." Key recommendations were for block grants (to give recipients flexibility in meeting needs) and per capita revenue sharing ("general support") payments.[52] Many, many federal programs directly fund local governments, under severe federal "guidelines" (i.e., regulations and thus controls),[53] priorities, and "a comprehensive plan" covering multi-jurisdictional areas or problems. States may not even know what is happening. This is the routine Great Society funding approach. The new Department of Housing and Urban Development is the archetype of this new governmental technique, burgeoning out of the Bureau of the Budget.

Once started for a new funding program, this road is a one way street for states and local governments and leads to increasing subservience. Congress is hardly a routine action mechanism for their appeals. They have no choice but to go along, and few have the clout to do much about numberless petty decisions, paper work, duplications, and confusion. Pragmatically, they choose to save their clout for the big ones, and thereby default almost absolute power. They cannot allocate the money as they judge their needs; rather "the plan" controls. The end result is great and increasing federal control over local affairs, through funding, where the Constitution has never reached previously. Administrative costs mount and many programs bring precious little result to the life and neighborhoods of Americans.[54]

So more than crime control funding may have rounded the corner with the two crucial Safe Streets amendments: block grants and a change in emphasis from federal-local to federal-state-local funding. This was the first entirely new major federal funding program to be yanked totally out of the Administration's

---

52 Interestingly, a section of the main report released on Jan. 30, 1968, entitled "State Government—A New Frontier," concludes:

> It is becoming increasingly apparent that a considerable portion of the "infra-structure" of metropolitan problems is soluble only by state action . . . the independence or dependence provided in the inherent powers of local governments in metropolitan areas—all of these very crucial determinants of the social, political, and economic fate of central cities—is a matter of state constitutions or statutes. . . . COUNCIL OF STATE GOVERNMENTS, STATE GOVERMENT NEWS, Dec. 1957, at 11.

53 "And, whenever you have Federal money, you have Federal control." 113 CONG. REC. 9792 (daily ed. Aug. 2, 1967) (remarks of Representative Hebert).

54 Messrs. Piven and Cloward, both on the faculty of the Columbia School of Social Work, raise the interesting thesis that in the name of helping inner cities, these funding with guideline techniques actually will have a reverse effect:

> [T]he end result of this process is likely to be not "creative federalism" but the demise of local government and the submergence of the minority which now stands to gain most from localism—the Negro. THE NEW REPUBLIC, Oct. 7, 1967, at 19.

mushrooming pattern. Indeed, states should keep the pressure on to consolidate many other specialized federal grant-in-aid programs into simplified block grants to states. Their first task, however, is to make the new pattern serve crime control if the two funding bills become law.

IX. State and Local Priority Directions

The two basic critiques on crime control approaches in America point out the lack of coordination and integration within the crime control field.[55] While some diffusion is an inescapable price of federalism, there also is immense diffusion within each level of government. The latter is the point for concentration.

Divided command and operations are major weaknesses since the system elements are like a chain. A vast array of individual agencies operate the basic services: police forces, prosecutors' offices, criminal courts, probation offices, local jails and state institutions, parole boards, and additional numbers of auxiliary service agencies (coroners or medical examiners, medical and psychiatric services, and youth programs). Whatever their leadership or financing, all function in sequence; until the first has acted the others do not move. All are concerned with one defendant who passes from one service to another along with his files, for all need to know the same basic information about him (who he is, what he did, his backrgound). All are concerned with his one offense against society. And that system is no stronger than its weakest link. What good is magnificent police work if courts do not function, or vice versa? A disastrous correctional experience can wash out excellence in all prior action.

America's systems on all governmental levels, however, are characterized by a lack of direction, leadership or regulating mechanism. In countless ways, this defect has enormous consequences upon each of the systems. And as systems grow larger and more complex in every sense, this defect becomes more and more important. Attention to structure is so important it should precede what are, by comparison, relatively esoteric program suggestions. Our system organization, developed for other reasons in another day, is wholly diffused.[56] In no other major governmental function are we so fragmented, uninformed and wandering. Crime control is too important under present challenges in a free society to be left in this condition and unattended at its highest levels. No planning or co-ordination, however valuable or well meaning, can substitute for focusing responsibility and jurisdiction so as to end the "everybody's business" approach. Of greatest priority, therefore, is development of state entities to serve this purpose. There can be no perfect model. Alaska's needs are not those of California; Vermont's. not those of New York. As adapted, however, a state department of criminal justice (or crime control) is the first step. It would fulfill these functions and also serve as the agent for mandatory state-wide planning and federal

---

55 AMERICAN BAR ASSOCIATION REPORT, ORGANIZED CRIME AND LAW ENFORCEMENT (1952) and A. C. MILLSPAUGH, CRIME CONTROL BY THE NATIONAL GOVERNMENT (1937).
56 CRIME REPORT 279.

funding.[57] Specific organization should follow the state-local public education formula so well accepted by the public.[58] Thus, the operational scope of local government would remain unchanged to any great degree.

Involvement of such a proposed state agency necessarily would differ with each functional system service: independent criminal courts obviously are one thing (they could hardly object to participating in system information plans), local police another; correction is something else again. Varying forms could serve the important interests, so long as the department is informed of what is going on. Personnel and operating standards would characterize police and prosecution relationships; *all* services, after guilt is determined, should be mainly rehabilitative, and there are many, many reasons why they should be under one state agency.

Not only higher standards and more uniform quality of service could result from this new entity, but additional objectives could be realized for the whole crime control field. Instead of confining themselves to processing violators *after* crime has occurred, agencies could begin to work at the larger *preventive* issues — the most significant of all issues and which are now unattended happenstance. Broad generalities about eliminating slums, ending delinquency, improving education, and providing jobs are not sufficiently specific to be useful; after they are stated, who does what? We need more incisive analyses; they can never come from agencies concerned only with slivers of the whole system. One could read almost any police department annual report at random, for example, and find no specific causation recommendations to its community. And that is what the community most wants to know. How do particular crime problems, for example, relate to the local school, housing project, welfare case load and "problem-families"? Developing practical guidance will be as arduous and intellectually testing as any task in society. New people and new procedures will be needed for that effort. Yet society must try. There is no other way to go. Society cannot afford to give up in fatalism merely because "No single formula, no single theory, no single generalization can explain the vast range of behavior called crime."[59]

Besides establishing a state crime control department, other steps to modernize the fight against crime should include: (1) Resources, of all kinds (more manpower, facilities, etc.). (2) An end to proliferation of new police agencies. (Indeed, local communities may see their self-interest demands consolidated on, say, a county-wide basis.) (3) A pooling of data about crimes and offenders, thereby broadening the base of everyone's single raw material. (Regional agencies could serve several states.) (4) Full-time, qualified prosecutors, locally elected as an important check on the system, but also subject to state standards. (Ballots are no remedy in counties where no trials are held and all cases result in pleas to reduced charges.) (5) Large local governments developing an official agency, with status and free inquiry, for local planning and to constantly press for both *prevention* and *quality* system action. (6) In terms of causation, jobs and a

---

57 *See* the functional flow chart of the United States' crime system graphically set out at Crime Report 8-9.
58 *Id.* at 11.
59 *Id.* at v.

decent place to live, which affect one's life and attitudes so deeply as to be patently obvious.

Whatever leadership, planning or standard-setting approaches are taken by the state, the role of local government will be intense. Over a long period it will diminish somewhat as the states assume stronger leadership. But there is more than plenty to do: major responsibility for policing and prosecution under today's conditions presents challenges enough for anyone.

X. Conclusion

The American people want more effective crime control. To get it, many changes must occur. What to do is complex in the extreme. First, priorities should commence with basics, for the system badly needs money, people, equipment. These priorities also include gathering fragmented agencies into stronger and new types of government structures. Strengthening state-level action, the most important level for crime control direction in today's conditions, should start with establishing state departments of criminal justice that embrace all segments of the state's systems. These departments should truly lead and assist local law enforcement, whose role will remain largely the same, and serve as state recipient for new federal funding programs.

Today it is government which falls between the cracks in our system. It is government which loses its way in the maze, far more often than the violator. It is government which must be reformed if stronger crime control efforts are to be realized. Shoving new programs into the maw, before structural attention, will only compound some present difficulties and create frustrations and illusions of action.

Additional funding under new federal programs coming out of the President's Crime Commission proposals can make a real difference *if* the President's proposals are amended so as to provide meaningful funds and to give block grants to states. Some sleepy state capitols will be pushed into action. This is what the states want, though, as was made clear when Representative Gerald Ford of Michigan announced in the House of Representatives, February 8, 1968, that 49 governors had notified him of their support for amendments to accomplish those ends. Governors want the money and the responsibility that will go with it.

With those funds, states will have to involve themselves directly with the quality of urban crime control, a task they have not usually assumed in the past, although legal power was no restraint. Past disorderly adjustments will not placate the realities of today's crime pressures from the people upon the politicians. Urban crime is no picnic. Again, those states that have not zeroed in on crime control will have to do so now.

Elected chief executives — governors, mayors, county supervisors — have the key action positions. They have greatest control over the devices of real government power: budget, manpower, policy direction of administrative action. So they are most responsible for what happens. They have impetus in their hands and that is crucial to criminal justice efforts. Previously they have too often defaulted, by comparison with other governmental activities, to their staff or budget officials. Now crime control has burst out of this neglect and into the center arena. The states are under the spotlight and the proper crime control "mix" is of greatest moment to them.

Introduction to the Symposium: RIOTS*

Dean Joseph O'Meara**

"There is no grievance that is a fit object of redress by mob law." Abraham
Lincoln as quoted by President Johnson. South Bend Tribune,
March 29, 1968, at 1.

This is the tenth in our series of annual symposia, each dealing with a highly
controversial problem of urgent national concern. Of these ten symposia, this
is the third having to do with crime. The extent of our concern with this cancer-
ous problem is demonstrated by that fact. My own belief is that the rising incidence of crime is our country's number one domestic problem.

It is all too easy to ascribe this ugly phenomenon to the ugly phenomena
of poverty and unemployment among Negroes. The fact is that crime is increasing more rapidly in well-to-do neighborhoods than in the colored sections of our
cities;[1] and, referring to "[t]he typical rioter in the summer of 1967," the National
Advisory Commission on Civil Disorders found: "Economically his position was
about the same as his Negro neighbors who did not actively participate in the
riot."[2]

As for the riots, that plague of the 1960's, the first thing to say is that every
effort should be made to prevent them.[3] Once a riot has started, however, it is
the *obligation* of the authorities to stop it. As President Eisenhower has said:

> These riots are a growing danger to our nation and must be handled with-
> out temporizing. When the police cannot cope with the situation, there
> should be no hesitancy in calling out the National Guard. And the culprits,
> when their guilt is clear, must be dealt with as any other criminals, regardless
> of their race or their grievances against society. People simply must be taught
> that personal or social problems cannot be solved by violence and defiance
> of authority.[4]

There is no excuse for a riot that lasts for four or five days with the atten-
dant injuries, loss of life, and damage to property. *A riot can be stopped before
it is twenty-four hours old* and should be. Law and order are a precondition
of civilized society.

Please note that what I have to say has to do only with riots — not with
peaceful demonstrations. The march on Selma, the march on Washington —
these were peaceful demonstrations inspired by a deep conviction of injustice.
In no sense could they be characterized as riots. On the other hand, none

---

* In this paper I speak neither for the University of Notre Dame nor for the Notre Dame
Law School but only for myself.
** Dean Emeritus, Notre Dame Law School.
1 *See* FBI, UNIFORM CRIME REPORTS FOR THE UNITED STATES — 1966, tables 6-7, at
92-94 (1967) (shows a higher rate of crime increase in suburban areas than in major cities).
2 REPORT OF THE NATIONAL ADVISORY COMMISSION ON CIVIL DISORDERS 128 (Bantam ed.
1968).
3 *Id.* at 2.
4 READER'S DIGEST, Aug., 1967, at 70.

of the riots in recent years was the product of a sense of injustice, as the Selma and Washington demonstrations were.

Some will disagree, of course, and point to Harlem, Watts, and other violent episodes. They were not race riots, they were *youth* riots.[5] Those who challenge that assertion will have to explain the riots by young *white* people in Oregon, New Hampshire, Florida, Wisconsin, and on university campuses, beginning with the riot at that seed bed of youthful lawlessness, the University of California at Berkeley.[6] For these young white rioters were not giving vent to a bottled-up sense of outraged justice. They were responding, I assume, to the pressures of the Age, but so are we all. To be sure, the most damaging riots have occurred in blighted areas inhabited by Negroes. Understandably, therefore, the focus is on them, and I accept that focus in the rest of what I have to say.

Four years of worsening riots are enough — riots which were not put down, mark you, but simply ran out of steam after four or five days of terror. Crime must be suppressed; riots must be put down and put down fast, as they can be. To accomplish that, however, requires stern measures and, so far, the officials of our city and state governments have been too timid to do what the situation requires. Timidity — official timidity — almost as great a problem as the riots.

It may be even a greater problem for, unless the rioting by young Negroes is stopped, inevitably the wild ones in the white community will respond in kind and that will mean the worst horror yet — guerrilla warfare between whites and blacks. Then no neighborhood will be immune, nobody will be safe. Peaceful people in quiet neighborhoods will be gunned down from passing cars; their homes will be fire-bombed in hit-and-run attacks. Every city in the land will become another Algiers — worse than Algiers, in fact, because the Algerians did not resort to burning. God forbid.

The message comes through loud and clear to all who do not close their ears: *Disarm*. Rioters should be disarmed forcibly — and it can be done. But that is only a beginning. All possible pressure must be brought to bear for effective weapons-control legislation — national, state and local.

The fine record of young Negroes in Viet Nam indicates that they have as much to contribute to this nation's welfare as their white counterparts. How to bring this promise to fruition is a question of utmost complexity, whose answer I think no man fully understands. Whatever the remedy or remedies may be, however, one thing is sure: no remedy can be applied until the rule of law has been recognized and order has been restored. That can be accomplished only by the prompt and courageous use of effective measures. But it *can* be

---

5 Referring to the riots of 1967, the National Advisory Commission found that "The typical rioter in the summer of 1967 was a Negro, unmarried male *between the ages of 15 and 24 . . . ." supra* note 2, at 128 (emphasis added).

John P. Spiegel, Director of the Lemberg Center for the Study of Violence at Brandeis University, commenting on recent disorders, said:

Kids, often very young kids — I call it "youth phenomena" — started the trouble and then if the adults joined, it was because they gave in to the temptation of looting. After all, they liked a colored television set as much as anyone. South Bend Tribune, April 10, 1968, at 12, cols. 5-6.

6 *See* Moore, *Anarchy on the Campus: The Rebels . . . and the Law*, THE POLICE CHIEF, April, 1965, at 10.

accomplished; and those city and state officials who fail to accomplish it should be held responsible by their constituents.

How can it be accomplished? How can a riot be stopped within 24 hours — less than a quarter of the time span of virtually all the riots of the last few years? Assuming that the mayor and the governor cooperate and that they are willing to use strong medicine, it can be done as follows. In the first place, the National Guard should be mobilized immediately, that is to say, as soon as it is plain that a serious riot is in progress.[7] And the rule should be better too soon than too late.[8] Moreover, someone other than the police should decide the question, for the police will hesitate to admit they can't handle the situation. What I have said doesn't mean that *some* Guardsmen should be sent to the scene, or that *all* Guardsmen should be alerted. It means that an adequate number of Guardsmen should be mobilized and dispatched to the riot area *at once*. And, again, the rule should be better too many than too few.[9]

As soon as the Guardsmen arrive, the riot area (that is, the area where the rioting is taking place and/or from which bands of marauders erupt to carry the rioting to other areas until resistance drives them back to the riot core) — the riot area, to repeat, should be sealed off absolutely and no one permitted in or out except the Guardsmen themselves and emergency vehicles, such as ambulances, convoyed by Guardsmen.

An around-the-clock curfew should be put into effect immediately and announced every few minutes by loud speakers at strategic points. This would allow no one on the streets. To enforce the curfew the streets should be patrolled by Guardsmen in tanks. They should be used to protect the Guardsmen from snipers. Anybody violating the curfew should be arrested or, if he resists arrest, shot.[10] And if a little imagination were used, perhaps some of the Guardsmen could be armed with sawed-off shotguns using shells having a reduced charge of powder. It should be possible to reduce fatalities in this way, especially if the Guardsmen are ordered to shoot low, that is, at the ankles of the rioters.

Strategic buildings in the area should be rushed in order to get at snipers on the roofs, along with those using the primitive but deadly Molotov cocktail. With these preparations made, Guardsmen *in force* should systematically search every building in the area and confiscate all weapons found, including bottles and gasoline. There would be some resistance, of course; and those with arms (including bottles, etc.) who refuse to give them up and resist being deprived of them, should be arrested or, if necessary, shot. The new and apparently effective chemical weapon called "Mace" should be used at close quarters, since it

---

7   Orlando Wilson, one of the nation's leading criminologists, has said:
        "There is no substitute for force in quelling civil disturbances, and if the police are unable to provide the manpower to restore normalcy, then there is no alternative but to put in a call for the National Guard — and as quickly as possible." This is my view in a nutshell.
Wilson, *Civil Disturbances and the Rule of Law*, 58 J. CRIM. L.C. & P.S. 157 (1967).
    8   *See* HOUSE COMM. ON ARMED SERVICES OF THE SPECIAL SUBCOMM. TO INQUIRE INTO THE CAPABILITY OF THE NATIONAL GUARD TO COPE WITH CIVIL DISTURBANCES, 90th Cong., 1st Sess., 5652 (Dec. 18, 1967) (recommending the judicious early commitment of adequate National Guard forces).
    9   *See* text accompanying notes 7-8 *supra*.
    10   *See* text accompanying note 11 *infra*.

subdues without injuring.[11] There should be no hesitation, however, about using deadly weapons if the Guardsmen are fired on from a distance beyond the range of "Mace."

Strong medicine? Assuredly, but that is exactly what is needed. Consider what has happened in city after city across the country. Fires are set and the firemen who respond are attacked with rocks and bottles — even fired upon. More and more the rioters are armed with shotguns, rifles, and other deadly weapons. Motorists in peaceful neighborhoods are fired upon from passing cars. The police are shot at. Looting is growing in areas outside the riot core. Who is safe, either in his person or in his property? Are not citizens, black as well as white, entitled to protection from these increasing outbursts of mass violence?[12]

Milder measures have been tried for four years, but the riots spread and the violence increases. It is time and past time for tough tactics.[13] To repeat, strong medicine is exactly what is needed. Needed or not, many will be horrified by my suggestion that armed persons in a riot area, who disregard the curfew, refuse to surrender their weapons or turn them on the police or Guardsmen, should be shot. To those who find this a shocking suggestion I put this question: Is it not better to kill some malefactors than to allow them to kill innocent persons?

That question will not stop those who are horrified by my suggestions. Regardless of the evidence to the contrary, they will insist that Harlem, Watts, and subsequent violent episodes were the product of a sense of injustice. Even if that were true, even if a riot (whether by whites or blacks) were churned up by a deep feeling of outraged justice, there would still be a moral as well as a legal obligation to use *effective* measures to protect the community. The "community" is not just an abstraction but *an aggregation of people, people whose rights as individuals are just as sacred as the rights of those few individuals who resort to violence.* Why is it so hard for some persons to understand this?

---

11 South Bend Tribune, Jan. 7, 1968, at 25, col. 3.
12 Consider the words of a young Negro Marine, wounded in Viet Nam, flying back to Detroit only to learn of the riot in progress there.

> This is my first time home in almost two years and look what the hell I come home to. I just hope nobody hurt my family. They live on the West Side. I heard it was pretty bad there.
> It's not like that in Vietnam. I'm a Marine. You know, Marines have a thing: I take care of the next guy, he takes care of me. It's beautiful.
> . . . .
> I was in pre-med school before I went into the Marines. My mother's a pediatrician. I wanted to be a pediatrician. But when I get out, I'm going to be a cop. I left my application in Los Angeles.
> . . . . Boy I sure hope they didn't hurt my family. I don't care who it is, I'll fight to save my family.

South Bend Tribune, July 25, 1967, at 8.
13 The *Restatement (Second) of Torts* says of the tactics that may be used in riot control:

> The use of force or the imposition of a confinement which is intended or likely to cause death or serious bodily harm for the purpose of suppressing a riot or preventing the other from participating in it is privileged if the riot is one which threatens death or serious bodily harm.

RESTATEMENT (SECOND) OF TORTS § 142(2) (1965). The commentary on this section clarifies this permissible use of force.

> If the riot itself threatens death or serious bodily harm, it is sufficiently serious to justify the use of deadly means to suppress it. It is not necessary that the avowed purpose of the riot be to inflict such harm. It is enough that the conduct of the rioters is such as to create the probability or even the possibility of such consequences.

RESTATEMENT (SECOND) OF TORTS, Comments § 142, comment g, at 257 (1965).

When a lone sniper is surrounded and shot down, nobody is outraged. In a riot there are many snipers. And every person bearing arms in the riot zone is a potential sniper. So, I submit, the real question is: Whom should we protect? The snipers and those who beat and kill and burn and loot — or their victims?

Cities and neighborhoods differ from one another to a greater or lesser extent. Thus I recognize that modifications of the plan of operations I have outlined briefly might, almost certainly would be called for in some instances.

One final thought. A woman whose husband or son has been killed, the owner of property whose premises have been burned down, a merchant whose store has been looted — why are they not entitled to compensation from the municipality and/or state which could have protected them, but was too timid to do so? The city solicitors, corporation counsel (or whatever else they may be called) would do well, I suggest, to start preparing whatever defense they may think they have against the damage suits that are bound to be filed and are being filed.[14]

---

14 The Supreme Court has spoken to this point of public liability for riot damage, as follows:

> The State is the creator of subordinate municipal governments. It vests in them the police powers essential to the preservation of law and order. It imposes upon them the duty of protecting property situated within their limits from the violence of such public breaches of the peace as are mobs and riots. *This duty and obligation thus entrusted to the local subordinate government is by this enactment emphasized and enforced by imposing upon the local community absolute liability for property losses resulting from the violence of such public tumults.*
> The policy of imposing liability upon a civil subdivision of government exercising delegated police power is familiar to every student of the common law. We find it recognized in the beginning of the police system of Anglo-Saxon people. Thus, "The Hundred," a very early form of civil subdivision, was held answerable for robberies committed within the division. By a series of statutes, beginning possibly in 1285, in the statutes of Winchester, 13 Edw. I, c.1, coming on down to the 27th Elizabeth, c.13, the Riot Act of George I (1 Geo. I, St. 2) and Act of 8 George II, c.16, we may find a continuous recognition of the principle that a civil subdivision entrusted with the duty of protecting property in its midst and with police power to discharge the function, may be made answerable not only for negligence affirmatively shown, but absolutely as not having afforded a protection adequate to the obligation. Chicago v. Sturges, 222 U.S. 313,323 (1911) (emphasis added).

A majority of the relatively small number of cases appear to be contra. But Chicago v. Sturges never has been overruled·or qualified. *See also* County of Allegheny v. Gibson, 90 Penn. St. 397, 35 American 670 (1879). These two cases, especially the latter, sketch the historical background of the legislative enactments about to be mentioned.

Nearly half of the states have statutes imposing liability or government subsidies for riot damage. Most of these are collected in Note, *Riot Insurance*, 77 YALE L.J. 541, 552 n.75 (1968). Another relevant statute is: W. VA. CODE § 61-6-12 (1966). It goes without saying, of course, that these enactments are not uniform in their provisions. The extent and conditions of liability vary considerably.

SURVEY

The Long, Hot Summer: A Legal View

I. Riot Prevention

A. Introduction

The number and severity of race-related disturbances has increased steadily from 1961 to 1967.[1] In the search for the causes of this violent civil disorder, the conclusion most often reached is that the riots are a direct attack on the conditions of slum ghetto existence.[2] Therefore, the most effective anti-riot legislation is undoubtedly that in the form of social and economic measures designed to eliminate the root causes of poverty and discrimination.

However, as long as the conditions which spawn the riots exist, it is essential that law enforcement officials be prepared to suppress the disturbances promptly whenever they occur. The purpose of this Note is to examine selected legal problems that arise in the context of mass urban disorder and to suggest possible solutions. First considered is an analysis of the legal foundations of the police and military functions pertinent to riot prevention and control. Then, the scope of the suppression power during the actual riot situation is delineated. Finally, an in-depth treatment is offered on the possible sources of recovery for riot victims who attempt to assert their claims in the aftermath of the disaster.

B. State Statutory Controls

1. State Powers and Duties

The primary responsibility for keeping the peace by the prevention and suppression of disorder falls upon state and local law enforcement agencies. This is in accord with the principle that the general duty of the administration of

---

1 For a comprehensive city-by-city outline of racial disturbance from 1961 to September 25, 1967, see P. Downing, "Race Riots, 1961 to September 25, 1967," Civil Disorder (Legislative Reference Service of Library of Congress, Aug. 4, 1967). As of July 27th, 1967, the total riot costs for the year 1967 were summarized as follows:

Number of riots:	42
Killed:	78
Injured:	3,120
Arrests:	7,050
Property Damage:	$524 million

These figures were gathered from newspaper reports and reprinted in 36 Cong. Q. 1707 (Sept. 8, 1967).

2 President's Commission on Law Enforcement and Administration of Justice, The Challenge of Crime in a Free Society 37 (1967). See generally Governor's Commission on the Los Angeles Riots, Violence in the City — An End or a Beginning? (1965). The National Advisory Commission on Civil Disorders has pointed out that one of the most "bitter fruits" of "white racism" has been the formation of Black ghettos. These ghettos are an integral part of the "explosive mixture which has been accumulating in our cities since the end of World War II." National Advisory Commission on Civil Disorders, Report of the National Advisory Commission on Civil Disorders 203-04 (Bantam ed. 1968) (hereinafter cited as Riot Commission Report).

criminal justice rests with the states.[3] The riot itself, and any crimes committed during its course, such as murder, assault, arson, theft and vandalism, are all violations of state law. Therefore, it is necessary to examine and evaluate the existing legal machinery that states employ to cope with urban racial violence.

State provisions dealing with the riot situation generally follow a pattern formulated by the common law. Three distinct common-law crimes pertaining to the disruption of public order were recognized by Blackstone. "Unlawful assembly" occurred when three or more persons assembled with the common intention of performing an unlawful act in a violent and tumultuous manner.[4] If action was taken to further this illegal cause, the activity was characterized as a "rout."[5] "Riot" itself was committed when the mob actually employed force or violence to accomplish its illegal purpose.[6] Several states have no statutory provisions relating directly to riot[7] and thus still rely primarily on these common-law definitions. Other states maintain the common-law crimes as a supplement to their statutory enactments.[8] These riot statutes themselves, although varying in form, incorporate the common-law dichotomy between unlawful assembly and riot.[9] The crime of rout is usually either abandoned or merged with unlawful assembly.[10] Thus, the fundamental state legal tools for the protection of the public order from violence are based on the common-law conception of riot, supplemented by statutory prohibitions against disorderly conduct and breach of the peace.[11]

2. State Statutory Scheme

a. Unlawful Assembly

Unlawful assembly statutes have as a basic requirement the assemblance of at least two,[12] and usually three,[13] persons with the common purpose of performing an unlawful act. The states are divided as to whether there must be an intention to perform the planned activity in a violent manner. Many states require the presence, or at least the threat, of force or violence disruptive of public order. The Iowa statute is a typical example of this class:

> When three or more persons in a violent or tumultuous manner assemble together to do an unlawful act, or, when together, attempt to do an act, whether lawful or unlawful, in an unlawful, violent, or tumultuous

---

3 Jerome v. United States, 318 U.S. 101, 104-05 (1943). *See also* United States v. Cruikshank, 92 U.S. 542, 556 (1876); 41 Op. Att'y Gen. 313, 322-23 (1963).

4 4 Blackstone, Commentaries *146.

5 *Id.*

6 *Id.*

7 For example, the laws of Mississippi, Tennessee, and Wyoming do not specifically define and prohibit a "riot."

8 *See, e.g.,* Commonwealth v. Frishman, 235 Mass. 449, 455, 126 N.E. 838, 840 (1920).

9 *E.g.,* Iowa Code Ann. § 743.1 (unlawful assembly), § 743.2 (riot) (1950).

10 *See, e.g.,* N.Y. Penal Law §§ 240.00-.10 (McKinney 1967). *Contra* Cal. Penal Code § 406 (West 1955).

11 Disorderly conduct and breach of the peace offenses are considered in the context of demonstration controls in Part C see text accompanying notes 89-140 *infra.*

12 *E.g.,* Ala. Code tit. 14, § 407 (1959); Cal. Penal Code § 407 (West 1955).

13 *E.g.,* Del. Code Ann. tit. 11, § 361 (1953); N.Y. Penal Law § 240.10 (McKinney 1967); Ore. Rev. Stat. § 166.040(2) (1953).

manner, to the disturbance of others, they are guilty of an unlawful assembly. . . .[14]

In other jurisdictions, however, the element of force or violence need not be present to sustain a conviction if the purpose of the assembly is unlawful. The California unlawful assembly provision is representative of this latter category of statutes:

> Whenever two or more persons assemble together to do an unlawful act, and separate without doing or advancing toward it, . . . such an assembly is an unlawful assembly.[15]

In addition to raising constitutional difficulties,[16] such a formulation tends to obscure the basic common-law conception of unlawful assembly as an anticipatory act to a riot.

The Supreme Court has upheld state legislation that prohibits assemblies having as their purpose the execution of an unlawful act by means of force or violence. In *Cole v. Arkansas*[17] the Court stated that there was "no abridgment of free speech or assembly for the criminal sanctions of the state" to be fastened upon persons "promoting, encouraging and aiding an assemblage the purpose of which is to wreak violence."[18] However, convictions under some of the statutes containing vague terminology have been reversed on the ground that the statute's overly broad language failed to establish adequate standards for distinguishing between constitutionally permissible and constitutionally impermissible suppression.[19] These difficulties usually arise when the offense of unlawful assembly is employed in specific cases against conduct that does not pose an immediate threat to public safety.[20] Presumably, this argument would not be available to participants who assemble with the intention of creating or furthering the type of disorder that has characterized a modern urban riot.

Historically, unlawful assembly statutes were used chiefly to suppress the violence that has often accompanied labor disputes.[21] During the early period of the civil rights movement, at least one Southern state employed this sanction against sit-in demonstrators assembling at lunch counters and department stores.[22] Although the terminology of most state provisions is broad enough to cover almost any type of unruly gathering,[23] the antiquated forms in which the statutes are cast indicate that they were not intended to cope with modern mass urban

---

14 Iowa Code Ann. § 743.1 (1950).
15 Cal. Penal Code § 407 (West 1955).
16 In State v. Bulot, 175 La. 21, 142 So. 787 (1932), an unlawful assembly statute was struck down because the lack of a requirment for violence gave police officers too much discretion in applying the provision to peaceful assemblies.
17 338 U.S. 345 (1949).
18 *Id.* at 353-54.
19 *E.g.*, Wright v. Georgia, 373 U.S. 284, 292 (1963).
20 In the *Wright* case, the statute in question had been applied to six Negroes whose "unlawful assembly" consisted of playing basketball in a public park that had traditionally been segregated for "whites only." There was no evidence of any activity that could be characterized as a breach of the peace. *Id.* at 285.
21 *E.g.*, Cole v. State, 214 Ark. 387, 216 S.W.2d 402, *aff'd*, 338 U.S. 345 (1949).
22 *See generally* Pollitt, *Dime Store Demonstrations: Events and Legal Problems of First Sixty Days*, 1960 Duke L.J. 315, 334.
23 *See* the cases collected in Annot., 71 A.L.R.2d 875 (1960).

disorder. However, by modernizing the language of the statutes, an effective riot-prevention tool can be forged.

In the context of an urban riot, a modern unlawful assembly provision should be so formulated so as to place a legal sanction on each member of a mob that forms with the intention of doing violence. The special efficacy of such a formulation is that it would enable the police to arrest violators for the offense even before any violence actually occurs.[24] For example, such a law would be of great value in a situation where a demagogue exhorts a crowd of fifteen or twenty persons in a slum area to stone a passing police car. Once the group acquiesces in this common purpose, the people comprising the crowd can all be held guilty of unlawful assembly, whether or not the project is actually accomplished.[25]

The recently adopted New York Penal Code incorporates an unlawful assembly provision that is specifically designed to achieve this purpose:

> A person is guilty of unlawful assembly when he assembles with four or more other persons for the purpose of engaging or preparing to engage with them in tumultuous and violent conduct likely to cause public alarm, or when, being present at an assembly which either has or develops such purpose, he remains there with intent to advance that purpose.[26]

The Practice Commentary to the New York Penal Code states that the statute is designed to make unlawful assembly an "inchoate or anticipatory offense" with respect to an actual riot.[27] Conceivably, the provision might have been constitutionally strengthened by replacing the broad phrase, "likely to cause public alarm," with a more explicit "clear and present danger" test, keying upon the probability that grave violence would result if immediate action were not taken. In this way, the first amendment rights of free speech and assembly would be better insulated from abuse, and more emphasis would be placed on the preventive nature of the law. However, even as it is presently phrased, the New York statute illustrates the useful function that a modern unlawful assembly provision can perform in the prevention of urban disorder: it provides legal authority to arrest each member of a threatening mob before violence breaks out.

b. Riot

The statutory riot provisions have the same general purpose as the common law upon which they are based: the maintenance of public order. The essence of riot implies the idea of lawless mobs bent on accomplishing some object in a violent and tumultuous manner.[28] Although the statutes vary widely in form, their basic framework is similar.

---

24   The actual commission of the intended violence is not an element of the offense of unlawful assembly, but rather it is the distinction between unlawful assembly and the crime of riot. BLACKSTONE, *supra* notes 4 & 6.

25   *See* Denzer & McQuillan, *Practice Commentary*, N.Y. PENAL LAW § 240.08, at 121-22 (McKinney 1967).

26   N.Y. PENAL LAW § 240.10 (McKinney 1967).

27   Denzer & McQuillan, *supra* note 25, § 240.10, at 122.

28   People v. Edelson, 169 Misc. 386, 7 N.Y.S.2d 323 (Kings County Ct. 1938).

The essential elements of the crime as defined by statute are: (a) An assemblage of three or more persons for any purpose; (b) use or attempted use of force or violence against property or persons . . . ; and (c) a resulting disturbance of the public peace.[29]

Although many of the statutes remain couched in archaic language, the typical form is illustrated by the Minnesota provision:

> When three or more persons assembled disturb the public peace by an intentional act or threat of unlawful force or violence to person or property, each participant therein is guilty of riot . . . [30]

At least three states have varied this traditional pattern by placing the crime of riot in the more explicit context of illegal mob action.[31] Here again, the primary focus is upon the preservation of peace and order. Mob action is defined in the same terms as riot, but the penalties are structured so as to be most severe when actual injury to persons or property results from the disorder.[32]

There is no doubt that the states have the constitutional power to punish individuals for participation in riotous assemblies. When the statutes have been challenged on constitutional grounds, the main thrust of the argument has centered on the vagueness of the terminology as applied to a particular factual situation. A three-judge federal district court in *International Longshoremen's and Warehousemen's Union v. Ackerman*[33] held the riot statute of Hawaii unconstitutional because the criterion of "striking terror or tending to strike terror into others"[34] was necessarily one that must be "purely subjective and hence objectionable."[35] Such a rationale could cast doubts on nearly all state riot acts, since "public alarm,"[36] "disturbing the public peace,"[37] or "terror"[38] is the language commonly employed to differentiate riot from other types of permissible assemblies. However, the *Ackerman* case was reversed on other grounds on appeal without a discussion of the subjective standard point.[39] More recently, in *Carmichael v. Allen*,[40] an attempt was made to secure a federal injunction to prevent enforcement of the Georgia riot statute on the ground that it was "too vague and uncertain to state any ascertainable standard of guilt."[41] The threat-

---

29 State v. Winkels, 204 Minn. 466, 468, 283 N.W. 763, 764 (1939).
30 MINN. STAT. ANNOT. § 609.71 (1964).
31 N.H. REV. STAT. ANN. § 609-A:1 (Supp. 1967); N.J. STAT. ANN. § 2A:126-1 (1953); OHIO REV. CODE ANN. § 3761.01 (Page 1954).
32 *E.g.*, N.H. REV. STAT. ANN. §609-A:2,3 (Supp. 1967).
33 82 F. Supp. 65 (D. Hawaii 1948), *rev'd on other grounds*, 187 F.2d 860 (9th Cir.), *cert. denied*, 342 U.S. 859 (1951).
34 HAWAII REV. LAWS § 11571 (1945), as quoted in 82 F. Supp. at 96 n.60.
35 *Id.* at 101.
36 N.Y. PENAL LAW § 240.05-.06 (McKinney 1967).
37 CAL. PENAL CODE § 404 (West 1955).
38 DEL. CODE ANN. tit. 11, § 361 (1953).
39 International Longshoremen's & Warehousemen's Union v. Ackerman, 187 F.2d 860 (9th Cir.), *cert. denied*, 342 U.S. 859 (1951), *rev'g on other grounds*, 82 F. Supp. 65 (D. Hawaii 1948).
40 267 F. Supp. 985 (N.D. Ga. 1967).
41 *Id.* at 995. The state riot statute in question provided:
    Any two or more persons who shall do an unlawful act of violence or *any other act in a violent and tumultuous manner,* shall be guilty of a riot . . . . GA. CODE ANN. § 26-5302 (1953) (emphasis added).
Petitioner argued that the statute was unconstitutional in that there were many presumably

ened riot indictment in this case came as a result of activities engaged in by the petitioners during a violent racial disturbance in Atlanta on September 6th and 10th, 1966. The court, in refusing to issue the injunction, held that the acts charged in the indictment were obviously within the power of the state to punish as a type of hard-core public misconduct that would be prohibited under any construction of the statute.[42] Thus, it appears that a constitutional argument based on vagueness would not be available to participants in mass urban violence who were being prosecuted under the standard form of riot statutes.

As was the case with unlawful assembly provisions, the riot statutes have traditionally found their most prolific application in the area of labor disputes.[43] Although the common-law concept of riot embodied in the statutes is broad enough to cover urban violence, the effective use of statutory riot provisions in this field could be hampered by their archaic form.[44] In the more recent racial disturbances, it appears that there were relatively few prosecutions under the riot statutes. Instead, most rioters were indicted for crimes that were committed incidentally to the riot itself, such as arson, assault and battery, resisting arrest, and larceny.[45] Nevertheless, a well-drafted riot statute can still serve a vital function in the context of modern urban disorder. Under such a provision, an individual engaging in mob violence could be prosecuted for a felony offense when it would be difficult to indict him personally for one of the more traditional incidental crimes committed during the course of the riot.

The new New York riot provisions are designed to accomplish this very purpose. The crime of riot is divided into two offenses. The lesser offense, riot in the second degree, focuses on riotous conduct that is terminated before actual injury results, and it renders participants guilty of a misdemeanor.

> A person is guilty of riot in the second degree when, simultaneously with four or more other persons, he engages in tumultuous and violent conduct and thereby intentionally or recklessly causes or creates a grave risk of causing public alarm.[46]

The crime of riot in the first degree increases the penalty to a felony offense if the proscribed conduct actually results in personal injury or property damage.

> A person is guilty of riot in the first degree when (a) simultaneously with ten or more other persons he engages in tumultouous [sic] and violent conduct and thereby intentionally or recklessly causes or creates a grave

---

legal acts done in a violent and tumultuous manner that were beyond the power of the legislature to proscribe. However, the prosecution recognized this weakness in the statute and was careful to charge only unlawful acts in the indictment. Carmichael v. Allen, 267 F. Supp. 985, 995 (N.D. Ga. 1967). *See also* Remarks of Lewis R. Slaton, Greenbrier Conference of the National District Attorneys Association, Aug., 1967, printed in *Riot Panel,* 3 THE PROSE-CUTOR 282, 285 (1967).

42   Carmichael v. Allen, 267 F. Supp. 985, 996 (N.D. Ga. 1967).
43   *E.g.,* People v. Brown, 193 App. Div. 203, 184 N.Y.S. 165 (Sup. Ct. App. Div. 1920).
44   *See, e.g.,* CONN. GEN. STAT. ANN. § 53-169 (Supp. 1967).
45   During the August, 1965 Watts riot in Los Angeles, 71% of the 3,438 adults and 81% of the 514 juveniles arrested were charged with the crimes of burglary and larceny. GOV-ERNOR'S COMMISSION ON THE LOS ANGELES RIOTS, *supra* note 2, at 24.
46   N.Y. PENAL LAW § 240.05 (McKinney 1967).

risk of causing public alarm, and (b) in the course of and as a result of such conduct, a person other than one of the participants suffers physical injury or substantial property damage occurs.[47]

As explained in the Practice Commentary to the New York Penal Code, this latter formulation of the crime of riot is drafted to conform to the usual conception of a "genuine" urban riot. The minimum number of people required to constitute a riot is increased from three to eleven, and the violence produced must now result in actual harm.[48] The phrase, "tumultuous and violent conduct," is described as meaning more than just loud noise or disturbance and is designed to include "frightening mob behavior involving ominous threats of injury, stone throwing or other such terrorizing acts."[49] Presumably, "public alarm" would also be construed in such a fashion that its existence would depend on grave danger to life and property, rather than mere annoyance or inconvenience. As such, the New York statute stands as an example of the necessary function that a riot provision must serve: it shifts the emphasis from retribution for the commission of some incidental crime and imposes a direct legal penalty on intentional and active participation in the riot itself.

c. Inciting to Riot

An inciting to riot provision focuses upon the instigator of the disorder, rather than upon the participants. Its function is to provide a legal basis for silencing demagogues who create a clear and present danger of serious public disorder by going beyond the boundaries of protected speech in an attempt to stir an assemblage into the use of illegal force or violence. Action can be taken against the agitator even before the requisite number of persons necessary for unlawful assembly acquiesce in the proposed riotous activity.[50]

Obviously, the major problem encountered in this area is defining the crime of inciting to riot in such terms so as to take it out from under the free speech guarantees of the first amendment. Although the Supreme Court has made it clear that the fundamental rights of the first amendment are so vital that they are to be accorded the utmost protection,[51] the Court has recognized that there are limits to the exercise of these liberties. Words which by their very utterance tend to incite an immediate breach of the peace have been placed in "well-defined and narrowly limited classes of speech, the prevention and punishment of which have never been thought to raise any Constitutional problem."[52] Even more explicitly, the Court stated in *Cantwell v. Connecticut*[53] that

> [n]o one would have the hardihood to suggest that the principle of freedom of speech sanctions incitement to riot . . . . When clear and present danger of riot, disorder, . . . or other immediate threat to public safety,

---

47   *Id.* § 240.06.
48   Denzer & McQuillan, *supra* note 25, § 240.06, at 121.
49   *Id.* § 240.05, at 118-19.
50   *Id.* § 240.08, at 121-122.
51   United States v. Carolene Prods. Co., 304 U.S. 144, 152 n.4 (1938); *see* Dombrowski v. Pfister, 380 U.S. 479, 486-87 (1965).
52   Chaplinsky v. New Hampshire, 315 U.S. 568, 571-72 (1942).
53   310 U.S. 296 (1940).

peace, or order, appears, the power of the state to prevent or punish is obvious.[54]

The factual pattern in *Feiner v. New York*[55] most closely approximates the type of situation that is likely to occur in a modern urban ghetto. Feiner made an inflamatory speech to a group of about seventy-five or eighty Negroes and whites gathered on a city street. Both the thrust of his remarks and his manner of speaking were directed at arousing the Negro audience to rise up in arms and fight against the whites. When the crowd's reaction, both for and against the speaker, threatened to erupt into violence, the police attempted to disperse the assembly. Because Feiner refused to step down, he was placed under arrest for the offense of breaching the peace. In upholding Feiner's conviction, the Court noted that when a "speaker passes the bounds of argument or persuasion and undertakes incitement to riot,"[56] the police are not powerless to act if "motivated solely by a proper concern for the preservation of order and protection of the general welfare."[57]

Both *Cantwell* and *Feiner* were cited with apparent approval in a more recent decision in *Cox v. Louisiana.*[58] Although the Court in *Cox* distinguished them on their facts, it pointed out that nothing said in the opinion was "to be interpreted as sanctioning riotous conduct in any form."[59] Thus, it is clearly within the power of the state to proscribe speech that intentionally threatens to incite violence, provided that the customary test of "clear and present danger"[60] is satisfied.

State courts have not been hesitant to uphold convictions based on inciting to riot against the agitators who played a part in the more recent urban disturbances. During a disturbance in Philadelphia in August, 1964, the defendant in *Commonwealth v. Hayes*[61] was observed leading a large crowd in directing chants against the police and attempting to hinder the dispersal of an unruly gathering. Evidently there was no violence when the defendant first appeared on the scene, but after he began to lead the assembly, a witness testified that:

> [E]verything just seemed to cave in at once. Bottles and bricks and whatever kind of missiles that could be thrown started to rain down from the air, and windows started breaking all over the place.[62]

The Supreme Court of Pennsylvania concluded that evidence of this nature was sufficient to support a conviction of inciting to riot. Apparently this court assumed that speech that is intentionally used to incite such illegal activity is

---

54   *Id.* at 308.
55   340 U.S. 315 (1951).
56   *Id.* at 321.
57   *Id.* at 319.
58   379 U.S. 536, 551, 554 (1965). Here, the judgment of the Supreme Court of Louisiana, upholding the convictions of demonstrators under a breach of the peace statute and an obstructing public passages statute, was reversed on the grounds that the statutes were unconstitutionally applied and enforced. *Id.* at 552, 558.
59   *Id.* at 559, 574.
60   Dennis v. United States, 341 U.S. 494, 505 (1951). *See also* Yates v. United States, 354 U.S. 298, 321 (1957).
61   205 Pa. Super. 338, 209 A.2d 38 (1965).
62   *Id.* at 342, 209 A.2d at 40.

conclusively within the power of the state to punish, because it did not even discuss the conviction in the context of the first amendment. In *Lynch v. State*,[63] however, the Court of Special Appeals of Maryland, in upholding an inciting to riot conviction, made a point of specifically distinguishing the type of remarks that had been made by the defendant from the classes of speech protected by the Constitution.[64] Relying primarily on *Feiner v. New York*,[65] the court held that such exhortations as "Rise up and unite white man and fight" following a diatribe against Negroes, Jews, and other minority groups were a factor in inciting some of the estimated three thousand listeners to commit the acts of violence which ensued.[66]

It is interesting to note that in both *Lynch* and *Hayes* the arrests, which were based not on statutes but on the common-law crime of inciting to riot,[67] were made after the speeches had brought about actual riotous conduct. By pointing to this actual result, the courts could easily conclude that the language employed posed a clear and present danger to public order. However, the eruption of violence after an inflammatory speech should not be a condition precedent to prosecution if the crime of inciting to riot is to serve as a preventive as well as a punitive measure. A legal basis for silencing the intentional agitator is created once a clear and present danger situation arises. Although dispensing with the requirement that actual disorder must result from the inciter's activity makes the offense more susceptible to arbitrary abuse, the Supreme Court has recognized the need for such discretion and has upheld its exercise when performed with the sole motive of preventing serious violence.[68]

Many states have failed to enact an inciting to riot provision in addition to the normal statutory prohibitions against riot and unlawful assembly. As has been seen in *Hayes* and *Lynch*, there is a common-law basis for the crime that can be employed in those states lacking a statutory prohibition. However, probably as a direct result of the widespread occurrence of racial violence, the distinct trend among these states is toward adoption of a specific inciting to riot statute.[69] The recent Georgia provision illustrates the form into which the offense is usually cast:

> Any person who, with intent to cause a riot, does an act or engages in conduct which urges, counsels, or advises others to riot, at a time and place and under circumstances which produce a clear and present danger of a riot, shall be guilty of a misdemeanor.[70]

Although there have been no reported cases under these new statutes, they

---

63   236 A.2d 45 (Md. 1967).
64   *Id.* at 48-54.
65   340 U.S. 315 (1951).
66   Lynch v. State, 236 A.2d 45, 43-54 (Md. 1967).
67   *Id.* at 55; Commonwealth v. Hayes, 205 Pa. Super. 338, 341, 209 A.2d 38, 39 (1965).
68   Feiner v. New York, 340 U.S. 315, 319 (1951).
69   *E.g.*, CAL. PENAL CODE § 404.6 (West Supp. 1967); GA. CODE ANN. § 26-5304 (Supp. 1967); N.Y. PENAL LAW § 240.08 (McKinney 1967); TEX. PEN. CODE art. 466a (Supp. 1967).
70   GA. CODE ANN. § 26-5304 (Supp. 1967). The General Assembly of Georgia is expected to increase the penalty for inciting to riot from a misdemeanor to a felony in 1968. Remarks of Lewis R. Slaton, *supra* note 41, at 285.

seem to emphasize sufficiently the preventive nature of an inciting to riot measure and are couched in the judicially acceptable terms of clear and present danger.

d. Conspiracy

As yet, there is no evidence that some form of nationwide conspiracy has been responsible for the planning and execution of the recent urban violence.[71] Nevertheless, on the local scene, various radical organizations have been quick to seize upon discontent growing out of a spontaneous incident and to enkindle it into full scale disorder.[72] Often the individuals in the organizations so involved do not take part in the actual riot activity, yet it is their behind-the-scene manipulations that determine the course and extent of the violence. Such conduct falls within both the spirit and the letter of the law proscribing criminal conspiracies.

In *People v. Epton*[73] a conviction based on conspiracy to incite riot was upheld by the New York Court of Appeals. Evidence produced at the trial established that, during the Harlem riots of July, 1964, Epton and his co-conspirators did their utmost to stir into violence the unrest caused by the shooting of a fifteen-year-old boy by an off-duty police lieutenant. The court clearly distinguished the conspiracy charge from the crime of riot itself:

> The essence of a conspiracy is an agreement or plan among two or more persons to commit a crime in the future. The crime of riot, however, is not committed until three or more persons, actually assembled, have disturbed or immediately threatened the public peace. A previous agreement or plan is not a necessary element of the crime. . . . One who agrees with others to organize a riot sometime in the future and who commits an overt act pursuant to that agreement is guilty not of riot but of conspiracy to riot.[74]

Although Epton argued that his conviction could not stand because the bulk of the evidence against him centered on his speech, this contention was rejected as a misunderstanding of the gravamen of a conspiracy to riot charge.[75] It was not speech, but the illegal agreement that constituted the essence of the crime. Furthermore, while recognizing the first amendment limitations upon prosecution for non-speech crimes when the evidence consists solely of speech, the court concluded that the language employed fell outside the scope of constitutional protection. It created a "clear and present danger" of attempting or accomplishing the prohibited crime.[76]

---

71 RIOT COMMISSION REPORT, *supra* note 2, at 202.
72 In People v. Epton, 19 N.Y.2d 496, 227 N.E.2d 829, 281 N.Y.S.2d 9 (1967), *cert. denied,* 88 S. Ct. 824 (1968), the defendant, convicted of conspiracy to incite riot, was president of the Harlem club of the Progressive Labor Movement. *Id.* at 501, 227 N.E.2d at 831-32, 281 N.Y.S.2d at 12. Other radical organizations that advocate violence to achieve desired goals include the Revolutionary Action Movement and the Nation of Islam. *See* Excerpts from the Testimony of J. Edgar Hoover before the House Subcommittee on Appropriations, reprinted in 36 CONG. Q. 1711 (Sept. 8, 1967).
73 19 N.Y. 2d 496, 227 N.E.2d 829, 281 N.Y.S.2d 9 (1967), *cert. denied,* 88 S. Ct. 824 (1968).
74 *Id.* at 508, 227 N.E.2d at 836, 281 N.Y.S.2d at 18.
75 *Id.* at 507, 227 N.E.2d at 835, 281 N.Y.S.2d at 18.
76 *Id.,* 227 N.E.2d at 836, 281 N.Y.S.2d at 18.

The case illustrates the useful function that a conspiracy charge can perform in the prevention of mass urban violence. This penal sanction can be applied to the activities of conspirators even before their illegal plan is executed. The overt act required for a conspiracy indictment does not have to be the riot itself, but can consist of any preliminary independent action performed by one of the conspirators in order to bring the planned disturbance into existence.[77] If violence does erupt as a result of the agreement, the agitators can be prosecuted both for the conspiracy and the substantive crime of riot, even though they may not be physically present at the riot scene.[78]

e. Emergency Powers

State legislatures often grant to cities various emergency powers that can be employed to preserve public health and safety during periods of natural disaster or civil disorder.[79] If the rioting in a city becomes intensive or threatens to spread, authority can be found in these provisions for such tactical measures as the imposition of a curfew, restrictions on the sale of gas and liquor, and a blockade of the riot area.[80] The local district attorney should keep a catalogue of the emergency powers available to the various public officials in order to insure that the required action can be taken without undue delay.[81] As in the other areas of riot legislation, the usefulness of many of these emergency powers is hindered because they were not drafted to cope with the problems of mass urban racial violence.[89] One state, Ohio, has recently passed a statute that is expressly designed to delegate to local authorities the power to impose necessary restrictions during a period of riot:

> The chief administrative officer of a political subdivision with police powers, when engaged in suppressing a riot or when there is a clear and present danger of a riot, may cordon off any area or areas threatened by such riot and prohibit persons from entering such area or areas . . . and may prohibit the sale . . . or transportation of firearms or . . . other dangerous explosives in, to, or from such areas. . . . [83]

---

77 Although something more than mere conversation among conspirators forming and planning the riot would be necessary, one federal court has gone so far as to designate the making of a telephone call as an "overt act" sufficient to sustain a conspiracy conviction. Bartoli v. United States, 192 F.2d 130, 132 (4th Cir. 1951).

78 Pinkerton v. United States, 328 U.S. 640, 645-47 (1946).

79 *E.g.,* WIS. STAT. ANN. § 66.325 (1965):
  (1) Not withstanding any other provision of law to the contrary, the common council of any city of the first class is empowered to declare, by ordinance or resolution, an emergency existing within such city whenever conditions arise by reason of . . . riot or civil commotion . . . .
  (2) The emergency power of the common council herewith conferred shall include such general authority to order, by ordinance or resolution, whatever is necessary and expedient for the health, safety, welfare and good order of such city in such emergency . . . .

80 RIOT COMMISSION REPORT, *supra* note 2, at 524-25. The National Advisory Commission on Civil Disorders has recognized the efficacy of the measures and has recommended that states adopt legislation that will specifically authorize their employment in emergency situations. *Id.* at 524-27.

81 Remarks of Melvin G. Rueger, Greenbrier Conference of the National District Attorneys Association, Aug. 1967, printed in *Riot Panel, supra* note 41, at 287.

82 *E.g.,* CONN. GEN. STAT. ANN. § 53:169 (Supp. 1967).

83 OHIO REV. CODE ANN. § 3761.16 (Page Current Material Binder 1967).

If properly implemented by local officials, such a statute appears to be a legitimate exercise of emergency police power. Although freedom of movement is probably not accorded the same degree of importance as the basic first amendment guarantees, it has received recognition as a significant right.[84] Nevertheless, considering the efficacy of a curfew and other related measures in riot suppression and control, a vital state interest can be recognized in their utilization during such disorders.[85] The clear and present danger test incorporated into the statute serves to insure a reasonable and acceptable standard by which the necessity for the emergency restrictions can be judged.

3. Conclusion

The major defect hindering the effective application of state riot provisions is the archaic terminology employed in the statutes. The existence of common-law formulations of the crimes in the statutes often results in one of two extremes: the wording is so vague as to be susceptible to constitutional challenge[86] or the elements are specified in technical terms that have little relation to the factual pattern of a modern urban riot.[87] However, by modernizing the language of existing statutes and adding, when necessary, a well drafted inciting to riot provision, a state can provide an adequate legal foundation for prosecuting those who attempt to cause or actually participate in urban violence. Proper utilization of the conspiracy and inciting to riot statutes can serve to silence agitators whenever their activity intentionally causes a clear and present danger of grave public disorder. The unlawful assembly and riot provisions place a blanket legal sanction on all who participate in mob action that threatens or in fact produces a riot situation. Finally, in addition to the above offenses, a state can also indict a rioter for any of the substantive incidental crimes, such as arson or looting, that he may personally commit during the course of the riot.[88]

C. State Power Over the Right to Demonstrate

1. Scope of Power

Although the majority of the recent riots were characterized as "spontaneous

---

84   Kent v. Dulles, 357 U.S. 116, 125-27 (1958). *See also* Edwards v. California, 314 U.S. 160, 177-181 (1941) (concurring opinion of Justice Douglas).

85   Roadblocks and a curfew used in conjunction with massive force sweep tactics were credited with an important role in bringing the August 11-17, 1965 Watts riot in Los Angeles under control. GOVERNOR'S COMMISSION ON THE LOS ANGELES RIOTS, VIOLENCE IN THE CITY — AN END OR A BEGINNING? 20, 21 (1965).

86   *See* International Longshoremen's & Warehousemen's Union v. Ackerman, 82 F. Supp. 65, 101 (D. Hawaii 1948), *rev'd on other grounds*, 187 F.2d 860 (9th Cir.), *cert. denied*, 342 U.S. 859 (1951); *cf.* Baker v. Binder, 274 F. Supp. 658, 661 (W.D. Ken. 1967).

87   *E.g.*, MASS. ANN. LAWS ch. 269, § 1 (Supp. 1966). The National Advisory Commission on Civil Disorders has recognized the need for updating and strengthening state riot control statutes. RIOT COMMISSION REPORT, *supra* note 2, at 523-24.

88   The National Advisory Commission on Civil Disorders concluded as a result of a survey that there was "no basic lack of legal tools available to control disorders." RIOT COMMISSION REPORT, *supra* note 2, at 522. The Commission has recommended, however, the adoption of certain additional state legislation to cover specific problem areas. It cited the need for measures designed to restrict the sale of firearms, proscribe the manufacture or possession of ·incendiary devices ("Molotov cocktails") and prohibit forceful interference with the work of firemen or other emergency workers. *Id.* at 522-23.

outbursts,"[89] there have been instances when planned demonstrations have degenerated into mob action resulting in serious violence.[90] The purpose of this section is to outline the legal procedure that a state governmental agency can employ to prohibit or control such demonstrations in racially tense areas. The basic problem is structured by the conflict between first amendment rights granting freedom of speech and assembly and the police power of the state to preserve public peace and order.

There is no doubt that peaceful assemblies are protected under the Constitution. The ability to demonstrate en masse has proved to be a vital tool for minorities wishing to air their grievances in public view. Such conduct has been upheld, even when the views expressed by the demonstration were extremely unpopular.[91] Often it is the only recourse for groups who find publication in the mass media either ineffective or prohibitively expensive.[92]

Nevertheless, the right to demonstrate is not accorded the same privilege as communication by "pure speech." In *Cox v. Louisiana*[93] the Supreme Court stated that

> [W]e emphatically reject the notion urged by appellant that the First and Fourteenth Amendments afford the same kind of freedom to those who would communicate ideas by conduct such as patrolling, marching, and picketing on streets and highways, as these amendments afford to those who communicate ideas by pure speech.[94]

Obviously, when a demonstration loses its peaceful character, the state can intercede and effect dispersal of the demonstrators.[95] A more complex problem results when the demonstration itself remains peaceful, but its presence in a racially tense area incites spectators to violence. In such a situation, the general rule is that the right of assembly cannot be abridged merely because of a hostile audience reaction.[96] Rather, it is the duty of the state to provide adequate police protection to insure the safety of the demonstrators.[97] However, if the magnitude of the impending disorder poses a serious danger to life and property, suppression or regulation of the demonstration may be warranted.[98] Thus, whether it be the

---

89 PRESIDENT'S COMMISSION ON LAW ENFORCEMENT AND ADMINISTRATION OF JUSTICE, THE CHALLENGE OF CRIME IN A FREE SOCIETY 37 (1967).

90 The wave of violent demonstrations which occurred in Chicago during the summer of 1966 is chronicled in City of Chicago v. King, 86 Ill. App. 2d 340, 343-49, 230 N.E.2d 41, 42-46 (1967). During 1966 and 1967, demonstrations in the following cities resulted in riots or serious disorder: Birmingham, Ala. Jan. 11, 1966; Lorman, Miss. April 4, 1966; Philadelphia, Miss. June 21, 1966; Jacksonville, Fla. July 18-19, 1966; Louisville, Ky. April 20, 1967; Houston, Texas May 16-17, 1967; Boston, Mass. June 2-4, 1967. 36 CONG. Q., *supra* note 72, at 1710-12.

91 Cox v. Louisiana, 379 U.S. 536, 551-52 (1965). *See generally* H. KALVEN, JR., THE NEGRO AND THE FIRST AMENDMENT 140-60 (1965).

92 *See* Adderley v. Florida, 385 U.S. 39, 50-51 (1966) (dissenting opinion of Justice Douglas); Williams v. Wallace, 240 F. Supp. 100, 106 (M.D. Ala. 1965).

93 379 U.S. 536 (1965).

94 *Id.* at 555.

95 *E.g.*, Pritchard v. Downie, 326 F.2d 323 (8th Cir. 1964); State v. Leary, 264 N.C. 51, 140 S.E.2d 756 (1965).

96 *See* the cases cited in note 125 *infra* and accompanying text.

97 *See* Hague v. CIO, 307 U.S. 496, 516 (1939); Kelly v. Page, 335 F.2d 114, (5th Cir. 1964); Williams v. Wallace, 240 F. Supp. 100, 110 (M.D. Ala. 1965).

98 *See* City of Chicago v. King, 86 Ill. App. 2d 340, 346-47, 230 N.E.2d 41, 44 (1967); *cf.* Walker v. City of Birmingham, 388 U.S. 307, 315-17 (1967).

demonstrators themselves or the spectators who pose the threat of uncontrollable riot, the essential questions remain the same: at what point in time, and by what legal methods, can the state act to restrict freedom of assembly?

2. Timing of State Action

In *Cantwell v. Connecticut*[99] the Supreme Court pointed out that a state has the power not only to punish, but also to prevent, immediate threats to public safety, such as riots and similar disorders.[100] Thus, if an otherwise legal demonstration threatens to erupt into riot, it would seem that the state can act to disperse it before the violence actually occurs. In an analogous situation occurring during a labor dispute, the Court sustained an injunction against all picketing, including that which was peaceful, when the past activity was marred by violence that threatened to recur.[101] This is basically an application of the "clear and present danger" test to the right of free assembly.

The major problem with the clear and present danger doctrine inheres in its application to a specific set of circumstances. For example, in *Terminiello v. Chicago*[102] both Justice Douglas speaking for the majority and Justice Jackson in dissent agreed that the doctrine should be employed, but they differed as to whether the particular conduct in question posed the requisite menace to justify state action.[103] However, when a threatening urban demonstration is considered in the context of the recent wave of serious disorders that have swept the country, the need for state regulation is readily apparent. One commentator has suggested that a demonstration in such an area as the Watts section of Los Angeles during a period of unrest could by its very presence induce violence.[104] In such a case, it would seem that the state could act to prevent or at least stringently control that presence before any disorder occurred.

3. Methods of Control

a. Breach of the Peace Statutes

Statutes and ordinances proscribing breach of the peace or disorderly conduct have traditionally been the primary tools employed by the states to regulate demonstrations. However, in a series of cases beginning with *Edwards v. South Carolina*[105] and culminating in *Cox v. Louisiana*,[106] the Supreme Court has cast grave doubts on the constitutionality of these measures when they are used for that purpose. The primary objection centers on the vague terminology used in such statutes to define the offenses, because the language "sweeps within its broad scope activities that are constitutionally protected free speech and assembly."[107] It is important to note, however, that in the cases where the statutes

---

99   310 U.S. 296 (1940).
100   *Id.* at 308.
101   Milk Wagon Drivers Local 753 v. Meadowmoor Dairies, Inc., 312 U.S. 287 (1941).
102   337 U.S. 1 (1949).
103   *Id.* at 4-5, 26. *See* Comment, *Freedom of Assembly,* 15 DePaul L. Rev. 317, 321-23 (1966).
104   Note, *Regulation of Demonstrations,* 80 Harv. L. Rev. 1773, 1774 (1967).
105   372 U.S. 229 (1963).
106   379 U.S. 536 (1965).
107   *Id.* at 552.

were struck down, the conduct to which they had been applied was in fact
protected. The demonstrations were essentially peaceful, or at the least they
did not pose the clear threat of violence characterized by an urban riot.[108]

In the last few years there has been a shift in the philosophy of the Negro
movement. The theory of non-violence embedded in the early sit-in demonstrations has been replaced to some degree by the more militant views of the
vociferous advocates of "Black Power." The transition has been manifested by a
marked increase in "community harassment" and, in some cases, has led to
actual riot.[109] The question arising from this change in tactics is whether the
type of the breach of the peace statutes that the Court held void when applied
to peaceful civil rights demonstrations will also be struck down when employed
to regulate militant demonstrations threatening the more violent forms of the
recent urban disturbances.

As yet, the Supreme Court has not passed on this issue. But it would seem
that, even if the statutes were vague in wording, they would still be effective to
proscribe the hard-core conduct that is encompassed by even the strictest type
of statutory interpretation. In *Carmichael v. Allen*[110] a federal district court
employed this rationale to uphold Georgia's riot statute, but it declined to
afford the same treatment to a broadly worded municipal disorderly conduct
ordinance.[111] Although the conduct in question was clearly within the power of
the state to proscribe under the state riot statute, the court enjoined the employment of the municipal ordinance because its vague terminology readily permitted
the executive and judiciary "to make a crime out of what is protected
activity."[112]

This decision suggests that the standard breach of the peace and disorderly
conduct provisions may be too vaguely worded to be an adequate tool in the
regulation of demonstrations, even when violence is threatened or actually erupts.
However, because of the broad spectrum of conduct that can validly be prohibited as a "breach of the peace," it is virtually impossible to draft the definitions in precise terms.[113] Thus, although states should reexamine the language
of such statutes in an attempt to eliminate the more obvious ambiguities, the
primary test of validity should turn on the conduct to which they are in fact
applied. A certain amount of discretion on the part of law enforcement officials
is a necessity. It is the state's responsibility to exercise this discretion in such a
manner as to prohibit only that type of activity that is clearly beyond the pale
of constitutional protection.

---

108 In both *Edwards* and *Cox,* the demonstrators engaged in singing and cheering, but
the Court made an independent examination of the record and found that the conduct
could not constitutionally be prohibited as a breach of the peace. Edwards v. South Carolina,
372 U.S. 229, 233-35 (1963); Cox v. Louisiana 379 U.S. 536, 545-51 (1965).
109 H. ABRAHAM, FREEDOM AND THE COURT 298-99 (1967). *See generally* Costanzo,
Public Protest and Civil Disobedience: Moral and Legal Considerations, 13 LOYOLA L. REV.
21, 50-53 (1967).
110 267 F. Supp. 985 (N.D. Ga. 1967).
111 *Id.* at 996, 997-99. See note 41 *supra* for the language of the state riot statute.
112 267 F. Supp. at 999.
113 DENZER & McQUILLAN, *Practice Commentary,* N.Y. PENAL LAW § 240.20(7), at 129
(McKinney 1967).

b. Parade Permits

Many municipalities maintain ordinances requiring those who wish to use the public streets for the purpose of staging a demonstration to acquire prior approval in the form of a parade permit. Although the Supreme Court upheld this type of regulation in *Cox v. New Hampshire*,[114] it was careful to delineate the exact limits of such authority. The undoubted power of the municipality to control the use of its streets for parades was recognized, but the inherent discretion could only be exercised with a " 'systematic, consistent and just order of treatment, with reference to the convenience of public use of the highways . . . .' "[115] It is important to note that the ordinance in *Cox,* as narrowly construed by the state court, was strictly a measure for traffic control. The city had no power to deny a permit because of the content of the message that the demonstration sought to convey.[116]

The rhetoric of "public convenience" in a parade permit ordinance could conceivably be extended to authorize the denial of a parade permit because the demonstration would create a clear and present danger of serious public disorder.[117] However, such a determination would necessarily involve a subjective judgment on the part of the official issuing the permit. The Supreme Court has been extremely reluctant to tolerate this type of administrative discretion on the grounds that it often results in either a prior restraint of the rights of free speech and assembly or a denial of equal protection. In *Cox v. Louisiana*[118] the Court pointed out that

> [i]t is clearly unconstitutional to enable a public official to determine which expressions of view will be permitted and which will not or to engage in invidious discrimination among persons or groups . . . by use of a statute providing a system of broad discretionary licensing power . . . . [119]

Hence, it appears that parade permits are valid insofar as they are restricted to the purely empirical function of traffic regulation. But when an official has the power to deny a permit because he believes that the demonstration will cause a serious danger of riot, his decision necessarily incorporates a personal appraisal of the content of the message to be conveyed.[120] Such discretion is clearly prone to the type of abuse condemned in *Cox v. Louisiana.*[121] Thus, although a state or city has the authority to suppress demonstrations that pose a serious threat to public safety, this power should not be exercised by means of the permit system. Because of the subjective elements involved, a more

---

114   312 U.S. 569 (1941).
115   *Id.* at 576, adopting the language of the New Hampshire Supreme Court in State v. Cox, 91 N.H. 137, 143, 16 A.2d 508, 513 (1940).
116   312 U.S. at 575-76.
117   In *Walker v. City of Birmingham,* 388 U.S. 307 (1967), the Court, in discussing a parade permit, implied that a properly drafted and enforced permit system could be employed to prevent "public disorder and violence." *Id.* at 315-17. *See* notes 131-136 *infra* and accompanying text.
118   379 U.S. 536 (1965).
119   *Id.* at 557.
120   *See* Hague v. CIO, 307 U.S. 496 (1939), where a permit ordinance was held void on its face partly because "[i]t enable[d] the Director of Safety to refuse a permit on his mere opinion that such refusal will prevent 'riots, disturbances or disorderly assemblage.' " *Id.* at 516.
121   379 U.S. 536 (1965).

formal judicial process should be required for ascertaining the facts in each case and weighing them in the context of the "clear and present danger" doctrine.

c. Judicial Control

The equity power of a court can be effectively employed as a means of exercising state control over demonstrations. Upon a showing of clear and present danger, a court can lay down specific regulations as to the size, place and time of the proposed demonstration in order to insure that it can be kept under proper police control. Such an injunction can be based either on the power of the court to enjoin violations of a statute, such as a breach of the peace provision,[122] or on the general equity power to meet with an emergency situation.[123] The validity of the decree will depend upon the extent to which it meets · the exigencies of the particular situation without needlessly infringing upon protected conduct.[124]

Although the Supreme Court has continually stated that the exercise of constitutional rights cannot be infringed because of hostile audience reaction,[125] there is some authority for the proposition that an injunction can be issued when the magnitude of anticipated disorder threatens to exceed effective police control.[126] Such a situation arose in Chicago during the summer of 1966. Civil rights leaders had embarked upon a program of "creative tension," and the result was several million dollars of property damage, the death of 27 persons and injury to 374 others, including 61 police officers.[127] Much of this violence seemed to emanate from mobs of spectators who constantly harassed the demonstrators, even though the police department strained to provide adequate protection.[128] Finally, the City of Chicago applied for and received a temporary injunction severely limiting the size of future demonstrations, restricting them to daylight hours (exclusive of rush-traffic periods), and requiring twenty-four hours' advance notice of their location.[129] In discussing the necessity of these regulations, the Appellate Court of Illinois seemed impressed with the allegation unless the demonstrations were subject to such measures, the burden placed

---

122 *See* Walker v. City of Birmingham, 388 U.S. 307, 309, 315 (1967).
123 *See* City of Chicago v. King, 86 Ill. App. 2d 340, 353-54, 230 N.E.2d 41, 47-48 (1967).
124 *E.g.,* Milk Wagon Drivers Local 753 v. Meadowmoor Dairies, Inc., 312 U.S. 287, 298 (1941).
125 Cox v. Louisiana, 379 U.S. 536, 551-52 (1965); Wright v. Georgia, 373 U.S. 284, 292-93 (1963); Watson v. City of Memphis, 373 U.S. 526, 535 (1963); Cooper v. Aaron, 358 U.S. 1, 16 (1958); Brown v. Board of Educ., 349 U.S. 294, 300 (1955). *See generally* Pollitt, *Free Speech for Mustangs and Mavericks,* 46 N.C.L. Rev. 39 (1967).
126 City of Chicago v. King, 86 Ill. App. 2d 340, 346-47, 230 N.E.2d 41, 44 (1967); *cf.* Walker v. City of Birmingham, 388 U.S. 307, 315 (1967).
127 City of Chicago v. King, 86 Ill. App. 2d 340, 342-47, 230 N.E.2d 41, 42-45 (1967).
128 Chicago's Superintendent of Police, O. W. Wilson, charged that in fact the demonstrators did not want adequate police protection.

I believe that it was the aim of these marchers to subject themselves to violence. If the marches were conducted without incident, nothing would be gained. The violence which occurs is in fact their bargaining wedge. If violence occurs, they can make demands upon the city administration and in return for the granting of those demands agree to end the marches and thereby end the violence. Otherwise they have no bargaining power. For this reason, those in charge of the marches do not really want adequate police protection . . . . Wilson, *Civil Disturbances and the Rule of Law,* 58 J. Crim. L.C. & P.S. 155, 159 (1967).

129 City of Chicago v. King, 86 Ill. App. 2d 340, 342-43, 230 N.E.2d 41, 42 (1967). *See* Pollitt, *supra* note 125, at 41-42; Note, *supra* note 104, at 1787 n.86.

on the police department would seriously hinder its ability to preserve peace and prevent crime throughout the entire city of Chicago.[130]

The point of discussing this case is not to call for a general reappraisal of the "hostile audience" doctrine. The right to protest against the majority — peacefully, but with force and vigor — obviously cannot be suspended because of the existence of civil rights tensions in the major cities. However, when the demonstrations that provoke the hostility are carried on in such a fashion as to seriously endanger the safety of not only those who demonstrate, but also the entire community, a state must be permitted to regulate such demonstrations after balancing the interest of the individual against that of society itself.[131] In such a situation, it is both reasonable and necessary to allow a court to subject a demonstration to stringent regulations designed to protect the rights of all persons who are both directly and indirectly affected by the activity.

Once an injunction is granted, the demonstrators are bound to obey it until its expiration or its dissolution through the ordinary methods of appeal. There is no right to engage in the proscribed activity under the theory that the decree was erroneous and then attack it collaterally when cited for contempt.[132] This familiar principle was reaffirmed by a severely divided Court in the recent case of *Walker v. City of Birmingham.*[133] A state circuit court had granted an injunction prohibiting the petitioners from violating a local parade ordinance by engaging in unlicensed demonstrations. Alleging that the decree was clearly unconstitutional, the petitioners proceeded to conduct their demonstrations as planned and were later convicted of contempt. Justice Stewart, speaking for the majority, conceded that the breadth and vagueness of the language employed in both the parade ordinance and the injunction would certainly be subject to substantial constitutional question.[134] However, after pointing out that the state court clearly had jurisdiction over the petitioners and the subject matter of the dispute, he refused to characterize the injunction as "transparently invalid or [having] only a frivolous pretense to validity."[135] Thus the contempt convictions were upheld because the litigants failed to test the injunction according to the prescribed procedure for review. Although there may be doubts as to the ultimate wisdom of the policy embraced by the majority,[136] it does have the advantage of forcing demonstrators whose conduct could validly be proscribed to fight their battle in the courts and not in the streets.

---

130 City of Chicago v. King, 86 Ill. App. 2d 340, 345-46, 230 N.E.2d 41, 43-44 (1967).
131 *See* Wilson, *supra* note 128, at 159. The Chicago Police Superintendent attributed the marked increase in crime in the entire city during periods of civil disorder to the fact that "a tremendous amount of police personnel and effort had been diverted from crime fighting to dealing with civil disturbances." *Id.* at 158.
132 Howat v. Kansas, 258 U.S. 181, 189-90 (1922).
133 388 U.S. 307 (1967).
134 *Id.* at 316-17.
135 *Id.* at 315.
136 In dissent, Justice Brennan pointed out that
     [w]e cannot permit fears of "riots" and "civil disobedience" generated by slogans like "Black Power" to divert our attention from what is here at stake — not violence or the right of the State to control its streets and sidewalks, but the insulation from attack of *ex parte* orders and legislation upon which they are based even when patently impermissible prior restraints on the exercise of First Amendment rights, thus arming the state courts with the power to punish as a "contempt" what they otherwise could not punish at all. *Id.* at 349 (dissenting opinion).

d. Police Discretion

There is no doubt that the police have the power to suppress a demonstration when it crosses the bounds of peaceful protest and erupts into violence.[137] The more subtle problem arises in those borderline cases in which actual disorder has not yet occurred, but there seems to be a clear and present danger that some violence will result. It is understandably difficult for police to make on-the-spot distinctions between validly proscribed disorderly conduct and that form of protected activity that "induces a condition of unrest, creates dissatisfaction with conditions as they are, or even stirs people to anger."[138] Nevertheless, the decision to characterize a demonstration as illegal is first made at the scene by the police, and they must be accorded the necessary discretion to act quickly in the interests of public safety.

The importance of extensive tactical training for police in the field of demonstration control cannot be overemphasized.[139] In the past, police activity during demonstrations has been marred by incidents of serious abuse by some police officers.[140] A peaceful demonstration should not be looked upon with disapproval by a police agency. Rather, it should be considered a safety valve possibly serving to prevent a riot. The spark that could transform a peaceful assembly into a violent mob could very easily be supplied by arbitrary and unwarranted police action. The power in the police to make on-the-spot decisions is present by reason of necessity, the ability to make these decisions correctly is just as essential.

4. Conclusion

The state has a valid interest in suppressing demonstrations that present a clear and present danger of riot or other serious public disorder. However, because of the first amendment rights involved, this authority cannot be employed arbitrarily. There is no doubt that the state can take all reasonable measures necessary to preserve public peace and safety. Nevertheless, unsubstantiated claims of riot prevention will not justify excessive restrictions on assemblies that are essentially peaceful in themselves, or do not pose an uncontrollable threat to the safety of the state. Thus, the fundamental element in demonstration control is the proper exercise of discretion in determining the need for regulation and in fashioning restrictions to meet the specific circumstances of each situation.

D. Federal Riot Statutes

1. The Anti-Riot Statute

On April 10, 1968, the Congress passed H.R. 2516,[141] a civil rights bill

---

137 *E.g.*, Pritchard v. Downie, 326 F.2d 323 (8th Cir. 1964); State v. Leary, 264 N.C. 51, 140 S.E.2d 756 (1965).
138 Terminiello v. Chicago, 337 U.S. 1, 4 (1949).
139 *See* RIOT COMMISSION REPORT, *supra* note 2, at 328-29. *See also* Leary, *The Role of the Police in Riotous Demonstrations*, 40 NOTRE DAME LAWYER 499 (1965).
140 *See* Note, *supra* note 104, at 1785 n.75.
141 114 CONG. REC. 2758-826 (daily ed. April 10, 1968). The entire bill, as passed by the Senate and adopted by the House, is reprinted in 114 CONG. REC. 2578-83 (daily ed. March 11, 1968).

that included a provision making it a federal crime to use any facility of inter-state commerce to incite or engage in a riot.[142] This measure was signed into law by the President on April 11, 1968.[143] Whereas state laws center primarily on the disturbance itself, the avowed purpose of the federal criminal statute is to focus on the individual who crosses a state line for the purpose of enkindling public disorder.[144] The section is patterned after the Anti-Racketeering Act[145] and is intended to supplement local law enforcement by assuring federal investi-gative and prosecutive jurisdiction over "out-of-state" inciters.[146]

The history of the anti-riot provision is rather intricate. Its nucleus can be found in H.R. 421,[147] which passed the House on July 19, 1967.[148] H.R. 421 was strongly criticized by certain Congressmen who pointed out that, among other defects, the definition of inciting to riot was so vague as to be unconstitu-tional under the first amendment.[149] The Senate did not act on H.R. 421 as such. However, when the Senate was in the process of strengthening the civil rights aspects of H.R. 2516, proponents of an anti-riot statute were able to in-corporate the basic features of H.R. 421 into the civil rights bill by means of amendments.[150] Although the present anti-riot statute closely parallels the pro-visions of H.R. 421,[151] an attempt was made in the Senate amendment to define the crime in more precise language so as to avoid any constitutional challenges.[152] Nevertheless, when the amended civil rights bill was returned to the House, there were still strong reservations concerning the anti-riot measure.[153] How-ever, because of the "realities of the parliamentary situation,"[154] which necessi-tated acceptance of the anti-riot amendment if the open housing and other civil rights provisions were to be accepted, the measure was passed without prolonged debate.[155]

One of the underlying rationales behind the federal anti-riot statute appears to be the assumption that outside agitators have played a major part in causing modern urban disturbances. As yet, the proof on this issue has certainly not been conclusive. There seems, however, to be no doubt that the immediate cause of nearly all the recent riots has been a spontaneous incident, usually involving police action in a ghetto area.[156] Once the rioting was under way, certain extremist elements became active, but often as not these groups were

---

142   H.R. 2516, 90th Cong., 2d Sess., ch. 102, §§ 2101-02 (1968), now 18 U.S.C. §§ 2101-02.
143   N.Y. Times, April 2, 1968, at 1, col. 1.
144   H.R. Rep. No. 472, 90th Cong., 1st Sess. 3 (1967).
145   18 U.S.C. §§ 1951-54 (1964).
146   H.R. Rep. No. 472, supra note 144, at 3.
147   H.R. 421, 90th Cong., 1st Sess., ch. 102 (1967).
148   113 Cong. Rec. 9010-11 (daily ed. July 19, 1967).
149   See, e.g., id., at 8953-54 (remarks by Rep. Conyers and Rep. Mathias and excerpt from letter of Lawrence Speiser, American Civil Liberties Union).
150   On March 5, 1968, the anti-riot amendment was added to S. 2516 on the floor of the Senate. 114 Cong. Rec. 2220-32 (daily ed. March 5, 1968).
151   114 Cong. Rec. 2764 (daily ed. April 10, 1968) (remarks of Rep. Celler).
152   Id. at 2815 (reprint of Memorandum on H.R. 2516 prepared by House Committee on the Judiciary).
153   Id. at 2794-95 (remarks of Rep. Ryan).
154   Id.
155   Id. at 2758-826.
156   See President's Commission on Law Enforcement and Administration of Jus-tice, The Challenge of Crime in a Free Society 37 (1967).

locally based and the crossing of state lines was not involved.[157] In the relatively few cases where outside agitators were present,[158] state criminal laws were adequate to proscribe their conduct.[159]

Of course, even a few inciters traveling interstate with the intention to create a disorder can produce tremendous harm. By being available in such situations, the federal statute can play an important, but limited, role in dealing with riots.[160] Nevertheless, the great majority of street disturbances will probably not be affected by the federal statute but will remain exclusively within the state's criminal jurisdiction.

However, even putting aside doubts cast upon its constitutionality or utility, the federal statute is still open to a basic objection. A criminal statute, whether federal or state, cannot come to grips with the underlying causes of civil disorder.[161] A truly effective congressional anti-riot act would aim at the real problems behind urban riots, such as slum housing, unemployment, and inadequate educational and vocational training programs.[162] These root causes do call for a program that is national in scope, whereas the less challenging task of drafting local police statutes can be relegated to the more appropriate hands of the states. It is to be hoped that Congress has not become distracted from its real obligation by the specific anti-riot section in H.R. 2516, but will come to realize that the most effective anti-riot measures in that law are the open-housing and other civil rights provisions.

2. Control of Riot Reporting by Mass Media

Certain members of Congress also expressed an interest in holding hearings to determine what role the mass communications media plays in inciting and spreading the riots. Charges were leveled that early on-the-spot coverage of the disturbances tended to foment further rioting.[163] Senator Hugh Scott suggested the formulation of a voluntary code under which the news media would

---

157 For example, the element of the Progressive Labor Movement that was active during the Harlem riots of July, 1964, seems to have been locally based. See People v. Epton, 19 N.Y.2d 496, 501, 227 N.E.2d 829, 831-32, 281 N.Y.S.2d 9, 12-13 (1967), cert. denied, 88 S. Ct. 824 (1968).

158 In a survey of the twenty-six major race riots between April 1 and July 21, 1967, outside agitators were conclusively found to be present in only seven of the disorders. P. Downing, S. Schlesinger & F. Wyman, "Riots, April 1 to July 21, 1967," Civil Disorder, 1-14 (Legislative Reference Service of Library of Congress Aug. 4, 1967).

The seven cases where the presence of outside agitators was conclusively established are as follows: Willie Ricks (Jackson, Miss., May 12-13, 1967). Id. at 2. Stokely Carmichael (Nashville, Tenn. April 8-10, 1967; Houston, Texas, May 16-17, 1967; Prattville, Ala., June 11, 1967; Atlanta, Ga., June 18-21, 1967). Id. at 1, 3, 4, 7. H. Rapp Brown (Cincinnati, Ohio, June 12-16, 1967; Dayton, Ohio, June 14-15, 1967). Id. at 5, 6. All the above-named individuals are officers of the Student Non-violent Coordinating Committee.

159 See note 88 supra and accompanying text. Stokely Carmichael's attempt to secure a federal injunction against state prosecution under the Georgia riot statute was thwarted in Carmichael v. Allen, 267 F. Supp. 985 (N.D. Ga. 1967). Notes 40-42 supra and accompanying text.

160 RIOT COMMISSION REPORT, supra note 2, at 224.

161 Id.

162 See 113 CONG. REC., supra note 148, at 8945-49 (remarks of Rep. Conyers and Rep. Ryan).

163 Representative Durward G. Hall stated:
   A Stokely Carmichael calling for insurrection on a street corner soapbox is a curiosity — a hippie talking to other hippies. But a Stokely Carmichael talking face-to-face to millions of people (via television) is immediately transformed from

balance the inflammatory statements of riot agitators by presenting at the same time appeals from moderates and government officials.[164] Most executives in the communications industry opposed any imposition of a code, but instead stressed that the best guideline would be the professional judgment of responsible newsmen.[165] At present, it does not appear that any congressional action will be taken to impose restraints on the television or press coverage of riots. Senator Scott has been reported to have abandoned further action on the matter, since "his letters had perhaps served the purpose of causing the industry to examine itself and that this introspection might be sufficient for the time being."[166]

Some of the criticism leveled at the media, at least during the first wave of riots, probably was justified since reporters were inexperienced in handling such situations. The McCone Report, which attempted to dissect the causes of the 1965 Watts riot in Los Angeles, pointed out a lack of balance in the coverage of the early stages of that disorder.[167] Mayor Richard Daley, speaking of disturbances in Chicago during the summer of 1966, claimed that the very presence of the mass media tended to incite rioting. He stated that "in disturbances resulting from protest marches, the television cameras didn't seek the violence, the violence sought the camera."[168] Public officials in Toledo, Ohio, and Newark, New Jersey, also attributed to television a contributing role in their riots.[169]

In an attempt to limit these adverse effects, certain principles of responsible riot coverage have been articulated by the School of Journalism and the Department of Telecommunications of the University of Southern California. These measures have been incorporated into a model code containing sixteen provisions that emphasize the common-sense factors of balanced coverage, inobtrusive presence and prudent reporting of inflammatory incidents.[170] Voluntary adherence to such guidelines is probably the most effective method for insuring that riots are reported in a reasonable manner. Moreover, any form of government-imposed regulations that are enforced by sanctions, such as suspension of

---

an oddball to a national figure. Reprinted in 36 CONG. Q. 1756 (Sept. 8, 1967). Representative Torbert H. Macdonald expressed interest in learning whether news coverage operated to put police at a tactical disadvantage.

> I . . . am very concerned whether or not spot coverage of riots tends to foment further rioting. There is some question as to whether those intent on criminal actions use the news media to ascertain where the police are — or are not. 113 CONG. REC. 11265 (daily ed. Aug. 25, 1967).

164   Senator Scott's suggestion is reported in Younger, Roll a Car — You're on TV!, 3 THE PROSECUTOR 424, 425 (1967). See also 36 CONG. Q., supra note 163, at 1756.
165   See 36 CONG. Q., supra note 163, at 1757; Younger, supra note 164, at 425-26.
166   36 CONG. Q., supra note 163, at 1757.
167   Discussing a meeting widely covered by the press, radio, and television which occurred immediately before the major outbreak of rioting, the Commission points out that

> one Negro high school youth ran to the microphones and said the rioters would attack adjacent white areas that evening. This inflammatory remark was widely reported on television and radio, and it was seldom balanced by reporting of the many responsible statements made at the meeting. GOVERNOR'S COMMISSION ON

THE LOS ANGELES RIOTS, VIOLENCE IN THE CITY — AN END OR A BEGINNING? 13 (1965).
168   Mayor Daley is quoted in Haddad, A Code for Riot Reporting, 6 COLUM. JOURNALISM REV. 35 (Spring 1967).
169   36 CONG. Q., supra note 163, at 1756.
170   Haddad, supra note 168, at 35. See generally RIOT COMMISSION REPORT, supra note 2, at 362-86.

the broadcasting license by the Federal Communications Commission,[171] would have to be very precisely drafted to avoid infringement of first amendment rights. Therefore, it is submitted that the most practical course at the present time would be to avoid imposing any restrictions that might hinder the media's essential role of carrying news to the public accurately and to trust the media to recognize its responsibility to the community in riot coverage.[172]

II. Riot Control and Suppression

A. Introduction

It is essential that a state equip itself in advance for the quick and orderly suppression of domestic violence occurring within its borders. The formulation of a sound system of constitutional riot-control laws, however, is not, of itself, sufficient equipment. Because laws are meaningless if not enforced, the state must also be prepared to act surely and swiftly to quell any disturbance that causes their breakdown. It must be prepared to protect or restore immediately the operation of law and order.

An obstacle to the rapid implementation of control measures in riot situations has been the uncertainty fostered by the fact of federalism. The hazy distinction between state and federal responsibility leads to severe consequences in terms of destruction of life and property.[173] Unfortunately, as the recent squabble between President Johnson and Michigan's Governor Romney forcefully indicates,[174] the confusion continues to exist. If needless destruction at the hands of rioters is to be avoided, these problems of uncertain governmental responsibility — and the separate problems of command and control that arise once military assistance is utilized[175] — must be reviewed and resolved in advance. This portion of the Note will address itself to such a resolution.

Suppression of riots and other domestic violence is primarily a state respon-

---

171   Suspension of licenses was suggested as a possible sanction by Evelle J. Younger, District Attorney of the County of Los Angeles. Younger, *supra* note 164, at 426.

172   The positive aspect of riot reporting is often overlooked. In a speech to the Rice Institute in Houston during the week of Nov. 8, 1967, Deputy Attorney General Warren Christopher noted that rumors were often instrumental in spreading the violence. He cautioned against unreasonable bans on reporting racial incidents, pointing out that "[f]ast accurate reporting of the true state of affairs is probably the best antidote to poisonous rumors in the ghetto." 2 CRIM. L. RPTR. 2119 (1967).

173   The actions of the federal government have generally embodied the spirit of Theodore Roosevelt's assertion that "twenty-four hours of riot, damage, and disorder" are preferable to the illegal use of troops. Comment, *Federal Intervention in the States for the Suppression of Domestic Violence: Constitutionality, Statutory Power, and Policy*, 1966 DUKE L.J. 415, 460 n.162. It is alarming to note that the confusion as to responsibility appears to leave only these unhappy alternatives.

174   The following newspaper articles report the history of the Detroit riot and the ensuing controversy: N.Y. Times, July 24, 1967, at 1, col. 6; *id.*, July 25, 1967, at 1, col. 8; *id.*, July 30, 1967, § 1, at 1, col. 2, & at 1, col. 3, & at 52, col. 1.

175   Note, *Riot Control and the Use of Federal Troops*, 81 HARV. L. REV. 638, 642 (1968). The importance of advance planning and carefully developed systems of command and control was highlighted recently by the experience of events at Watts, Newark, Detroit and Milwaukee. HOUSE COMM. ON ARMED SERVICES, REPORT OF SPECIAL SUBCOMM. TO INQUIRE INTO THE CAPABILITY OF THE NATIONAL GUARD TO COPE WITH CIVIL DISTURBANCES, 90th Cong., 1st Sess. 5662 (December 18, 1967) [hereinafter cited as REPORT ON NATIONAL GUARD CAPABILITY].

sibility, because riots and their incidental crimes are violations of state law.[176] Moreover, since state officers are constitutionally obliged to support the Constitution and to uphold federal laws,[177] the suppression of riots continues to be a state responsibility despite the fact that federal laws may in some way become involved in the riot or its consequences.[178]

In contrast to the states, the federal government does not have the general power or duty to maintain public order. It is not, however, totally without responsibility in this regard. The constitutional provision that "[t]he United States shall guarantee to every State . . . a Republican Form of Government, and shall protect each of them . . . against domestic Violence"[179] provided the basis for an early Supreme Court decision[180] which held that "[i]f a State cannot protect itself against domestic violence, the United States may . . . lend their assistance for that purpose."[181] In addition to this power to assist a state in suppressing domestic violence, the federal government can act when it is itself the target of insurrection, or when unlawful obstructions or assemblages hinder the execution of federal laws or threaten federal property.[182] The constitutional foundation in these instances is the responsibility of the President to take care that the laws be faithfully executed.[183] The statutes that implement these constitutional provisions and thereby form the basis for federal aid in domestic disturbances[184] are discussed below in the context of federal intervention.[185] For present purposes, it is only necessary to understand that the primary responsibility for riot suppression rests with the state, that the state must plan its riot-control operation before any riots break out, and that such planning must recognize and provide for the delicate problems caused by federalism. The necessity of this basic degree of preparation has been acknowledged by a special subcommittee of the House Committee on Armed Services[186] which conducted

---

176   41 Op. Att'y Gen. 313, 324 (1963).
177   Cooper v. Aaron, 358 U.S. 1, 18-19 (1958).
178   41 Op. Att'y Gen. 313, 324 (1963).
179   U.S. Const. art. IV, § 4.
180   United States v. Cruikshank, 92 U.S. 542 (1876).
181   *Id.* at 556.
182   F. Wiener, A Practical Manual of Martial Law 43 (1940). For a detailed historical study of federal military aid, see S. Doc. No. 263, 67th Cong., 2d Sess. (1922).
183   U.S. Const. art. II, § 3.
184   10 U.S.C. §§ 331-34 (1964).
185   See notes 229-348 *infra* and accompanying text.
186   The subcommittee expressed the view that
     law enforcement and maintenance of law and order in individual communities remain the primary responsibility of State and local officials. Therefore, the subcommittee cannot emphasize too strongly its view that State and local law enforcement agencies must review and agree upon acceptable plans for contingencies that may arise in the event of future local disorders. Included in this preplanning must be adequate provision for the integration of police and military forces, communications problems, protection of firefighting personnel, handling of prisoners, and a myriad of other details which are essential if a State is to have a truly effective contingency plan for meeting local disorders.

     . . . . .
     State planning for these contingencies must envision the utilization of Federal support only as a last resort. These plans must nonetheless contemplate the utilization of Federal support in extraordinary contingencies . . . . Report on National Guard Capability, *supra* note 175, at 5663.

hearings that touched on several areas of civil disturbance.[187] A succinct statement of this need was given at a recent conference of the National District
Attorneys Association:

> Riots — mob violence — insurrection — call it what you will, everyone
> should be aware of the fact that virtually every community is vulnerable.
> Thus although the potential problem is not pressing, it is incumbent on
> each one of us to at least prepare for the eventuality.[188]

B. Civilian Law Enforcement Measures

Since local law enforcement agencies constitute the first line of defense
against outbreaks of domestic violence, planning should be initiated at the local
level. In the formulation of a city plan, problems of command are virtually
nonexistent. The mayor is the chief executive; his orders are enforced by the
city police force under the immediate direction of the chief of police. The
chain of command that normally operates in the city continues to prevail in
the riot situation.

The police force is the basic law enforcement agency of any city. This
agency is subjected to strenuous demands when a riot occurs, because it must
provide sufficient force to calm the disorder while still carrying on its ordinary
function of crime prevention throughout parts of the city not struck by violence.
This demand for manpower flexibility requires the implementation of specific
riot procedures carefully tailored to fit the needs and circumstances of the particular city.[189] Proper utilization of the task force concept,[190] by which a specially
trained and equipped task force of police officers can be moved into a given
area on short notice, would seem to maximize flexibility. This concept has the
added advantage of providing a "continuity and unity of command and the
solidarity which hastily gathered forces lack."[191]

The city plan should further attempt to alleviate any anticipated manpower shortage by providing for assistance to the police from other municipal
resources such as the Fire Department, the Public Utilities Department, the
Highway Department, and the Department of Health. However, despite these
and other means of supplying additional manpower,[192] there are certain physical
limits on every local police department which must be recognized.

---

187 *Hearings Before Special Subcomm. to Inquire into the Capability of the National
Guard to Cope with Civil Disturbances of the House Comm. on Armed Services,* 90th Cong.,
1st Sess. (1967) [hereinafter cited as *Hearings on National Guard Capability*].
188 Remarks of Melvin G. Rueger, Greenbrier Conference of National District Attorneys
Association, Aug., 1967, printed in *Riot Panel,* 3 THE PROSECUTOR 282, 286 (1967).
189 Conscious of manpower requirements, President Johnson's Riot Commission prepared
model plans, adaptable to varying local needs and circumstances, for police mobilization and
operations, and recommended that the Department of Justice disseminate them to police
throughout the country. RIOT COMMISSION REPORT, *supra* note 2, at 485-88.
190 For a discussion of Chicago's implementation of the task force concept, see Wilson,
Civil Disturbances and the Rule of Law, 58 J. CRIM. L.C. & P.S. 155, 157 (1967). This
article also contains a definition of the police role and an excellent discussion of police tactics
and techniques in civil disturbances. *Id.* at 156-58.
191 *Id.* at 157.
192 Wilson also suggests the possibilities of "requiring men to work into the next watch,
canceling days off, and putting the force on 12-hour shifts." *Id.*

Riots can reach proportions that exceed the control capabilities of local law enforcement agencies. Therefore, it is essential that a city plan beyond its own limited resources. It can eliminate a great deal of indecision by making an advance determination of the emergency powers of the governor, the county sheriff, the state police force, the National Guard, and the federal troops.[193] Likewise, the assistance available from other state and county sources should be ascertained and catalogued during the planning stage. Advance cooperation agreements should be arranged with law enforcement agents of neighboring political subdivisions. While these agreements must necessarily remain somewhat flexible, they should be specific at least on the point of assigning tasks to the personnel of the cooperating agencies. Insofar as it is possible, such "borrowed" personnel should be utilized in the nonviolent areas of the city. They should assume the routine functions of the local police, such as directing traffic and manning police lines to isolate the affected area. This peripheral use observes the important designation of riot-control as a local responsibility by freeing the local police to participate in the actual suppression of the disturbance. This procedure also simplifies control by leaving suppression of the riot to police officers who are familiar with the area and simplifies command by leaving it to commanders and forces who are used to working with each other.

Another possible means of localizing the force employed in a riot to the greatest extent possible is the use of a *posse comitatus*. It was early recognized that a sheriff has the power to summon the entire population of his county to assist him in keeping the peace.[194] Those summoned were bound to participate under pain of fine and imprisonment.[195] Although this ancient power has had only infrequent use in present-day America, its recent attempted revival in Cook County, Illinois, by Sheriff Joseph Woods[196] has caused considerable interest in its vitality as a riot-control measure.[197] In Illinois, a sheriff is vested with the power to summon a *posse comitatus* "when necessary" to keep the peace.[198] Stressing his "legal right in the time of emergency to deputize a posse comitatus,"[199] Sheriff Woods' plan to train the posse in advance but not to deputize it "until 'Detroit-type' trouble occurs"[200] seems to stretch the statutory requirement of necessity beyond permissible limits. Not surprisingly, the plan has been ruled illegal as being violative of a number of Illinois constitutional and statu-

---

193   Remarks of Melvin G. Rueger, *supra* note 188, at 287. Although this determination must be made on an individual state basis, the Riot Commission generally found state police or highway patrol to be of little practical assistance. In addition to their lack of experience and training in the control of civil disorders, most state police forces cannot be mobilized in significant numbers because their primary duty to police the entire state has already diluted their strength. RIOT COMMISSION REPORT, *supra* note 2, at 496-97.
194   1 BLACKSTONE, COMMENTARIES *343.
195   *Id.* at *343-44.
196   This plan envisioned a volunteer force of 1,000 men. NEWSWEEK, Feb. 26, 1968, at 26.
197   Law enforcement officials from six counties in six different states have contacted Woods seeking information about his plan. Chicago Sun-Times, Feb. 20, 1968, at 3, col. 3.
198   ILL. ANN. STAT. ch. 125, § 18 (Smith-Hurd 1967) provides:
        To keep the peace, prevent crime, or to execute any writ, warrant, process, order or decree, he [sheriff] may call to his aid, when necessary, any person or the power of the county.
199   Chicago Sun-Times, Feb. 20, 1968, at 3, col. 1.
200   *Id.*

tory provisions and Sheriff Woods has been permanently enjoined from recruiting any persons for use in such a posse.[201] In addition, the concept has been widely criticized as "unnecessary," "vigilante," and the prelude to a "blood bath."[202] Another serious drawback is that such a plan would cause difficult problems in the determination of liability for civil and criminal violations by members of the deputized posse. The objections and resentment to Sheriff Woods' plan clearly outweigh its obvious benefit as a ready source of additional manpower. Therefore, regardless of the usefulness of a pre-trained *posse comitatus,* the utilization of recognized state law enforcement agencies, the National Guard or even federal troops would still seem to be a more desirable solution to the problem of riot control.[203]

Although assistance from state and local law enforcement agencies can be separately arranged between political subdivisions, a state-level assistance plan offers the advantage of insuring assistance to all local areas including those that have failed to make any prior arrangements. California has led the way in this area by the implementation of its Mutual Aid Law Enforcement Plan,[204] and many of the other states are either presently formulating state assistance plans of their own or revising their existing plans.[205] Additionally, some conditions may lend themselves to the adoption of mutual assistance programs between two or more states. Interstate compacts would seem to be particularly appropriate where large metropolitan areas extend across state borders. Indeed, analogous precedent for the execution of such interstate agreements is found in the congressionally approved military aid compact signed by New York, New Jersey, and Pennsylvania.[206]

The important objectives of all state and interstate plans are to establish procedures for requesting assistance and to define authority for granting such assistance. Although the same specific procedures may not be suitable for every state, some basic policies would seem to be of universal application.

Control over state resources must be centralized. Authority to dispatch state assistance should therefore reside in the governor of the state from which assistance is sought, and all requests by local officials should be made directly to him. The plan should further provide for the state-wide or interstate coordination of law enforcement operations and planning and for the coordinated transportation of law enforcement personnel and equipment to local areas in response to requests for assistance. It should develop and outline a system of accountability for law enforcement personnel and equipment. A communica-

201 *Id.,* March 1, 1968, at 2, cols. 1-4. The Illinois State's Attorney's office has indicated that it does not intend to appeal this order. *Id.,* March 13, 1968, at 10, col. 3.
202 NEWSWEEK, *supra* note 196, at 26.
203 Speaking for the Urban League, Deputy Director Alvin J. Prejean expressed the feeling that "professional police matters are best left to professional people." Chicago Sun-Times, Feb. 16, 1968, at 22, col. 2.
204 *See* Letter from Major General Glenn C. Ames, Adjutant General of the State of California, to the House Committee on Armed Services, Sept. 1, 1967, in *Hearings on National Guard Capability, supra* note 187, at 6144, 6150.
205 *See* Letters from Adjutants General of the various states, concerning their ability to cope with local disorders, to the House Committee on Armed Services, in *id.,* at 6135-255 *passim.*
206 Act of June 4, 1956, ch. 365, 70 Stat. 247, *amending* Act of July 1, 1952, ch. 538, 66 Stat. 315.

tions system should be established for the transmission of pertinent law enforcement information between local, state, and federal officials. Finally, the plan
should resolve the command and control arrangements that will apply upon
the occurrence of the contingency. In this latter regard, it is necessary that
some degree of operational control remain in the local officials because of their
familiarity with the affected area. The exact arrangement will be dependent
upon the structure of the local government and upon the capabilities of the
individual officials involved. Whatever arrangements are finally made, all
participants should have advance knowledge of who is to make what decision
and when, and under whose control and direction forces are to be employed.

A final nonmilitary measure of state law enforcement would be the establishment of a defense force, in addition to, or as a substitute for, the state
National Guard, for use within the jurisdiction of the state.[207] In view of the
present National Guard strength and availability,[208] however, this tool appears
to be of little practical value. When the riot reaches a stage beyond the control
of civilian law enforcement agencies at the state level, the obvious step is to look
to the military for assistance.

C. Martial Law

An analysis of the declaration and effect of martial law will provide a
helpful background against which to consider the use of military force to quell
domestic violence. Such an analysis must necessarily define the framework in
which the term "martial law" is used in this Note, because the term

> has been justifiably criticized as obscure. However, its dominance in lay
> and legal parlance makes acceptance of any other terminology seem hope-
> less. The trouble lies in the fact that "martial law" has been employed to
> cover the entire spectrum of use of military for civil purposes, from total
> subversion of civil government to selling tickets at football games.[209] (Cita-
> tions omitted.)

It will facilitate a grasp of the concept to draw a basic distinction between
"absolute" and "qualified" martial law. Absolute martial law refers to the
replacement of every civil instrumentality by a corresponding military agency.[210]
By definition, therefore, civil courts do not function in a state of absolute martial
law; military tribunals function in their stead. Qualified martial law, on the
other hand, exists when military instrumentalities carry on certain governmental
activities, but civil courts continue to operate.[211] One authority has noted that
the "vast distinction" between the two is that absolute martial law

> replaces the former civil law whereas military aid [qualified martial law]

---

207   States are authorized to enact such legislation by the provisions of 32 U.S.C. § 109
(1964).
208   *See* REPORT ON NATIONAL GUARD CAPABILITY, *supra* note 175, at 5647-52.
209   Note, *Rule by Martial Law in Indiana: The Scope of Executive Power,* 31 IND. L.J.
456 n.3 (1956). For an excellent discussion of the various meanings that are attached to
"martial law," see F. WIENER, *supra* note 182, at 6-15.
210   F. WIENER, *supra* note 182, at 11.
211   *Id.* at 12.

furnishes no body of law whatsoever but merely the force of arms to ensure that the civil law will remain supreme and not degenerate into military rule. Thus the military forces exercise no legal jurisdiction over offenses committed by civilians or over their persons.[212]

Much of the confusion that has typified the treatment of martial law by the commentators and by the courts seems to result from their failure to observe this distinction. Decisions and treatises alike have gathered widely differing attributes into the general category of "martial law."[213] Looking beyond the label, however, the message is clear and consistent. It is that instances of absolute martial law will, and should, be rare.[214] The reasons for abhorring the imposition of such a state are diverse and compelling. They are an outgrowth of the attitude of a free society that is historically reluctant to give military tribunals the authority to try civilians for non-military offenses.[215] A study of the birth, development, and growth of our governmental institutions reveals that the extension of military jurisdiction to try civilians charged with crime is foreign to our political traditions and our belief in the procedural safeguards of a jury trial.[216] Such an attitude and tradition has caused the American people to regard "[t]he substitution of military, for the civil law, in any community . . . [as] an extreme measure. Socially, economically and politically, it is deplorable and calamitous."[217]

This is not to say that absolute martial law should never exist in our society. Necessity remains the basis and the justification for martial law,[218] whether absolute or qualified. In the event of a sufficiently dire necessity, absolute martial law may be warranted.[219] The determination of necessity is a question of fact; the exact degree required to justify the imposition of martial law is difficult to predict. It is clear, however, that the substitution of military tribunals for civil courts should be the last and most extreme step taken to suppress domestic disturbances and that such a step is not justified as long as the courts are open[220]

---

212 Farrell, *Civil Functions of the Military and Implications of Martial Law*, 22 U. KAN. CITY L. REV. 157, 159 (1954).
213 *Compare* language of *Ex parte* Milligan, 71 U.S. (4 Wall.) 2, 127 (1866):
  [T]here are occasions when martial rule can be properly applied. If, in foreign invasion or civil war, the courts are actually closed, and it is impossible to administer criminal justice according to law, *then,* on the theatre of active military operations, where war really prevails, there is a necessity to furnish a *substitute* for the civil authority . . . ; and *as no power is left but the military,* it is allowed to govern by martial rule until the laws can have their free course. (Emphasis added.)
with language of Note, *Riot Control and the Fourth Amendment,* 81 HARV. L. REV. 625, 632 (1968): "[S]tatutes provide that the governor may declare any county to be under martial law, thus effecting a *partial suspension* of civil government . . . ." (Emphasis added.)
214 F. WIENER, *supra* note 182, at 13.
215 Lee v. Madigan, 358 U.S. 228, 232-33 (1959).
216 Duncan v. Kahanamoku, 327 U.S. 304, 319-24 (1946).
217 *Ex parte* Lavinder, 88 W. Va. 713, 716, 108 S.E. 428, 429 (1921).
218 This point is universally conceded by courts and commentators. *See, e.g.,* Duncan v. Kahanamoku, 327 U.S. 304, 335 (1946) (concurring opinion of Chief Justice Stone); *Ex parte* Milligan, 71 U.S. (4 Wall.) 2, 126-27 (1866); F. WIENER, *supra* note 182, at 16; 45 MICH. L. REV. 86, 87 (1946).
219 *Ex parte* Lavinder, 88 W. Va. 713, 719, 108 S.E. 428, 430 (1921).
220 Frederick Wiener elaborates, saying that " 'open' and 'closed' must be understood as referring not to the mere physical condition of the court house but to the execution and effectiveness of process . . . ." F. WIENER, *supra* note 182, at 120. Applying this definition,

and able to operate. Indeed, the Supreme Court of the United States has recognized that martial law was never intended to supersede the civilian courts, but only to assist the government in keeping those courts open.[221] Frederick Bernays Wiener, a leading authority on martial law, has expressed the belief that no case in the history of the United States has presented a situation of sufficient necessity to warrant the imposition of absolute martial law.[222] His contention is strongly supported by the Supreme Court's holding in *Ex parte Milligan*[223] that military commissions set up to try civilians during the Civil War — certainly this country's hour of most drastic need — were without jurisdiction.[224] Speaking for the *Milligan* Court, Justice Davis used strong language in rejecting the validity of that attempt to institute absolute martial law:

> It is claimed that martial law covers with its broad mantle the proceedings of this military commission. The proposition is this: that in a time of war the commander of an armed force (if in his opinion the exigencies of the country demand it, and of which he is to judge), has the power, within the lines of his military district, to suspend all civil rights and their remedies, and subject citizens as well as soldiers to the rule of *his will;* and in the exercise of his lawful authority cannot be restrained, except by his superior officer or the President of the United States.
>
> If this position is sound to the extent claimed, then . . . the commander . . . can, if he chooses, within his limits, on the plea of necessity, with the approval of the Executive, substitute military force for and to the exclusion of the laws, and punish all persons, as he thinks right and proper, without fixed or certain rules.
>
> The statement of this proposition shows its importance; for, if true, republican government is a failure, and there is an end of liberty regulated by law. Martial law, established on such a basis, destroys every guarantee of the Constitution, and effectually renders the "military independent of and superior to the civil power" . . . . Civil liberty and this kind of martial law cannot endure together; the antagonism is irreconcilable; and, in the conflict, one or the other must perish.[225]

Qualified martial law is far more acceptable to the people because it does not deprive them of their constitutional rights under civil law. On the contrary, in its ordinary characterization as the intervention of National Guard or federal troops to suppress domestic violence, qualified martial law is intended as a means of protecting constitutional rights by keeping the civil courts open.[226] Its use in this capacity has not been infrequent in recent years,[227] a fact that bears testimony to its effectiveness as a riot-control measure and to its general acceptability within the limits of necessity that demand and justify its imposition.

---

he goes on to say that trial of civilians by military tribunals would seem to be proper "where conditions are so thoroughly disturbed that the courts are not only closed but there is no likelihood of their opening in the immediate future . . . ." *Id.*
221   Duncan v. Kahanamoku, 327 U.S. 304, 324 (1946).
222   F. WIENER, *supra* note 182, at 120.
223   71 U.S. (4 Wall.) 2 (1866).
224   *Id.*
225   *Id.* at 124-25.
226   *In re* McDonald, 49 Mont. 454, 476, 143 P. 947, 954 (1914).
227   *See* REPORT ON NATIONAL GUARD CAPABILITY, *supra* note 175, at 5648-49.

A governor's power to declare martial law is a local question with each state.[228] In this regard, state constitutional and statutory provisions are in a state of hopeless confusion. In Indiana, for example, the state attorney general has stated that the governor's power to declare martial law is implied from other specific mandates outlined in the state constitution,[229] namely that the governor is commander-in-chief of the armed forces[230] and, as such, is chargeable with the execution of state law.[231] Contrary to this position, it has been asserted that the governor does not have the power to declare martial law in Indiana.[232] This latter argument views the statutory responsibility for execution of the laws as giving the governor power to use troops in civil disturbances and requiring him to use as much force as is necessary to quell the lawlessness, but denies that it encompasses the "power to suspend civil government."[233]

In some states, statutes specifically bestow upon the governor the power to declare martial law[234] and stipulate that this declaration must be made by proclamation.[235] Even under such statutory authorization, general confusion results from a failure to attribute one definite meaning to the "martial law" label. Attorneys and government officers cannot expect any general certainty in this area; they can only try to ascertain the construction given the elusive term by the courts and legislatures of their particular state.

It is suggested that the rule of necessity provides the only touchstone common to all states in this realm of martial law. If this rule were accepted as a binding criterion — and it should be for the sake of uniformity and certainty — state statutes requiring the formal proclamation of martial law would not be necessary.[236] Under the rule of necessity, "martial law proclaims itself."[237] The proclamation is unnecessary where there is necessity, and useless where there is none.

Whether his power is by implication, by specific statutory provision, or by basic rule of necessity, the governor is the person responsible for the institution of martial law at the state level. The amount of legal significance to be accorded to his declaration has long been the subject of controversy. A series of Supreme Court cases[238] had established and upheld the "doctrine of conclusiveness" as to the use of the military by a governor in quelling civil disorders. In disallowing judicial review of the governor's actions, this doctrine proved to be particularly

---

228 Sterling v. Constantin, 287 U.S. 378, 395-96 (1932).
229 1967 IND. ATT'Y GEN. OP. No. 66, § III, at 8.
230 IND. CONST. art. 5, § 12, provides: "The Governor shall be commander-in-chief of the military and naval forces, and may call out such forces, to execute the laws, or to suppress insurrection, or to repel invasion."
231 IND. CONST. art. 5, § 16, provides: "He [the Governor] shall take care that the laws be faithfully executed."
232 Note, *supra* note 209, at 473.
233 *Id.*
234 *E.g.*, N.J. REV. STAT. § 38A:2-3 (Supp. 1967) provides:
    Whenever the militia, or any part thereof, is employed in aid of civil authority, the Governor, if in his judgment the maintenance of law and order will thereby be promoted, may by proclamation, declare any county or municipality, or part thereof, in which the troops are serving to be subject to martial law.
235 *Id.*
236 F. WIENER, A PRACTICAL MANUAL OF MARTIAL LAW 19-20 (1940).
237 *Id.* at 20.
238 Moyer v. Peabody, 212 U.S. 78 (1909); Luther v. Borden, 48 U.S. (7 How.) 1 (1849); Martin v. Mott, 25 U.S. (12 Wheat.) 19 (1827).

obnoxious to American beliefs in a republican form of government and undoubtedly caused added invective to be written into the Court's opinion in *Ex parte Milligan*.[239]

The doctrine of conclusiveness first appeared in 1827 in the Supreme Court decision of *Martin v. Mott*.[240] In that case conclusive legal effect was accorded the exclusive discretion of the President to call out the militia in cases of actual invasion or the imminent danger of invasion.[241] Twenty-two years later, the Court extended the doctrine to state officials in the celebrated case of *Luther v. Borden*.[242] In *Luther* a group acting under the leadership of a man named Dorr set itself up under a claim of rightful authority in competition with the established government of Rhode Island. A series of arrests, including the arrest of one of the rebels in his own home, followed the declaration of martial law by the older government. In this resulting action in trespass, the Court avoided a decision as to which government was lawfully in power on the ground that, as a political question, it was not proper for judicial review.[243] The Court did say, however, that a state could

> unquestionably . . . use its military power to put down an armed insurrection, too strong to be controlled by the civil authority. The power is essential to the existence of every government, essential to the preservation of order and free institutions, and is as necessary to the States of this Union as to any other government. The State itself must determine what degree of force the crisis demands. And if the government of Rhode Island deemed the armed opposition so formidable, and so ramified throughout the State, as to require the use of its military force and the declaration of martial law, we see no ground upon which this court can question its authority.[244]

In *Moyer v. Peabody*[245] the Court, in language that "went altogether too far,"[246] upheld the conclusiveness of a governor's declaration that an insurrection existed.[247] It chose to test the governor's liability for the arrests made as a precaution against domestic violence by inquiring into his good faith in ordering the arrests rather than by examining their reasonableness. Applying this test of "good faith," Justice Holmes announced for the Court that "[p]ublic danger warrants the substitution of executive process for judicial process"[248] and denied the lower court jurisdiction.[249]

The dangerous precedent established by *Moyer* gave unbridled license to state executives to use the military as a means of accomplishing their own designs. As was predictable in light of the weakness of human nature, the governors

---

239   *See* quotation set out in text accompanying note 225 *supra*.
240   25 U.S. (12 Wheat.) 19, 29-32 (1827).
241   *Id*. at 29. In now famous dicta, the Court stated that this power "is to be exercised upon sudden emergencies, upon great occasions of state, and under circumstances which may be vital to the existence of the Union." *Id*. at 30.
242   48 U.S. (7 How.) 1 (1849).
243   *Id*. at 47.
244   *Id*. at 45.
245   212 U S. 78 (1909).
246   F. WIENER, *supra* note 236, at 109.
247   Moyer v. Peabody, 212 U.S. 78, 83 (1909).
248   *Id*. at 85.
249   *Id*. at 86.

patently abused this privilege. Indeed, before the trend was checked, the "over-exuberant rhetoric" employed by Holmes in *Moyer* was "relied upon to justify what may with moderation be called some of the most curious pages in American jurisprudence."[250]

The controversy was finally put to rest in *Sterling v. Constantin*.[251] In that case, the governor declared martial law in certain Texas counties in which the plaintiffs had oil interests. By making this declaration and directing the National Guard to assume supreme command over the area, he attempted to reduce the depletion of oil reserves by the plaintiffs. Acknowledging a governor's discretion to determine the existence of an exigency requiring military aid, the Court nevertheless held that the reasonableness of his determination is a proper matter for judicial review.[252] The decision incorporated, to an extent, the "good faith" test of *Moyer* by allowing a governor a "permitted range of honest judgment" as necessary to the timely exercise of his duty to maintain peace.[253] The real significance of the case, however, derives from its recognition that this discretion cannot be unlimited. The decision reversed the snowballing doctrine of conclusiveness by declaring that "the allowable limits of military discretion, and whether or not they have been overstepped in a particular case, are judicial questions."[254]

In upholding the propriety of reviewing a governor's exercise of discretion, *Sterling* and later cases that reaffirmed it[255] recognized that the rights guaranteed by the Federal Constitution must be protected against unchecked gubernatorial actions that were possible under the conclusiveness doctrine. These cases complemented the "good faith" test of legality enunciated in *Moyer* with a "direct relation" test.[256] The latter test requires a balancing of the purpose of the action and the reasonableness of the means employed against the gravity of the resulting invasion of individual rights. Because martial law is so drastic and oppressive a measure, the cases require a high degree of necessity to carry the balance in favor of its justification.[257]

The *Sterling* decision also makes actions taken by a military commander pursuant to a declaration of martial law subject to judicial review. Such actions no longer remain lawful simply because martial law was properly declared. The criterion for legality, as always, is necessity; it is framed in the context of "whether or not the particular act in question was required by the public safety."[258] In the suppression of civil disorders, only reasonable force can be used and military commanders are liable for excesses.[259]

The application of the reasonableness test presents a danger of confusion

---

250   F. WIENER, *supra* note 236, at 110.
251   287 U.S. 378 (1932).
252   *Id.* at 400-01.
253   *Id.* at 399.
254   *Id.* at 401.
255   For a citation and discussion of cases reaffirming *Sterling,* see 41 OP. ATT'Y GEN. 313, 320 n.2 (1963).
256   Note, *supra* note 213, at 634.
257   Note, *supra* note 209, at 472.
258   Anthony, *Hawaiian Martial Law in the Supreme Court,* 57 YALE L.J. 27, 54 (1947).
259   Commonwealth *ex rel.* Wadsworth v. Shortall, 206 Pa. 165, 173, 55 A. 952, 955 (1903).

spawned by another misuse of labels.[260] Courts have carelessly referred to martial law situations interchangeably as "war" or "insurrection" despite the fact that the two concepts are clearly distinct, and differing degrees of authority are allowed to a military commander under each.[261] "Insurrection" is not "war," and costly pitfalls may await the military officer who equates the two. The safest course for military personnel employed in aid of civil authority is to recognize the limitations on their power. According to Wiener, any attempt to justify the use of war powers in an insurrection would never stand the test of review in the Supreme Court.[262] On the other hand, although it is persuasively argued that the word "insurrection" itself is not technically accurate[263] as a description of the circumstances justifying the use of the military,[264] this seeming error in terminology has been largely ignored as a practical matter. In determining the lawfulness of the military force used to quell a domestic disturbance, courts are not troubled by whether or not the disturbance was literally an insurrection. If sufficient necessity is present, military force will be upheld.

This discussion of martial law has attempted to show that the subject is fraught with misunderstanding. In summary, it may be said that a few definite principles stand out. Marital law is justified by necessity. Necessity confines it in area and limits it in duration. Necessity, therefore, provides the measure by which the courts determine the lawfulness of a governor's declaration of martial law and its subsequent implementation by the military. In its absolute form, martial law is a most extreme measure because it suspends civil courts in favor of military tribunals. As such, it is warranted only in a most extreme necessity; indeed, the requisite degree of necessity arguably has not been experienced in the history of this country. A qualified form of martial law, however, which consists in the supplanting of *some* governmental agencies by military counterparts, does have substantial precedent and can be prudently utlized by state governors in times of civil disorder. It is in this latter context that subsequent references to "martial law" should be understood.

D. The National Guard

> "There is no substitute for force in quelling civil disturbances, and if the police are unable to provide the manpower to restore normalcy, then there is no alternative but to put in a call for the National Guard — and as quickly as possible." This is my view in a nutshell.[265]

---

260   The confusion originates in dicta used by the Supreme Court in *Luther*. In finding that Rhode Island rightfully used military power to "put down an armed *insurrection*," the Court said: "It was a state of *war*; and the established government resorted to the rights and usages of *war* to maintain itself, and to overcome the unlawful opposition." Luther v. Borden, 48 U.S. (7 How.) 1, 45 (1849) (emphasis added).

261   For a general discussion of the differences between war and insurrection, see F. WIENER, *supra* note 236, at 28-35.

262   *Id.* at 78.

263   Wiener contends that the Civil War, the Dorr Rebellion in Rhode Island, and the Whiskey Rebellion in Pennsylvania present the only instances of actual insurrection in this country's history. *Id.* at 30.

264   State prescriptions for the utilization of military force against civil disorder usually allow it, *inter alia*, "to suppress insurrection." *E.g.*, IND. CONST. art. 5, § 12, set out in note 230 *supra*.

265   Wilson, *Civil Disturbances and the Rule of Law*, 58 J. CRIM. L.C. & P.S. 155, 157 (1967).

This tribute to the National Guard by Orlando Wilson, one of the country's leading criminologists, suggests that state and local authorities would be wise to familiarize themselves with the capabilities of their state militia and the procedures by which they can summon its assistance.

The National Guard is the modern descendant of the original militia reserved to the states by the Constitution.[266] Although it is federally equipped and its members are federally compensated, the National Guard is a state force subject to the control of the governor in accordance with state law and is ordinarily administered by the state adjutant general.[267] Its officers are officers of the state and not of the United States.[268] The Constitution makes no provision for a state to use its own militia, but it has been made clear that a state may do so for the purpose of suppressing riots:

> While a State has no right to establish and maintain a permanent military government, it is not to be inferred that it has no power over the militia resident within its borders. Unquestionably a State may use its military power to put down an armed insurrection too strong to be controlled by the civil authorities. The power is essential to the existence of every government . . . and is as necessary to the States of this Union as to any other government.[269]

The use of the National Guard as an emergency force available to a state governor for the maintenance of law and order is not without restriction. Indeed, state use has been partially preempted by federal statutory provisions that permit federalization of the National Guard in the interests of national security[270] or to suppress insurrections.[271] During the periods when Guard units are federalized, they are subject to control solely by the federal government and their members are governed by federal law.[272] They revert to state status under the authority of their governor only upon their discharge from active federal service.[273]

Additional encroachment upon the historical use of the National Guard as a state resource seems to have occurred through recent legislation that shapes the force structure of the National Guard and other reserve components pri-

---

266 Maryland *ex rel.* Levin v. United States, 381 U.S. 41, 46, *vacated on other grounds,* 382 U.S. 159 (1965).
    U.S. CONST. art. I, § 8, provides in part:
       The Congress shall have Power . . .

       . . .

       To provide for calling forth the Militia to execute the Laws of this Union, suppress Insurrections and repel Invasions;
       To provide for organizing, arming, and disciplining, the Militia, and for governing such Part of them as may be employed in the Service of the United States, reserving to the States respectively, the Appointment of the Officers, and the Authority of training the Militia according to the discipline prescribed by Congress;

       . . .

267 Maryland *ex rel.* Levin v. United States, 381 U.S. 41, 47, *vacated on other grounds,* 382 U.S. 159 (1965).
268 United States *ex rel.* Gillett v. Dern, 74 F.2d 485, 487 (D.C. Cir. 1934).
269 S. Doc. No. 263, 67th Cong., 2d Sess., 219 n.a (1922).
270 32 U.S.C. § 102 (1964).
271 10 U.S.C. §§ 331-33 (1964).
272 *Cf.* Houston v. Moore, 18 U.S. (5 Wheat.) 1, 16 (1820); United States *ex rel.* Gillett v. Dern, 74 F.2d 485, 487 (D.C. Cir. 1934).
273 *Id.*

marily according to federal requirements.[274] However, a special subcommittee
appointment by the House Committee on Armed Services believes that "appropriate recognition and support of State mission requirements is completely compatible with the concept of establishing the National Guard force structure based
initially upon only Federal mission requirements."[275] The subcommittee's view
indicates that the Guard will be as available to the state as it has traditionally
been; apparently, only the presumption as to its first duty has changed.

The capability of the National Guard as a riot control force appears to
be more than adequate in terms of personnel strength. This factor is borne out
by experience. A study of state use of the National Guard between 1957 and
1967 revealed that, on the average, only nine percent of the available force
was deployed for the purpose of suppressing a local disorder.[276] More significant,
perhaps, is the fact that only twice during that period were more than fifty
percent of the state troops employed.[277] In addition, the states themselves generally believe that their respective National Guard forces are sufficient to handle
local problems.[278]

Thus, there seems to be no need for any increase in the existing strengths
of the various National Guard units,[279] despite the fact that any given riot might
conceivably exceed the presently existing capability margins. The excess requirements could be easily handled by assisting forces from neighboring states
pursuant to interstate mutual aid compacts,[280] or by calling in federal troops.
It would be unrealistic and unnecessary to try to achieve a situation in which
each state could handle every possible contingency that might arise, especially
since the same end can be simply and less expensively accomplished by cooperation and joint planning with neighboring states.

The National Guard's capability to control civil disturbances reaches beyond
mere manpower considerations. The special subcommittee found, on the basis
of a study made of thirty-eight representative cities, that an average of fifty-nine
percent of the states' strength is located within a hundred mile radius of metropolitan areas.[281] This proximity of the bulk of National Guard strength to the
probable centers of disorder indicates that the state forces are in a good position
to respond rapidly to local urban problems. In fact, the National Guard can
generally be committed in significant force within four to six hours after the

274 REPORT ON NATIONAL GUARD CAPABILITY, supra note 175, at 5646.
275 Id.
276 Id. at 5649. For a table depicting the use of Army National Guard by states in civil
disturbances from 1957-1967, see id. at 5648-49.
277 The two instances were the 1965 Watts riot when sixty-two percent of the California
strength was used and the 1967 Detroit summer when eighty-five percent of the Guard
strength was utilized. In the latter situation, however, twenty to twenty-five percent of the
forces sent to the city were never committed. It is further significant to note in this regard
that in the recent riots in Newark and Milwaukee, only thirty-one and forty-three percent
of the available state force were used respectively. Id. at 5649.
278 Id. at 5650.
279 The internal composition of the National Guard, however, could be profitably changed
by immediately increasing the number of Negro Guardsmen. The Riot Commission found
that one significant factor that contributed to the superior effectiveness of the army troops in
Detroit vis-à-vis the National Guard was that the former had a proportionately greater number
of Negroes. RIOT COMMISSION REPORT, supra note 2, at 499.
280 Congressional acts approving an existing agreement of this sort between New York,
New Jersey and Pennsylvania are cited at note 206 supra.
281 REPORT ON NATIONAL GUARD CAPABILITY, supra note 175, at 5651.

time it is alerted.[282] Furthermore, the response will be increasingly effective with each passing month as a result of nationwide implementation of an intensified training program for Guard personnel in civil disturbance and riot-control techniques.[283]

In light of the Guard's mission in instances of civil disorder, there must be prior planning for the call-up and use of the National Guard. It was dramatically illustrated in Watts that "the goal of the military is to complement rather than replace civil authority"[284] and that the military is to assist in maintaining law and order, but is not to "take over" as a means to accomplishing that end.

The riot-control plan must necessarily stipulate procedures whereby local authorities can initiate a call for National Guard assistance. Accordingly, the plan should vest certain local officials with authority to directly request such assistance, and should designate the governor, or another individual in his absence, as the proper authority to grant the request. A general policy decision should be made and implemented in the plan to assist the governor in the exercise of his discretion in employing the state force. It is obvious that the National Guard, as an organized and trained riot-control unit, should be committed to assist at the scene of the riot only when the uprising increases beyond the control of local law enforcement agencies. Within this very general guideline, however, the governor should understand that the containment of civil disorders of the type that have recently rocked major cities throughout this country is utterly dependent on the *judicious early commitment* of adequate National Guard forces.[285]

Also in this regard, the plans should provide phases of preparation for the Guard so that the amount of the time lapse before its readiness for commitment will be minimized. There must necessarily be an alert phase in which the Guard is first notified to proceed toward a state of readiness. There may then be subsequent intermediate phases, each indicative of a higher stage of preparation than the prior one. Finally, there must be the commitment phase, which involves the actual engagement in riot-control activities. The decision on this final phase is subject only to the discretion of the governor or other appropriate official. To assure that Guardsmen will be available upon, and protected by, the governor's call, it should be made a legal requirement of each state that an employer grant a leave of absence to a Guardsman called to active duty because of a civil disturbance. Moreover, the states should require that the Guardsman's rights as an employee not be jeopardized in any way.[286]

---

282   *Id.* at 5652.
283   *Id.* at 5655. For a discussion of the requirements for and reaction to this new training program, see *id.* at 5655-57.
284   *Hearings on National Guard Capability, supra* note 187, at 5982.
>   Perhaps the most important lesson [of the Watts riot] for military and civil authorities alike is that troops can actually be committed in such [large] numbers, during a disturbance of this nature, with local law enforcement agencies remaining in full control of the situation. *Id.*
285   This view was strongly expressed by the subcommittee and every knowledgeable witness that appeared before it. REPORT ON NATIONAL GUARD CAPABILITY, *supra* note 175, at 5652.
286   *Cf.* IND. ANN. STAT. § 59-1022 (1961) which provides:
>   Any person who, as a reserve member of the armed forces of the United States, is called upon to receive temporary military training, shall be entitled to a

Separate support plans should be drawn up by the National Guard under the direction of the state adjutant general. These support plans should allocate responsibility among the different Guard units for the support of every locality within the state. At that point, each Guard unit should prepare its own plans based on the plans of the city or area that it supports. These plans must remain flexible so that Guard units can be moved with facility to other support areas, as needed.

This prior planning should include the actual utilization of National Guard troops once they have been committed to a riot situation. Since the military mission is one of cooperation to insure execution of the law, the military must operate within strict legal limits.[287] In this regard, the troops should be employed only in the immediate vicinity of the riot area, or in those areas that serve as potential targets for the rioters. Their purpose is to aid in quelling the disorder; it is not to police the entire city.

The uncertainty as to the exact relationship between the military commander and state law enforcement personnel during last summer's rioting in Detroit[288] dictates the necessity of solving the problem of command in advance. If the National Guard is federalized, it is subject to control by federal military superiors, and command is no longer a state responsibility. When acting as a state force, however, the Guard or any part thereof may be placed under the direction of any state or local officer designated by the governor for that purpose.[289] As a general rule, command over the Guard unit should be placed in the hands of local civilian leaders because their familiarity with local conditions best suits them for the job.

A related problem arises when the National Guard and federal troops are simultaneously called to the scene of a riot. In such a situation, the two military forces act independently.[290] Neither force has authority to order the other, although they cooperate as a matter of comity and in the common interest of rapidly and efficiently suppressing the disorder. They will observe each other's rank in a superior-subordinate relationship only if and when the Guard is federalized.

---

temporary leave of absence from his employer, not to exceed fifteen [15] days in any one [1] calendar year: . . . . Upon his return, such person shall be restored to his previous, or similar position, with the same status as he held before leaving for his training period. Such leaves may be granted with or without pay in the discretion of the employer.

Any temporary leave of absence so granted shall not affect the rights of the person to vacation leave, sick leave, or other normal benefits of his employment.
IND. ANN. STAT. § 59-1023 (1961) provides:

Any employer who refuses to grant an employee a temporary leave of absence, as provided in section 1 [§ 59-1022] of this act, shall be subject to a suit in damages for any damages sustained by the person denied such leave of absence.
While these statutes obviously differ from those proposed in the text both in purpose and in the extent of protection for the Guardsman, they nevertheless suggest a direction for the statutory enactment of pertinent requirements and sanctions.
287 Note, *Rule by Martial Law in Indiana: The Scope of Executive Power*, 31 IND. L.J. 456, 469 (1956).
288 REPORT ON NATIONAL GUARD CAPABILITY, *supra* note 175, at 5663.
289 Although the Riot Commission made no recommendation in this regard, it did emphasize that any plan of overall command must insure the utilization of National Guard units as units, each of which remains under the immediate command of a National Guard officer. RIOT COMMISSION REPORT, *supra* note 2, at 518-19.
290 F. WIENER, A PRACTICAL MANUAL OF MARTIAL LAW 53-54 (1940).

Almost of equal importance with the early commitment of the National Guard is its rapid withdrawal from the area once the riot has been effectively subdued. Request for removal of the Guard should be directed to the governor pursuant to a decision by local authorities, who act on the advice of the military commanders. The withdrawal may be staggered, but its rapidity is essential to easing tension in the area. Despite the immediate need for military force as a police auxiliary when rioting occurs, the value of its assistance is soon forgotten by the average citizen, and a continued military presence is upsetting and unwanted after order has been restored. It would appear advisable, however, to maintain the National Guard at an intermediate phase of readiness at a staging area not too distant from the recently disturbed city until the riot fever has had sufficient opportunity to cool. This provides a reserve force readily available to help suppress any further outbreaks that might occur.

Finally, the problems of liability that might arise from the commitment of the National Guard to suppress civil disorder must be reviewed and resolved in advance. A determination must be made as to the civil and criminal liability of the individual Guardsman under state law. This determination should reflect a policy consideration that the Guardsman, while performing his military duty, should be protected to the greatest possible extent within reasonable limits.. Indeed,

> [t]o deny this privilege is to create a state of apprehension about fulfilling and carrying out the orders of superiors in time of riot which will necessarily inhibit the guardsman's effectiveness. We should not ask a guardsman to protect the state if the state is unwilling to protect the guardsman.[291]

A state can and should protect its Guardsmen, first of all, by enacting legislation that requires the state to provide legal counsel for a Guardsman who is sued for his actions while on active state duty. Nevada statutes typify what is needed in this regard,[292] and other states have adopted similar legislation.[293] The obvious inequities of requiring a Guardsman to act in the state interest, while subjecting him to the concomitant threat of a possible civil or criminal suit at his own expense, would seem to obligate all states to provide such statutory relief.

Although many states further protect their Guardsmen by granting them statutory immunity from criminal liability for activities done in the line of their

---

291   1967 IND. ATT'Y GEN. OP. No. 66, § VI, at 18.
292   NEV. REV. STAT. § 412.740 (1963) provides in part:

> 2. When a suit or proceeding shall be commenced in any court by any person against any officer of the militia for any act done by such officer in his official capacity in the discharge of any duty under this chapter, or against any soldier acting under the authority or order of any such officer, or by virtue of any warrant issued by him pursuant to law, the attorney general shall defend such officer or soldier.
> 3. Where the action or proceeding is criminal the adjutant general shall designate the judge advocate general or one of the judge advocates to defend such officer or person.

293   E.g., CAL. MIL. & VET. CODE § 393 (West Supp. 1967); ILL. ANN. STAT. ch. 129, § 220.90 (Smith-Hurd Supp. 1967).

military duty,[294] such a degree of protection seems to go beyond the balance that must be struck. Placed in the hands of some Guardsmen, immunity from criminal liability can amount to license for committing otherwise illegal acts. If granted to Guardsmen, who despite their training in riot-control are not professional soldiers, it can have the dangerous effect of supplying approval to their natural reaction in the tension of a riot situation to counter any opposition with excessive or even deadly force. Rather, actions by the Guardsmen should be subject to review by the courts for a determination of liability based on the common-law tort notion of "reasonableness under the circumstances." Furthermore, immunity is not a proper solution to those who accept the seemingly better view that the use of military force against domestic disturbances amounts to the undeclared institution of a state of qualified martial law.[295] Consistent with basic martial law principles, use of the military to assist the civil authorities is reviewable[296] and can be justified only by necessity.[297] When the force applied exceeds the necessity, it becomes unreasonable; military personnel are not allowed to escape liability for such excesses.[298]

E. Federal Intervention

Although the suppression of domestic violence is primarily a responsibility of the individual states, the federal government is also constitutionally responsible in this regard.[299] This federal obligation is implemented by a series of statutes that prescribe the circumstances under which federal forces may be used to control riots,[300] and by a separate statute that imposes limitations on the use of federal forces.[301]

1. The Request Statute

If the dimensions of an urban riot expand beyond the state's capability to control, the state can request federal assistance under section 331 of title 10 of the United States Code.[302] Whether or not federal assistance will be granted upon

---

294   *E.g.*, CAL. MIL. & VET. CODE § 392 (West 1955); NEV. REV. STAT. § 412.740(1) (1963); N.Y. MIL. LAW § 235 (McKinney 1953).
295   See the general discussion under "Martial Law" in text accompanying notes 209-264 *supra.*
296   Sterling v. Constantin, 287 U.S. 378 (1932).
297   *See* note 218 *supra* and accompanying text.
298   Commonwealth *ex rel.* Wadsworth v. Shortall, 206 Pa. 165, 173, 55 A. 952, 955 (1903).
299   U.S. CONST. art. IV, § 4 provides:
     The United States shall guarantee to every State in this Union a Republican Form of Government, and shall protect each of them against Invasion; and on Application of the Legislature, or of the Executive (when the Legislature cannot be convened) against domestic Violence.
     U.S. CONST. art. II, § 3 provides in pertinent part: "[H]e [the President] shall take Care that the Laws be faithfully executed . . . ."
300   10 U.S.C. §§ 331-34 (1964).
301   Posse Comitatus Act, 18 U.S.C. § 1385 (1964) provides:
     Whoever, except in cases and under circumstances expressly authorized by the Constitution or Act of Congress, willfully uses any part of the Army or the Air Force as a posse comitatus or otherwise to execute the laws shall be fined not more than $10,000 or imprisoned not more than two years, or both.
302   10 U.S.C. § 331 (1964) provides:
     Whenever there is an insurrection in any State against its government, the President may, upon the request of its legislature or of its governor if the legisla-

receipt of a proper state application rests within the sole discretion of the President.[303]

An issue that arises in connection with the use of federal troops under this statute is that their use is authorized against "insurrection," whereas the constitutional basis for the statute uses the broader language of "domestic violence."[304] Although one commentator finds this is to be the basic issue,[305] it presents little practical difficulty. As a matter of precedent, any combination of words used to indicate widespread violence and disorder has generally been regarded by Presidents as sufficient for the dispatch of troops.[306] This problem of semantics was further lessened in late 1967 when Attorney General Ramsey Clark wrote a letter to state governors advising them of the "legal requirements for the use of federal troops in case of *severe domestic violence* . . . ."[307] (Emphasis added.) The practical result is that, as with martial law statutes,[308] "insurrection" is a label and not a literal prerequisite for the implementation of the statute.

The procedure whereby federal troops are sent to assist in putting down a riot under section 331 can be reduced to four distinct steps. For a full understanding of the workings of section 331, it will be helpful to consider the prerequisites and legal requirements that attach to each of them.

a. Application by the State

The state should apply for federal aid only when it is experiencing a condition of severe domestic violence that "cannot be brought under control by the law enforcement resources available to the Governor, including local and State police forces and the National Guard."[309] This prerequisite reflects the basic concept that riot control is primarily the responsibility of the state, and if the prerequisite is not satisfied before application is made the President will not be favorably inclined to honor the request.

The application must be made by the legislature of the state or by the governor in the event that the legislature "cannot be convened."[310] As a practical matter, the overwhelming difficulties of convening the legislature while a riot is in progress eliminate the former alternative, and the duty to make the request thus falls upon the governor by default. Current federal guidelines indicate that the gubernatorial request will ordinarily suffice.[311]

The request from either the legislature or the governor should be in writing and should set out the details that provide its justification. This requirement of writing is not an absolute essential, because the President will entertain an

---

ture cannot be convened, call into Federal service such of the militia of the other States, in the number requested by that State, and use such of the armed forces, as he considers necessary to suppress the insurrection.

303 Letter from Attorney General Ramsey Clark to the governors of the separate states, Aug. 7, 1967, in REPORT ON NATIONAL GUARD CAPABILITY, *supra* note 175, at 5669, 5670.
304 U.S. CONST. art. IV, § 4. See note 299 *supra* for the language of this section.
305 Poe, *The Use of Federal Troops to Suppress Domestic Violence*, 54 A.B.A.J. 168, 169-70 (1968).
306 Note, *Riot Control and the Use of Federal Troops*, 81 HARV. L. REV. 638, 644-45 (1968).
307 Letter from Attorney General Ramsey Clark, *supra* note 303, at 5669.
308 *See* text accompanying notes 260-4 *supra*.
309 Letter from Attorney General Ramsey Clark, *supra* note 303, at 5669.
310 10 U.S.C. § 331 (1964).
311 Letter from Attorney General Ramsey Clark, *supra* note 303, at 5669.

oral request in the event of extreme emergency.[312] If the application is made orally, however, a written communication to the President should follow immediately to furnish him support for the issuance of his proclamation pursuant to federal law.[313] While this final formal request should be addressed to the President, the state should direct all preliminary communications to the Attorney General.[314] Observance of this procedure will relieve the President of detailed and unnecessary burdens, but will nevertheless keep the federal government informed of current developments so that it can save valuable time by taking such preliminary steps as placing troops on alert.

Another requirement is that the language used in the request be unconditional. This will preclude a presidential decision not to send troops on the ground that the application is inadequate, as has been the case on the few occasions when the requesting governor used language that was less than unequivocal.[315] The justification for this requirement is not altogether clear, but it seems to be an extension of the policy that underlies the basic statutory requirement of a formal request. It recognizes, first of all, the advantages of providing local solutions to local problems. Further, the probability of cooperation between federal troops and state authorities is increased if the former operate in the riot area at the positive request of the latter. But the most important justification seems to be a political one — "a desire to have the governor on record as undeniably calling for federal aid so that he can not later recharacterize the nature of his request and criticize the President for sending troops."[316]

b. Exercise of Presidential Discretion

Following the President's receipt of a state request, he must deliberate as to whether the request merits federal intervention. A preliminary consideration revolves around both the form and substance of the request received. It has already been suggested that political considerations might cause the President to deny a conditional request or a mere recommendation that he send assistance. He must also evaluate the validity of the state's assertion that it is unable to control the riot, and he must do so with an awareness that

> [b]oth the Constitution and statute [section 331] recognize it to be the right and duty of the State to preserve its own order. The State's duty to itself as well as its duty to the United States requires that application be made for Federal assistance only when the strength of the State is exhausted or is inadequate. . . . The growing strength of the National Guard in each of the States warrants the belief that occasions for the employment of Federal power to suppress insurrection against a State will be less frequent in the future than in the past.[317]

---

312   *Id.* at 5670.
313   10 U.S.C. § 334 (1964) provides: "Whenever the President considers it necessary to use the militia or the armed forces under this chapter, he shall, by proclamation, immediately order the insurgents to disperse and retire peaceably to their abodes within a limited time."
314   Letter from Attorney General Ramsey Clark, *supra* note 303, at 5670.
315   Note, *supra* note 306, at 641. For a comparison between language used in state requests that have been granted and state requests that have been denied for inadequacy, see *id.* at 641 n.31.
316   *Id.* at 641.
317   S. Doc. No. 263, 67th Cong., 2d Sess., 318 (1922).

The requirement that a state be unable to control a riot despite the utilization of all of its force is a prerequisite to an affirmative decision to send federal troops. Its purpose

> is to limit the number of occasions for federal intervention upon the assumption that the unnecessary commitment of federal troops would discourage the states from using their own peace-keeping forces. The requirement also reflects a general distaste for using the army as a police force.[318]

Once the President has verified the state's claim of inability to control the riot, he must consider such factors as the size of the force required, when it should be sent, and whether to federalize the National Guard instead of, or in addition to, sending federal troops.[319]

c. Issuance of Proclamation

The above steps constitute procedural and substantive requirements that must be met before federal troops can be dispatched pursuant to section 331. Once the President has made an affirmative decision in regard to a state's request for federal assistance, he must issue a proclamation as required by section 334 of title 10 of the United States Code.[320] This proclamation is clearly distinguished from a proclamation of martial law, and its issuance must not be considered an imposition or justification of martial law measures. Although a requirement of law, this proclamation is void of legal effect; it is required as a means of giving notice of the dispatch of federal troops to the scene, and of emphasizing the seriousness of the situation.[321] Hopefully, as a final warning to the unlawful elements, it may help to successfully avoid the necessity of using federal troops.

d. Presidential Dispatch of Troops

Finally, the President causes formal instructions to be given to the commander of the Army troops or federalized National Guard units that he has selected to commit to the riot in response to the request. These instructions should provide guidance for the conduct and command of the troops at the scene of the riot.

The problems of control in such a situation are particularly difficult and delicate. Federal troops are an integral part of the military organization of the United States and, as such, are responsible to the President as their Commander-in-Chief. It would seem, therefore, that the President should retain control of the federal troops in the hands of their own military superiors, despite the fact that local control undeniably offers the unique advantage of familiarity with the riot area. First of all, federal control would seem to be dictated by the fact that the state failed in its attempt to successfully contain the riot and thus necessitated the presence of the federal troops in the first place. Because the troops of the United States have been sent in a discretionary response to the

---

318 Note, *supra* note 306, at 645-46.
319 Letter from Attorney General Ramsey Clark, *supra* note 303, at 5670.
320 10 U.S.C. § 334 (1964). See note 313 *supra* for the language of this section.
321 F. WIENER, *supra* note 290, at 50-51.

state's request, the state can really neither demand nor expect to control them. Furthermore, armed forces personnel and federal officers are presently without the protection of federal law, since current federal statutes do not prescribe criminal sanctions against rioters.[322] It seems, therefore, that the federal government is under a non-delegable duty to control them. Since it offers no statutory protection for its personnel, it should afford them the only remaining protection that it can — the exercise of proper and responsible command. A separate argument for the federal retention of control over federal troops is grounded in a desire to save the President the political embarrassment of being able to approve the requests for federal troops from only those governors to whom he feels he can safely entrust command of the federal troops.[323] This federal command would also prevent the possible misuse of federal troops by a partisan governor.[324] Although close cooperation between federal and state agencies must characterize the operation, the balance of the competing considerations clearly favors the retention of federal control over the federal forces.

2. The Non-Request Statutes

The federal government has an important interest of its own in the preservation of its property and the execution of its laws and cannot be totally dependent on the will of state governors to protect those interests. The Supreme Court has recognized that the national government has a constitutional power and responsibility to compel obedience to law and order:

> We hold it to be an incontrovertible principle, that the government of the United States may, by means of physical force, exercised through its official agents, execute on every foot of American soil the power and functions that belong to it. This necessarily involves the power to command obedience to its laws, and hence the power to keep the peace to that extent.[325]

In addition to this judicially recognized constitutional power, Congress has granted the President specific statutory power to deal, on a non-request basis, with civil disorder occurring within a state. The relevant statutes are sections 332[326] and 333[327] of title 10 of the United States Code.

---

322 REPORT ON NATIONAL GUARD CAPABILITY, *supra* note 175, at 5665. This is a deplorable situation, and the subcommittee strongly recommends the enactment of legislation enabling the federal government to criminally prosecute rioters for assaulting federal personnel who are acting in an official capacity to quell the disorder. *Id.*
323 Note, *supra* note 306, at 642.
324 *Id.* For a capsule discussion of the misuse of federal troops by the Idaho Governor during the Coeur d'Alene mining dispute of 1899 and the subsequent effects of that misuse, see *id.* at 642 n.33.
325 *Ex parte* Siebold, 100 U.S. 371, 395 (1880).
326 10 U.S.C. § 332 (1964) provides:
   Whenever the President considers that unlawful obstructions, combinations, or assemblages, or rebellion against the authority of the United States, make it impracticable to enforce the laws of the United States in any State or Territory by the ordinary course of judicial proceedings, he may call into Federal service such of the militia of any State, and use such of the armed forces, as he considers necessary to enforce those laws or to suppress the rebellion.
327 10 U.S.C. § 333 (1964) provides:
   The President, by using the militia or the armed forces, or both, or by any other means, shall take such measures as he considers necessary to suppress, in a

No state application for the use of federal troops is necessary for the operation of these statutes. Once the President decides that the execution of federal laws or the protection of constitutional guarantees is being hindered or obstructed, his duty to "take care that the Laws be faithfully executed"[328] authorizes him to dispatch federal troops to enforce those laws and guarantees, and he may do so even over protest by the state.[329] Upon an affirmative decision to act under either of the non-request statutes, the President is required to issue a proclamation pursuant to section 334.[330]

Section 332 and the second clause of section 333 clearly authorize the use of federal troops in a situation where domestic violence is interfering with the enforcement of a court order. The obvious illustrations of such an instance were the school desegregation cases in Little Rock, Arkansas, and Oxford, Mississippi, where federal troops were sent by Presidents Eisenhower and Kennedy, respectively, to subdue any possible mob violence that might prevent the execution of federal court injunctions ordering integration. These instances point out the necessity for non-request statutes, because the court orders sought to be enforced were directed against the governors themselves.

The use of federal troops under these statutory provisions can conceivably be extended to situations other than the enforcement of court orders,[331] but such an extension is beset with doubts and difficulties.[332] Because of these difficulties and because the first clause of section 333 seems a more promising justification for the presidential exercise of discretion under a non-request statute, sections 332 and 333(2) should generally be limited to use as a means of guaranteeing the enforcement of federal court orders.

Section 333(1), on the other hand, is a broad discretionary provision that may be employed by the President when the state is deemed to have denied the equal protection of the laws, and the federal objective is to accord that protection. As such, this provision is readily adaptable to situations where rioting is racially motivated. Specifically, the President can dispatch troops under this section to

> any State in which a civil disturbance not only impedes the administration of Federal and State laws but also has the effect, as a consequence of a

---

State, any insurrection, domestic violence, unlawful combination, or conspiracy, if it —
> (1) so hinders the execution of the laws of that State, and of the United States within the State, that any part or class of its people is deprived of a right, privilege, immunity, or protection named in the Constitution and secured by law, and the constituted authorities of that State are unable, fail, or refuse to protect that right, privilege, or immunity, or to give that protection; or
> (2) opposes or obstructs the execution of the laws of the United States or impedes the course of justice under those laws.
In any situation covered by clause (1), the State shall be considered to have denied the equal protection of the laws secured by the Constitution.

328 U.S. CONST. art. II, § 3.
329 REPORT ON NATIONAL GUARD CAPABILITY, *supra* note 175, at 5668.
330 10 U.S.C. § 334 (1964). See note 313 *supra* for the language of this section.
331 For a discussion of theories of presidential action under these sections without a court order, see Note, *supra* note 306, at 649.
332 *Id.*

default on the part of a State, of depriving inhabitants thereof of certain rights secured to them by the Constitution and laws of the United States.[333]

Section 333 (1) has been said to contemplate circumstances "where there has been such a complete breakdown of law and order that civilian law enforcement measures are overwhelmed and use of the armed forces is required."[334] This characterization likens it to section 331, but in apparently assuming that state inability is a prerequisite to its operation, this view seems too limited to be entirely accurate.[335] By its terms, federal troops may be dispatched to a state by the President under this section when state authorities "are unable, fail, *or refuse*"[336] to protect the constitutional rights of state citizens.

Section 333(1), in mitigating the harshness of the "state inability" requirement of section 331, broadens the area of permissible use of federal troops far beyond the contemplation of section 331. Furthermore, because the President can act under the former statute without having to await a state invitation, the obvious argument is made that it should be used as an alternative to the request statute to avoid problems of delay that can mean added bloodshed.[337] Equally meritorious is the argument that the state's failure to protect the constitutional rights of its inhabitants "constitutes grounds for taking appropriate remedial action."[338] However, caution must be advised against too free a use of section 333(1). The President must bear in mind that since *Sterling,* actions that he takes to use federal troops under this or other statutes are subject to judicial review and, if not justifiable thereunder, constitute a violation of the Posse Comitatus Act.[339] Also, he will naturally be reluctant to act too hastily in sending federal aid because of the likelihood of resulting criticism, such as charges of "federalism" in an area of state responsibility, which mirror the deep-rooted expectations of local autonomy and the traditional civilian distrust of the military supplanting civil authority.[340] Most importantly, the President should remember that suppression of disorder is primarily a state responsibility, and that if the federal government too frequently acts to protect constitutional rights in this manner, it will encourage the states to ignore that responsibility.

Some speculation exists as to the meaning of the "any other means" that the President can utilize to suppress domestic violence under section 333. Although the term may suggest the use of federal civil officials such as agents of the Federal Bureau of Investigation, such a construction is not in keeping with the "salutary policy that the agents . . . shall not be used as a national police . . . ."[341] One of the "other means" contemplated is the use of United

---

333 REPORT ON NATIONAL GUARD CAPABILITY, *supra* note 175, at 5668-69.
334 Letter from Deputy Attorney General Nicholas deB. Katzenbach to Representative John Lindsay, July 30, 1964, in 110 CONG. REC. 18662 (1964).
335 *Contra,* Comment, *Federal Intervention in the States for the Suppression of Domestic Violence: Constitutionality, Statutory Power, and Policy,* 1966 DUKE L.J. 415, 419 n.20.
336 10 U.S.C. § 333(1) (1964) (emphasis added). See note 327 *supra* for the full text of this section.
337 Poe, *supra* note 305, at 170.
338 *Id.*
339 18 U.S.C. § 1385 (1964). See note 301 *supra* for the language of this section.
340 Comment, *supra* note 335, at 459-60.
341 41 OP. ATT'Y GEN. 313, 328 (1963).

States marshals. A United States marshal has the power to appoint deputies[342] and to summon a *posse comitatus*.[343] Generally, in executing federal law, he may exercise those same powers that a sheriff may exercise in executing state law.[344] In this latter regard, the marshal's exercise of power to keep the federal peace within a state has been upheld by the United States Supreme Court.[345] Marshals would seem to be useful in instances where only a relatively small amount of force is necessary to enforce a federal court order or to preserve the peace. But where their strength is insufficient, and time does not permit the effective enlistment of the citizenry to assist them in their efforts to maintain law and order, it would seem that resort must be had to the use of federal troops.

A federal force that is likely to see action in future disorders is a specially trained Army unit whose existence has recently been reported in testimony before the Senate Armed Services Committee.[346] Under this scheme,

> seven special task forces of Regular Army troops — more than 15,000 men — have been assigned as an elite service to cope with urban disruption. The riot forces will be dispatched only if the National Guard — which has been undergoing special riot training since its woefully inept performances in Newark and Detroit last summer — cannot do the job.[347]

Although this force will ultimately be available to quell riots, the Army is seeking to lessen the chance of its being needed by establishing special schools in civil disorder for Guardsmen and by arranging to supply them with special riot-control equipment.[348] These plans commendably preserve responsibility for the suppression of domestic violence in its proper perspective, by supplying a federal reserve to be used only after a much improved state force has demonstrated its inadequacy.

3. Criminal Jurisdiction Over Federal Troops and Federalized Guardsmen

Once a National Guardsman or a regular member of the armed forces of the United States has been released from active federal service, he is no longer subject to trial by federal court-martial. The de-federalized Guardsman may be tried by court-martial under his state law, but the usual forums for trying alleged offenses committed by such troops while in active service for the federal government are the appropriate civilian courts.[349]

---

342   28 U.S.C.A. § 562 (Supp. 1967) provides: "The Attorney General may authorize a United States marshal to appoint deputies and clerical assistants. Each deputy marshal is subject to removal by the marshal pursuant to civil-service regulations."
343   28 U.S.C.A. § 569(b) (Supp. 1967) provides: "United States marshals shall execute all lawful writs, process and orders issued under authority of the United States, . . . and command all necessary assistance to execute their duties." For an early analysis of the power of a United States marshal to summon a *posse comitatus*, see 6 OP. ATT'Y GEN. 466 (1856).
344   28 U.S.C. § 570 (Supp. 1967) provides: "A United States marshal and his deputies, in executing the laws of the United States within a State, may exercise the same powers which a sheriff of the State may exercise in executing the laws thereof."
345   *Ex parte* Siebold, 100 U.S. 371, 394-96 (1880).
346   TIME, Feb. 23, 1968, at 20.
347   *Id.*
348   *Id.*
349   Letter from Martin F. Richman, First Assistant, Office of Legal Counsel of the Department of Justice, to Representative F. Edward Hebert, Chairman of Special Subcommittee on Civil Disturbances, House Committee on Armed Services, Sept. 1, 1967, in REPORT ON NATIONAL GUARD CAPABILITY, *supra* note 175, at 5666.

More difficult problems arise in the case of a regular soldier or a Guardsman who is in federal military status when charged with a criminal offense committed while on federal duty. Such an individual may clearly be tried by federal court-martial, but unless the civil courts are closed as a result of the improbable imposition of absolute martial law, this military jurisdiction is not exclusive. Civilian courts also have jurisdiction; however, it is important to note that unless civil authorities actually make the arrest of a defendant soldier, this jurisdiction can attach only after a decision by the military to honor the request of state officials that such defendant be made available for civil trial.[350] In the deliberations pursuant to such a request, the defendant himself is without a voice — "he is not entitled to demand either trial by court-martial or trial by a civil court to the exclusion of the other."[351] The military is not required to grant such a request, but a decision to do so recognizes that the offense may be a violation of state law, punishable by the courts of the state. In this light, the granting of this request would seem proper as a general matter of comity. Furthermore, an affirmative response to the request will not deprive the military of its court-martial jurisdiction. Because the same act may offend both state and federal law, it is clear that a defendant may be tried by federal court-martial and also by a state tribunal without violating the double jeopardy clause of the fifth amendment.[352]

Yet laws that allow a defendant to be twice tried and twice sentenced for a single act seem offensive to the public's sense of equity, notwithstanding the fact that the same act violated two sets of laws. The injustice seems even stronger in a situation where the defendant is subjected to state punishment for an offense he would not have been in a position to commit but for the inability of, or refusal by, that state to cope with a local problem that necessitated his presence there as part of a federal force. While the federal military laws may be criticized for lacking the jury trial as a procedural safeguard, this alleged drawback certainly does not work to the state's detriment in the sense of preventing the exaction of proper retribution from the defendant. Until there is a change in the present state of the law that allows this possibility of double trial, it would seem an advisable policy for the military to generally deny these state requests, particularly in instances of riot-connected offenses, and to try the federal offender once and for all by a court-martial.

Moreover, the applicable legal standards would be substantially the same in either a state civil court or a federal military tribunal. Standards of sound military conduct are prescribed by the Uniform Code of Military Justice.[353] The basic rule of military law is the rule of martial law — that troops may use whatever force is reasonably necessary to effectuate their orders to suppress unlawful violence. In employing such force as is "reasonably necessary," military personnel are allowed a "permitted range of honest judgment" but the reason-

---

350   *Id.* at 5667. Article 14 of the UNIFORM CODE OF MILITARY JUSTICE, 10 U.S.C. § 814 (1964), provides that "a member of the armed forces accused of an offense against civil authority may be delivered, upon request, to the civil authority for trial."
351   Letter from Martin F. Richman, *supra* note 349, at 5667.
352   *Cf.* Bartkus v. Illinois, 359 U.S. 121 (1959).
353   10 U.S.C. §§ 801-940 (1964), *as amended.*

ableness of their actions is nevertheless properly reviewable by the courts.[354]
What is justifiable under this basic rule cannot be articulated with a high degree
of precision, but must be decided on a case-by-case basis in light of the circumstances as they appeared to the actor at the time of his action.[355] It is generally
understood, however, that

> [i]n the context of a domestic riot, it may be necessary to use greater force
> than could lawfully be exerted for ordinary law enforcement purposes;
> this conclusion naturally follows from the fact that the military is not
> called upon in such cases until the resources of conventional law enforce-
> ment have proved inadequate to suppress the violence.[356]

Perhaps the largest area of protection given an individual soldier against
criminal liability is the defense of good faith obedience to orders. The courts
have even excused homicide when it was committed in obedience to an order
that was fair on its face.[357] However, unlawful orders will not justify their
execution when, to a reasonable man, they would clearly exceed the basic rule
of necessary force.[358]

If prosecution is brought in a state court, either directly or by military
release, against anyone in the military service of the United States for an act
done under color of his office, such a suit may be removed to the appropriate
federal district court.[359] The "color of office" test means that the act complained
of must somehow have been related to the defendant's official duties in such a
way that it was thereby within the general scope of his authority as an officer
or soldier. In the event that the military decides to follow the harsh policy of
releasing soldiers to state jurisdiction, this allowance of removal is essential to
insure the defendant a fair trial, free from local prejudice. In addition to this
statutory protection, the federal government should also support military defendants by providing them with counsel when their alleged offenses are found
by the district courts to have been done under color of office. According to
recent indications from the Department of Justice, this legal assistance will
ordinarily be given.[360] Yet even with these protective measures, the trial of
military personnel under state law for offenses that simultaneously violate

---

354 Sterling v. Constantin, 287 U.S. 378 (1932).
355 Mitchell v. Harmony, 54 U.S. (13 How.) 115, 134 (1851).
356 Letter from Martin F. Richman, *supra* note 349, at 5667.
357 *E.g.,* Commonwealth *ex rel.* Wadsworth v. Shortall, 206 Pa. 165, 55 A. 952 (1903).
358 *E.g.,* United States v. Bevans, 24 F. Cas. 1138 (No. 14,589) (D. Mass. 1816) (orders
given were to kill a man who had used opprobrious language).
359 Removal jurisdiction may be claimed under the applicable provision of either of two
statutes. 28 U.S.C. § 1442a (1964) provides in pertinent part:
> A civil or criminal prosecution in a court of a State of the United States against
> a member of the armed forces of the United States on account of an act done
> under color of his office or status, or in respect to which he claims any right, title,
> or authority under a law of the United States respecting the armed forces thereof,
> . . . may . . . be removed for trial into the district court of the United States for
> the district where it is pending . . . .
28 U.S.C. § 1442 (1964) provides in pertinent part:
> (a) A civil action or criminal prosecution commenced in a State court against
> any of the following persons may be removed by them to the district court of the
> United States for the district and division embracing the place wherein it is pending:
>   (1) Any officer of the United States or any agency thereof, or person
>   acting under him, for any act under color of such office . . . .
360 Letter from Martin F. Richman, *supra* note 349, at 5668.

federal law presents a poor alternative to the simpler and seemingly fairer justice afforded by a single trial in a military court.

III. Procedure and Practice of Law Enforcement Agencies During a Riot

A. Force Used in Quelling a Riot

Perhaps the first and most crucial problem faced by state and municipal officials when masses of urban ghetto dwellers take to the streets bent on violence and destruction is the question of what amount of force may be practically and lawfully utilized to suppress the disturbance. The problem is compounded for the conscientious official who is aware of the practical need to restore calm to the community while avoiding the harsh measures that may only lead to future riots. This latter consideration is especially significant in view of the fact that the conduct of the police in dealing with suspected lawbreakers has been the initial spark and motivating factor in many of the ghetto riots.[361] As one public official has pointed out: "The major civil disturbances in this country, Watts, Detroit, Jersey City [Newark], arose not out of a demonstration getting out of hand but rather out of law enforcement incidents."[362] Thus, in addition to the legal questions that will be treated in this Note, local officials must consider the far more serious social ramifications of their response to urban rioting.

If any generalizations can be made about so complex and unsettled an area of the law, they would be that "[i]n making an arrest, an officer may use whatever force is reasonably necessary"[363] and that the standard of reasonableness involved is that of the ordinarily prudent and intelligent person faced with the same situation as the policeman.[364] However, the policeman will run the risk of civil and/or criminal liability[365] should he use more force than ". . . reasonably appears to be necessary, or subject the person arrested to unnecessary risk of harm."[366] But it has further been recognized that this standard of reasonableness includes an additional consideration when the officer is acting under color of duty because

---

361 *See, e.g.,* Ransford, *Attitudes of Negroes Toward the Los Angeles Riot,* 3 LAW IN TRANSITION Q. 191 (1966).

> When asked [of Los Angeles Negroes], "What do you think caused the riot?" 42% named police brutality, 24% named police methods or bad police treatment. The fact that 66% of the total sample mentioned either police brutality or poor methods as a cause is a remarkably high proportion, when considering that the question was open-ended; that is, mention of the police was completely spontaneous.

Id. at 193.

The report of the National Advisory Commission on Civil Disorder listed the first and most intense grievance of ghetto dwellers as police practices. RIOT COMMISSION REPORT, *supra* note 2, at 143.

362 Comments by Louis Ancel (Corporation Counsel for the Village of Maywood, Illinois), Illinois State Bar Association Midyear Meeting, Symposium: Riots and Mass Demonstrations: The Problem and the Law, in Chicago, Illinois, January 25, 1968. A copy of this presentation is on file in the office of the NOTRE DAME LAWYER.

363 Breese v. Newman, 179 Neb. 878, 140 N.W.2d 805, 808 (1966).

364 *Id.*

365 Noback v. Town of Montclair, 33 N.J. Super. 420, 428, 110 A.2d 339, 343 (1954).

366 City of Miami v. Albro, 120 So. 2d 23, 26 (Fla. Dist. Ct. App. 1960).

[p]olice officers are not volunteers. They are armed and required to act to
enforce the law. They may err in their judgment and exceed their authority
in the sense that they misjudge the need for extreme measures or their right
to resort to them. Yet, where the purpose is to comply with duty, it would
be unreasonable to impose the measure of criminal responsibility applicable
to the citizen whose involvement does not originate in a legal compulsion
to act and who is free to turn away.[367]

Perhaps the primary distinction between the peace officer and the ordinary
citizen with regard to the force that they may impose is that the police officer
is under no duty to retreat when effecting an arrest. He may become the
aggressor and use all reasonable force to overcome what resistance the arrestee
may offer.[368]

1. Force Against Misdemeanants

Although the standards governing the use of force are often confusing,
some rules are quite clear. It has long been recognized at common law that a
peace officer could not kill a misdemeanant in order to effect an arrest.[369] The
reason for such a rule is that

> [t]he law values human life too highly to allow an officer to proceed to
> the extremity of shooting an escaping offender who in fact has committed
> only a misdemeanor or lesser offense, even though he cannot be taken
> otherwise.[370]

That the law on this point is quite settled was aptly demonstrated in *Noback v.
Town of Montclair*.[371]

> Police officers must learn, if they are not already aware, that there
> are definite limitations upon the amount of force that may be used by
> them in arresting a citizen charged with a crime or with a violation of
> the Disorderly Persons Act; that they may be held liable, both civilly and
> criminally, for the use of excessive force either in making a lawful arrest
> or in attempting to capture a fleeing offender; and that the law will not
> countenance the shooting or killing of a fleeing offender charged merely
> with a misdemeanor, breach of the peace, or violation of the Disorderly
> Persons Act.[372]

This rule has even been extended as far as to hold a policeman liable for wound-
ing a suspect after the suspect assaulted the officer and began to retreat.[373] The
Restatement (Second) of Torts supports the general proposition.[374]

---

367 State v. Williams, 29 N.J. 27, 36, 148 A.2d 22, 27 (1959).
368 *Id.* at 39, 148 A.2d at 28.
369 Davis v. Hellwig, 21 N.J. 412, 416, 122 A.2d 497, 499 (1956). *See also* Moreland,
The Use of Force in Effecting or Resisting Arrest, 33 NEB. L. REV. 408, 419 (1954).
370 Davis v. Hellwig, 21 N.J. 412, 419, 122 A.2d 497, 499 (1956).
371 33 N.J. Super. 420, 110 A.2d 339 (1954).
372 *Id.* at 428, 110 A.2d at 343; *accord*, Wimberly v. City of Paterson, 75 N.J. Super.
584, 594, 183 A.2d 691, 696 (1962).
373 Padilla v. Chavez, 62 N.M. 170, 306 P.2d 1094 (1957).
374 In the absence of legislative authority, neither a peace officer nor a private person
is privileged to use force against or impose confinement upon another for the purpose
of preventing the violation of a statute or a municipal ordinance or a continuance

These limitations on the use of force in dealing with misdemeanants are especially significant in the area of riot control since a substantial number of the persons apprehended during civil disturbances are merely misdemeanants. In the Detroit riot of 1967, of the 7,223 persons arrested, 1,652 were arrested for misdemeanor offenses[375] and 743 out of 3,356 arrests in the Watts riot of 1965 were for misdemeanors.[376] However, the law does recognize that under certain limited conditions a police officer, for his own protection, may be forced to resort to the use of more serious force than would otherwise be allowed[377] and that emergencies may arise ". . . when the officer cannot be expected to exercise that cool and deliberate judgment which courts and juries exercise afterwards upon investigations in court."[378] Likewise, the officer is privileged to threaten deadly force to deter and apprehend misdemeanants by firing warning shots so long as he does not intend to actually shoot the suspect[379] and exercises extraordinary care in the use of his firearms.[380]

Thus, when dealing with those suspected of, or in the act of, committing misdemeanor offenses, the police are strictly bound by the tradition that "[i]t is more in consonance with modern notions regarding the sanctity of human life that the offender escape than that his life be taken, in a case where the extreme penalty would be a trifling fine or a few days imprisonment,"[381] unless the circumstances are such that the officer must defend himself or his fellow officers against an attack by the misdemeanant.

2. Force Against Felons

Where the police are confronted with a felony offender, the law takes a much more liberal position with regard to the amount of force that may be used to effect his arrest. There are three basic approaches possible in analyzing

---

or commission of a misdemeanor other than an affray or equally serious breach of the peace.

RESTATEMENT (SECOND) OF TORTS § 140 (1965). When a breach of the peace is concerned, the *Restatement* goes further:

> Either a peace officer or a private person is privileged to use force against another or to impose confinement upon him for the purpose of terminating or preventing the renewal of an affray or an equally serious breach of the peace which is being or has been committed in the actor's presence or of preventing such other from participating therein, if
> (a) the other is or the actor reasonably believes him to be participating or about to participate in the affray, and
> (b) *the confinement or force is not intended or likely to cause death or serious bodily harm, and*
> (c) the actor reasonably believes that the force or confinement is necessary to prevent the other from participating in the affray or other equally serious breach of the peace. *Id.* § 141 (emphasis added).

375 Cahalan, *The Detroit Riot*, 3 THE PROSECUTOR 430, 432 (1967).
376 *See* LOS ANGELES POLICE DEPARTMENT 1965 ANNUAL REPORT 21 (1966). In a much smaller riot in Cincinnati, Ohio, July 3 through July 5, 1967, there were approximately 400 arrests, generally for misdemeanors. Remarks of Melvin G. Rueger, Greenbrier Conference of National District Attorneys Association, Aug., 1967, printed in *Riot Panel*, 3 THE PROSE-CUTOR 282, 287 (1967).
377 *E.g.*, People v. Wilson, 36 Cal. App. 589, 172 P. 1116 (1918); Hutchinson v. Lott, 110 So. 2d 442, 444 (Fla. Dist. Ct. App. 1959); Fugate v. Commonwealth, 187 Ky. 564, 219 S.W. 1069 (1920); Padilla v. Chavez, 62 N.M. 170, 306 P.2d 1094, 1095 (1957) (dicta).
378 Mead v. O'Connor, 66 N.M. 170, 344 P.2d 478, 480 (1959).
379 Hutchinson v. Lott, 110 So. 2d 442, 444 (Fla. Dist. Ct. App. 1959).
380 Wimberly v. City of Paterson, 75 N.J. Super. 584, 600, 183 A.2d 691, 699 (1962).
381 Wilgus, *Arrest Without a Warrant*, 22 MICH. L. REV. 798, 814-15 (1924).

the permissible force that can be used against a felon.[382] The first approach is that deadly force is allowed whenever the officer reasonably believes that a felony has been committed and reasonably believes that the person against whom the force is to be applied has committed it.[383] This view has received only limited judicial support. In reversing and remanding a judgment rendered against the city of Miami for damages caused by a police officer when he shot and killed a fifteen-year-old burglary suspect, the Florida District Court of Appeals said:

> The fact that the person has not actually committed a felony or that no crime of any sort has been committed makes no difference, as long as the appearances are such as to lead a police officer to reasonably believe that a felony has been committed and the person he is about to arrest or apprehend is the person who has committed the felony.
>
> . . . .
>
> Having reasonable grounds to believe J. C. Nelson had committed a felony, the officers were entitled to use force which was reasonably necessary to capture him, even to the extent of killing or wounding him.[384]

But the dangers inherent in this approach are such that it generally is, and should be, rejected.[385] It would give a policeman the discretion, based on his reasonable belief, to use whatever force he felt necessary under the circumstances. This would have the ultimate effect of allowing police to respond in numerous apparent felony cases, which are in fact either misdemeanors or no crimes at all, with the degree of force that has been traditionally reserved for felony offenses.[386]

The second approach for considering the use of force against felons holds that "[k]illing is privileged if a felony has been committed and the arresting officer reasonably believes that the person killed committed the felony."[387] This more widely accepted test was adopted in *Petrie v. Cartwright*[388] which stated that ". . . where there is only a suspicion of a felony the officer is not warranted in treating the fugitive as a felon."[389] Thus, the officer must know that a felony actually was committed and then must reasonably believe that the suspect actually committed it before he can resort to the use of deadly force.

By far the most severe restriction on the use of force by the police is that imposed by the third approach. The Pennsylvania Supreme Court adopted this approach in the celebrated case of *Commonwealth v. Duerr*,[390] which, like *Petrie,* insisted that a felony must have actually been committed before deadly

---

382   94 U. Pa. L. Rev. 327, 328 (1946).
383   *Id.*
384   City of Miami v. Nelson, 186 So. 2d 535, 537-38 (Fla. Dist. Ct. App. 1966). *See also* Dixon v. State, 101 Fla. 840, 132 So. 684 (1931); Note, *Killing a Suspected Felon Fleeing to Escape Arrest,* 38 Ky. L.J. 618, 619-21 (1950).
385   *E.g.,* Petrie v. Cartwright, 114 Ky. 103, 70 S.W. 297 (1902). *See also* Note, *Killing a Suspected Felon Fleeing to Escape Arrest,* 38 Ky. L.J. 609, 612 (1950).
386   *See* Note, *supra* note 385, at 616.
387   94 U. Pa. L. Rev. 327, 328 (1946) (footnote omitted).
388   114 Ky. 103, 70 S.W. 297 (1902).
389   *Id.* at 109, 70 S.W. at 299. *See also* Moreland, *supra* note 369, at 409-10.
390   158 Pa. Super. 484, 45 A.2d 235 (1946).

force may be used. The court, however, went one step further by holding that "[t]he right to kill an escaping offender is limited to cases in which the officer *knows* that the person whom he is seeking to arrest is a felon and not an innocent party."[391] (Emphasis added.)

Although the rule allowing the use of deadly force in dealing with *all* felony offenses is still followed by most jurisdictions, there is a rising trend of, and call for, modification of the rule to preclude such force in instances of minor, non-atrocious felonies.[392]

3. Force in Riot Situations

Under riot conditions, the courts seem to take a much more lenient attitude in regard to the permissible amount of force that may be employed by peace officers. Just as in a non-riot situation, should police officers find their lives endangered by lawless conditions existing on the streets, they are always privileged to use whatever force is necessary to protect themselves and their fellow officers.[393] This same right is extended to those military forces called in to aid in the restoration of order.[394] Thus, it would certainly appear that the officers are clearly justified in the *proper* and *reasonable* use of deadly force to deal with snipers and other rioters who are intent on inflicting serious bodily harm on the officers.

Even in dealing with the large street-crowds which may be looting or destroying during a riot, the police and military are justified, under the law, in using more force than would be allowed in dealing with like criminal offenses under ordinary, non-riot conditions. An extreme application of this proposition was seen in *Commonwealth v. Stewart*,[395] where a lower Pennsylvania court upheld the actions of the police in quelling a small civil disturbance by pointing out:

---

391 *Id.* at 492, 45 A.2d at 239.
392 *See* Moreland, *supra* note 369, at 412-15. That the law seems to be heading in just such a direction is demonstrated by the RESTATEMENT (SECOND) OF TORTS § 143 (1965).

> (1) Either a peace officer or a private person is privileged to use force against or impose confinement upon another which is not intended or likely to cause death or serious bodily harm for the purpose of preventing any felony which the actor reasonably believes the other is committing or is about to commit if the actor reasonably believes that commission or consummation of the felony cannot otherwise be prevented.
> (2) The use of force or the imposition of confinement intended or likely to cause death or serious bodily harm is privileged if the actor reasonably believes that the commission or consummation of the felony cannot otherwise be prevented and the felony for the prevention of which the actor is intervening is of a type threatening death or serious bodily harm or involving the breaking and entry of a dwelling place. *Id.*

393 *E.g.*, Gordy v. State, 93 Ga. App. 743, 92 S.E.2d 737 (1956) (dicta) which states: "A person making a lawful arrest is justified in killing under the fears of a reasonable man that a felony is about to be committed upon himself or his fellow officers." *Id.* at 739.
394 Manley v. State, 62 Tex. Crim. 392, 137 S.W. 1137 (1911), *aff'd on other grounds on second appeal*, 69 Tex. Crim. 502, 154 S.W. 1008 (1913). Speaking of the rights of National Guardsmen, the court said:

> If in the performance of his [National Guardsman's] duties his life becomes endangered, or it appeared to him under all the facts and circumstances in evidence that some person was about to assault him with the intention of killing him, or doing him some serious bodily injury, he would have the right to act in self-defense. 137 S.W. at 1141.

395 58 Dauphin County Reports 209 (Ct. of Quarter Sessions of Dauphin County, Pa. 1947).

In Commonwealth vs. Martin, 9 Kulp 69, it is said, with reference to the amount of force that may be used:

> Those who attend a sheriff in order to suppress a riot may take such weapons as are necessary to effectuate the purpose, and they may justify beating, wounding, or even killing such rioters as shall resist or refuse to surrender.

> The policemen of the city of Harrisburg have the same authority as a sheriff under such circumstances.[396]

Hopefully, courts today would not be so inhumane, but it does appear that, at least in Pennsylvania, the police are authorized to use the utmost force in suppressing a riot.

An earlier Pennsylvania decision adopted this same position with regard to the amount of force that the military may use in the suppression of rioting. In *Commonwealth ex rel. Wadsworth v. Shortall*,[397] which upheld the action of a National Guardsman on riot duty in his killing, pursuant to orders, a person who ignored his repeated commands to halt, the Pennsylvania Supreme Court reasoned that

> . . . while the military are in active service for the suppression of disorder and violence, their rights and obligations as soldiers must be judged by the standard of actual war. No other standard is possible, for *the first and overruling duty is to repress disorder, whatever the cost, and all means which are necessary to that end are lawful.* The situation of troops in a riotous and insurrectionary district approximates that of troops in an enemy's country, and in proportion to the extent and violence of the overt acts of hostility shown is the degree of severity justified in the means of suppression.[398] (Emphasis added.)

The harsh result reached in *Shortall* has received some support from one of the leading commentators on martial law, Frederick Bernays Wiener, who said:

> We may disagree with much of what the court said and still approve the decision. Dynamiters do not respond to sweet reasonableness, and the disturbed situation in the community while not amounting to a state of war or even calling for the application of the rules of war, certainly justified drastic measures.[399] (Footnote omitted.)

Even if one rejects the undesirable conclusion reached in *Shortall* that under riot conditions the National Guard enjoys war powers and adopts the more moderate view that the troops acting in aid of civil authorities to suppress a riot have only the powers of the local peace officers,[400] troops in Pennsylvania

---

396   *Id.* at 218.
397   206 Pa. 165, 55 A. 952 (1903).
398   *Id.* at 174, 55 A. at 956.
399   F. WIENER, A PRACTICAL MANUAL OF MARTIAL LAW 73 (1940).
400   *See* Franks v. Smith, 142 Ky. 232, 134 S.W. 484 (1911); Bishop v. Vandercook, 228 Mich. 299, 200 N.W. 278 (1924); State v. McPhail, 182 Miss. 360, 180 So. 387 (1938); Fluke v. Canton, 31 Okla. 718, 123 P. 1049 (1912).

would possess virtually the same amount of power under the doctrine advanced in *Commonwealth v. Stewart.*[401]

Fortunately, until the current rash of ghetto riots, the United States had not experienced enough civil disorder for the courts to demonstrate whether a more enlightened view of the law will reject the legal theories arising from *Stewart* and *Shortall.* But it does seem obvious that the law will allow greater force in the suppression of riots than in the control of ordinary crime. The *Restatement (Second) of Torts,* which is ordinarily most reluctant to sanction the use of force in controlling criminal conduct,[402] has adopted in section 142 a rather permissive standard with regard to the amount of force authorized in riot control.

> (1) Either a peace officer or a private person is privileged to impose confinement upon or use force against another for the purpose of suppressing a riot or preventing the other from participating in it if
>   (a) the other is or the actor reasonably believes him to be participating or to be about to participate in the riot, and
>   (b) such force or confinement is not intended or likely to cause death or serious bodily harm, and
>   (c) the actor reasonably believes that the riot cannot otherwise be suppressed or the other's participation in it otherwise be prevented.
>   (2) *The use of force or the imposition of a confinement which is intended or likely to cause death or serious bodily harm for the purpose of suppressing a riot or preventing the other from participating in it is privileged if the riot is one which threatens death or serious bodily harm.*[403]
> (Emphasis added.)

That the *Restatement* does countenance the use of deadly force in the suppression of riots, such as those this country has experienced in the urban ghettos during the past several summers, is made quite clear by comment *g* to subsection 2 of section 142:

> If the riot itself threatens death or serious bodily harm, it is sufficiently serious to justify the use of deadly means to suppress it. It is not necessary that the avowed purpose of the riot be to inflict such harm. It is enough that the conduct of the rioters is such as to create the probability or even the possibility of such consequences. Thus a riot the purpose of which is the wholesale destruction of structures or chattels usually involves something more than a bare possibility of serious bodily harm to persons in the vicinity.[404]

Hence, for better or for worse, there has been, and will probably continue to be, a tradition in the law of allowing a most severe use of force against rioters.

---

401   58 Dauphin County Reports 209 (Ct. of Quarter Sessions of Dauphin County, Pa. 1947).
402   *See* notes 374 & 392 *supra.*
403   RESTATEMENT (SECOND) OF TORTS § 142 (1965).
404   RESTATEMENT (SECOND) OF TORTS, Explanatory Notes § 142, comment *g* at 257 (1965).

B. Arrest Procedures During a Riot

1. Power to Arrest

During a major ghetto riot, large numbers of persons are arrested and detained by civil and military law enforcement officials. In the first of the major riots of this type, Watts in 1965, the Los Angeles Police Department reported that 3,356 persons were arrested.[405] In the week-long rioting in Detroit in 1967, 7,223 citizens were arrested.[406] Faced with the likelihood of such an inordinately large number of arrests, officials charged with the suppression of violence and the restoration of order must determine when and whom the law permits them to arrest.[407]

In the area of arrest without a warrant, the law again makes a distinction between felony and misdemeanor offenses. Generally, it can be said that "[a]n officer can make an arrest for a misdemeanor without a warrant only when the offense is attempted or committed in his presence."[408] According to its strictest interpretation, the requirement of an officer's presence means that " . . . the acts constituting the offense become known to him at the time they are committed through his sense of sight or through other senses."[409] Practically speaking, the requirement that the misdemeanor must have been committed in the officer's presence should not cause much difficulty for riot arrests. During a riot, the police confront the persons whom they will arrest directly on the city streets and can learn of the crime only through their senses. In Detroit, for example, most of the 1,652 misdemeanor arrests were for curfew violations[410] which clearly must be committed in the presence of the police if they are to be detected.

405　*See* LOS ANGELES POLICE DEPARTMENT 1965 ANNUAL REPORT 21 (1966).

406　Cahalan, *supra* note 375, at 430.

407　It is sufficient here to note that there are certain differences in the law with regard to arrest with and without a warrant. However, under riot conditions it is unthinkable that the police and military officers would be able or disposed to obtaining warrants to arrest persons they confront on the streets. Therefore, the discussion may safely be limited to situations in which arrests are made without the use of a warrant.

408　Coakley, *Restrictions in the Law of Arrest*, 52 NW. U.L. REV. 2, 11 (1957) (footnotes omitted). It might also be noted that often there is an additional requirement for arrest without a warrant in the case of a misdemeanor, namely, that the offense must involve a breach of the peace. Commonwealth v. Gorman, 288 Mass. 294, 297, 192 N.E. 618, 619 (1934); Comment, *The Law of Arrest*, 17 MERCER L. REV. 300, 303 (1965). However, such a requirement is meaningless during actual riot conditions since riot-related offenses, by their very nature, involve a breach of the peace. This is made quite clear by examining what constitutes a breach of the peace. The Supreme Court of North Carolina has said:

> As to what constitutes a breach of the peace within the meaning of the rules which authorize an arrest without a warrant in such cases, the better reasoned authorities emphasize the necessity of showing as an element of the offense a disturbance of public order and tranquility by act or conduct not merely amounting to unlawfulness but tending also to create public tumult and incite others to break the peace. State v. Mobley, 240 N.C. 476, 83 S.E.2d 100, 104 (1954).

The RESTATEMENT (SECOND) OF TORTS defines a breach of the peace as " . . . a public offense done by violence, or one causing or likely to cause an immediate disturbance of public order." RESTATEMENT (SECOND) OF TORTS § 116 (1965). From the definitions advanced by these authorities, it would be difficult to envision any riot-related offense that would not be a breach of the peace, with the possible exceptions of loitering and curfew violations (which may be considered "likely to cause an immediate disturbance of public order," when done in the context of a riot).

409　State v. Pluth, 157 Minn. 145, 151, 195 N.W. 789, 791 (1923).

410　Cahalan, *The Detroit Riot*, 3 THE PROSECUTOR 430, 432 (1967). Furthermore, most states now authorize a peace officer to arrest without a warrant for any offense committed in his presence. Comment, *supra* note 408, at 304.

The arrest requirements for a felony offense are somewhat more permissive; they give the police greater freedom as to whom they can arrest and on what basis. These less stringent requirements for felony arrests take on added significance when it is remembered that the majority of those arrested in the course of a riot are charged with felonies.[411] The basic requirement for such an arrest is that it be made only upon probable cause which ". . . exists if the facts and circumstances known to the officer warrant a prudent man in believing that the offense has been committed."[412] Mere ". . . suspicion is not enough for an officer to lay hands on a citizen,"[413] although "[e]vidence required to establish guilt is not necessary."[414] One commentator has stated:

> With respect to felony offenses, therefore, the officer can act upon the complaint or report of reliable citizens, or upon information from reliable informants, and upon observed facts and circumstances which, although short of the actual commission of a crime, give rise to reasonable cause to believe that the suspect did commit a felony offense.[415]

Thus, if the officer has probable cause to believe that a felony has been committed and that the suspect committed it, he is entitled to arrest without a warrant. There is no indication that this legal principle would be any different during a riot.

However, there is some authority for the proposition that the rules governing arrest without a warrant may be relaxed, in some undefined manner, for military forces charged with, or aiding in, the suppression of a civil disorder. As Wiener has pointed out, there are three schools of thought on the powers that may be exercised by the military in controlling a riot.[416] On one extreme is the theory that under such conditions, military forces enjoy the powers they would have in conditions of actual war.[417] This appears to be the approach adopted by the Supreme Court of Pennsylvania in *Commonwealth ex rel. Wadsworth v. Shortall*,[418] where the court said that ". . . while the military are in active service for the suppression of disorder and violence, their rights and obligations as soldiers must be judged by the standard of actual war. No other standard is possible . . . ."[419] Such a position has received support in several equally antiquated cases from other jurisdictions.[420] It grants troops the same flexibility

---

411   In the Detroit riot, 5,571 of the 7,223 arrests were for felonies. *See* Cahalan, *supra* note 410, at 430, 432. And in the Watts riot, of the 3,356 persons arrested, 2,613 were charged with felonies. *See* Los Angeles Police Department 1965 Annual Report 21 (1966).
412   Henry v. United States, 361 U.S. 98, 102 (1959).
413   *Id.* at 104.
414   *Id.* at 102.
415   Coakley, *supra* note 408, at 12. *See also* Comment, *supra* note 408, at 302-03.
416   F. Wiener, *supra* note 399, at 74-78.
417   *Id.* at 77, 78.
418   206 Pa. 165, 55 A. 952 (1903). Although Wiener, without any stated reason, says that the case does not confer such power, F. Weiner, *supra* note 399, at 77 n.61.
419   Commonwealth *ex rel.* Wadsworth v. Shortall, 206 Pa. 165, 174, 55 A. 952, 956 (1903).
420   United States *ex rel.* Seymour v. Fischer, 280 F. 208 (D. Neb. 1922) where it was said:
> When a state of war or insurrection exists, and the Governor has legally called into action the military forces of the state, the will of the commander becomes the controlling authority in the occupied territory, so far as he chooses to exert it, *subject to the laws and usages of war. Id.* at 210 (emphasis added).
See also Hatfield v. Graham, 73 W. Va. 759, 81 S.E. 533 (1914); *Ex parte* Jones, 71 W. Va.

to respond to the riot situation according to the severity of the disorder as if they were engaged in the occupation of enemy territory.[421] Apparently, this approach would give the troops unlimited discretion in making riot arrests.[422] Fortunately,[423] such a position would not likely be accepted today because

> . . . it is believed that this issue [military having war powers to suppress riots] is erroneous and unsound and that — perhaps more to the point — it will never stand the test of review in the Supreme Court of the United States. Pending . . . authoritative precedent, it is suggested that it is potentially both dangerous and costly for military personnel employed in aid of the civil power to imagine themselves at war. The safer course is to regard their powers as not unlimited.[424]

On the other extreme is the view that military men answering the call to control domestic disorder have no greater power than that of the civil peace officers.[425] This position likewise has received some smattering of support as was demonstrated by *State v. McPhail*[426] which stated that ". . . whatever the Governor does in the execution of the laws, or whatever members of the militia do under such authority, must be as civil officers, and in strict subordination to the general law of the land."[427] At least one commentator has adopted this position by saying: "In carrying out their mission the troops are bound to follow legal procedures. The extent of their power is that of any peace officer acting under similar circumstances."[428] Were such a restricted standard adopted, the federal troops and National Guardsmen would be compelled to abide by the same arrest requirements as do the local police.

However, the more generally accepted approach is to regard the military as having powers somewhere in between those of actual war and those of the local police.[429] The Supreme Court of Iowa exemplified the majority position in *State ex rel. O'Connor v. District Court*[430] where it said:

567, 77 S.E. 1029 (1913); State *ex rel.* Mays v. Brown, 71 W. Va. 519, 77 S.E. 243 (1912).

421 Commonwealth *ex rel.* Wadsworth v. Shortall, 206 Pa. 165, 174, 55 A. 952, 956 (1903).

422 Although the cases do not explicitly spell out the effect of war powers on the ability of the military to make arrests, this unlimited arrest power is implicit in the decisions. See *id.*; United States *ex rel.* Seymour v. Fischer, 280 F.208 (D. Neb. 1922); Hatfield v. Graham, 73 W. Va. 759, 81 S.E. 533 (1914); *Ex parte* Jones, 71 W. Va. 567, 77 S.E. 1029 (1913); State *ex rel.* Mays v. Brown, 71 W. Va. 519, 77 S.E. 243 (1912).

423 The possible horrors of such a position were graphically demonstrated by Charles Fairman when he said:

> Other jurisdictions have gone to the opposite extreme and conceded war powers to the governor. Paint Creek takes on the importance of Manassas, and militia officers controlling longshoremen at Galveston or strikers at Nebraska City are assimilated to Glorious Ben [appropriately nicknamed "Beast"] Butler in the plenitude of his exuberant military government in New Orleans in 1862. Fairman, *The Law of Martial Rule and the National Emergency*, 55 HARV. L. REV. 1253, 1273 (1942) (footnotes omitted).

424 F. WIENER, *supra* note 399, at 78. *See also* Fairman, *supra* note 423, at 1273-74.

425 F. WIENER, *supra* note 399, at 74-76.

426 182 Miss. 360, 180 So. 387 (1938).

427 *Id.* at 371, 180 So. at 390. *See also* Franks v. Smith, 142 Ky. 232, 134 S.W. 484 (1911); Bishop v. Vandercook, 228 Mich. 299, 200 N.W. 278 (1924); Fluke v. Canton, 31 Okla. 718, 123 P. 1049 (1912).

428 Note, *Rule by Martial Law in Indiana: The Scope of Executive Power*, 31 IND. L.J. 456, 473 (1956).

429 Fairman, *supra* note 423, at 1274.

430 219 Iowa 1165, 260 N.W. 73 (1935).

. . . we think that overwhelming weight of authority does extend to the military officers under such [riot] conditions much greater latitude in the exercise of their discretion as to what means it is necessary and proper for them to employ than is possessed by civil officers in time of peace.[431]

The commentators, for the most part, agree that the military does enjoy increased powers in dealing with domestic violence.[432] In the area of actual arrest procedure, this additional power remains undefined[433] and the actions must be judged on a case-by-case basis until the courts do announce the applicable standards.

2. Identification of Arrestees

Because of the large number of persons who may be arrested during a major riot, an arresting officer would be unable to remember the surrounding circumstances under which he arrested each of a number of persons.[434] Therefore, it has been suggested by several prominent prosecutors that the police obtain Polaroid cameras so that on-the-spot pictures may be taken of the officer and the arrestee for future reference.[435] This procedure was effectively utilized during the Detroit riot in 1967.

> The police knew that the individual police officer could not possibly remember all the persons whom he had arrested and the loot with which such persons were apprehended and the circumstances of the arrest when it came time to testify in court. In many precincts, therefore, the arresting officer and the accused were photographed with a Polaroid camera side by side with the loot piled on the floor before them. On the back of the photo, particulars of name, location of arrest, etc. were noted. These photos were placed in the police file folder of the case and were referred to by the arresting officer just before his taking the witness stand for the purpose of refreshing his recollection. They proved an invaluable aid to the police officers.[436]

The use of such a procedure violates none of the constitutional rights of the accused. In *Holt v. United States*[437] Justice Holmes said of fifth amendment safeguards:

> [T]he prohibition of compelling a man in a criminal court to be witness against himself is a prohibition of the use of physical or moral compulsion

431 *Id.* at 1187, 260 N.W. at 84. *See also* Herlihy v. Donohue, 52 Mont. 601, 161 P. 164 (1916); State *ex rel.* Roberts v. Swope, 38 N.M. 53, 28 P.2d 4 (1933).

432 F. WIENER, *supra* note 399, at 76, where he states ". . . a broader scope of action is permitted to the troops, and acts which if done by police officers would be without authority of law are considered legal when done by the military in situations involving violence." *See also* Fairman, *supra* note 423, at 1274; Fairman, *Martial Law, in the Light of* Sterling v. Constantin, 19 CORNELL L.Q. 20, 32-33 (1933).

433 However, there is some authority for the proposition that the military will be granted the power to detain rioters until the disorder is suppressed. This topic will be discussed later in text accompanying notes 487-97 *infra.*

434 Cahalan, *supra* note 410, at 430-31.

435 *See* Remarks of Melvin G. Rueger, Greenbrier Conference of National District Attorneys Association, Aug. 1967, printed in *Riot Panel*, 3 THE PROSECUTOR 282, 287 (1967); Remarks of Donald L. Knowles, *id.* at 286.

436 Cahalan, *supra* note 410, at 430-31.

437 218 U.S. 245 (1910).

to extort communications from him, not an exclusion of his body as evidence when it may be material.[438]

This reasoning has been developed in the law to mean that the privilege protects only against the compelling of the person to give evidence ". . . of a testimonial or communicative nature."[439] Finally, the Supreme Court has ruled that ". . . it [fifth amendment] offers no protection against compulsion to submit to fingerprinting, *photographing*, or measurements, to write or speak for identification . . . ."[440] (Emphasis added.)

However, in *United States v. Wade*,[441] the Supreme Court, after accepting the proposition that such practices as photographing the defendant do not violate fifth amendment rights,[442] vacated and remanded a conviction because the defendant's sixth amendment rights were violated.[443] Defendant's counsel was not present at a lineup where witnesses identified the defendant in a manner that could not be adequately challenged in court and could have been warped by the circumstances.[444] This identification procedure was deemed a "critical stage of the prosecution."[445] But it was further stated that the defendant need not have counsel present at non-critical stages where ". . . there is minimal risk that his counsel's absence . . . might derogate from his right to a fair trial."[446] It would appear obvious that this suggested initial photographing is such a non-critical stage since there would be no meaningful function for counsel to perform.[447]

A practical problem that may be confronted, however, arises from the fact that slight shifts in camera position or the relative distances of the photographed persons from the camera and from the surroundings may greatly distort the photograph.[448] Therefore, the police should receive prior training in the proper use of the camera; for example, the suspect should be photographed beside the arresting officer so that any distortions would be obvious when they appear in court. This policy would avoid any problems that may be raised by *Wade*.

---

438   *Id.* at 252-53.
439   Schmerber v. California, 384 U.S. 757, 761 (1966) (footnote omitted).
440   *Id.* at 764; *accord*, Kennedy v. United States, 353 F.2d 462, 466 (D.C. Cir. 1965); Smith v. United States, 324 F.2d 879, 882 (D.C. Cir. 1963); United States v. Amorosa, 167 F.2d 596, 599 (3d Cir. 1948); Williams v. State, 239 Ark. 1109, 396 S.W.2d 834, 837 (1965); Graef v. State, 1 Md. App. 161, 228 A.2d 480, 484 (1967); C. McCORMICK, TREATISE ON THE LAW OF EVIDENCE § 126 (1954).
441   388 U.S. 218 (1967).
442   *Id.* at 223.
443   *Id.* at 227-39.
444   This could occur, for example, in cases where all participants in the lineup except the suspect are known to the witness, the other lineup participants are "grossly dissimilar" to the suspect, only the suspect is made to wear the distinctive clothing worn by the actual criminal, and where the police inform witnesses that the actual criminal has been arrested. *Id.* at 233.
445   *Id.* at 237.
446   *Id.* at 228.
447   Haworth, *The Right to Counsel During Police Identification Procedures*, 45 TEXAS L. REV. 504, 515 (1967).
448   For an example of the photographic distortions possible from such shifting, See M. HOUTS, FROM EVIDENCE TO PROOF, 182-83 (1956).

3. Riot Arrests: *Gideon*[449] and *Miranda*[450]

Although there is some support for the proposition that "[d]ue process of law depends upon circumstances and varies with the subject-matter and the necessities of the situation . . . ,"[451] the strong wording of the Supreme Court in *Miranda*[452] leaves no doubt that the specified procedural safeguards must be applied in riots as well as in normal circumstances.

> It is impossible for us to foresee the potential alternatives for protecting the privilege [freedom from self-incrimination under the fifth amendment] which might be devised . . . . However, unless we are shown other procedures which are at least as effective in apprising accused persons of their right of silence and in assuring a continuous opportunity to exercise it, the . . . safeguards must be observed.[453]

In view of this language, if it became impossible, as a practical matter, to give the specified *Miranda* warnings in the manner prescribed, the police may be allowed to modify the rule so long as none of the accused's rights, as specified under *Miranda,* are violated. But in dealing with a riot, the police are undoubtedly too occupied with the situation on the streets to be concerned with interrogating arrested persons who were probably apprehended in the process of committing the crime for which they are charged. Therefore, the *Miranda* problem in the riot context is not as significant as it first might appear.

Gideon, however, does present a more serious problem for local officials.[454] That the Supreme Court considers the right to counsel to be absolute in criminal cases was demonstrated by its statement that

> . . . reason and reflection require us to recognize that in our adversary system of criminal justice, any person haled into court, who is too poor to hire a lawyer, cannot be assured a fair trial unless counsel is provided for him. This seems to be an obvious truth. . . . The right of one charged with crime to counsel may not be deemed fundamental and essential to fair trials in some countries, but it is in ours.[455]

The fact that the police themselves agree that the safeguards of *Gideon* and *Miranda* apply even under riot conditions is exhibited by a letter from the Los Angeles Police Department which reads in part:

> The safeguards of Gideon, Miranda, and Escobedo are applied under riot conditions. Interrogation of arrestees who do not have counsel is scheduled according to the availability of public defenders.[456]

---

449   Gideon v. Wainwright, 372 U.S. 335 (1963).
450   Miranda v. Arizona, 384 U.S. 436 (1966).
451   United States *ex rel.* Seymour v. Fischer, 280 F.2d 208, 210 (D. Neb. 1922).
452   The accused, before he can be subjected to police interrogation, must be advised that he has the right to remain silent, it must be made clear to him that the police will respect that right, he must be informed that anything he says will be used against him, he must be advised of his right to counsel, and must be told that free counsel will be provided him if he is unable to retain counsel on his own. Miranda v. Arizona, 384 U.S. 436, 467-73 (1966).
453   *Id.* at 467.
454   An accused indigent has an absolute right to counsel paid for by the state. Gideon v. Wainwright, 372 U.S. 335 (1963).
455   *Id.* at 344.
456   Letter from Capt. T. F. Janes, Commander, Public Affairs Division, Los Angeles Police Department, to James P. Gillece, Jr., January 2, 1968, on file with the NOTRE DAME LAWYER.

The problem with these safeguards, then, is not theoretical, but practical. Due to the large number of arrests during a riot[457] and the fact that most of those arrested are poor and without retained counsel,[458] it is quite difficult to supply them with the required legal advice. In Detroit, most of the persons arrested faced arraignment without the benefit of counsel, although attorneys from the bar association were often present as observers.[459] Many local attorneys freely volunteered their services — a necessary measure since the costs of providing appointed counsel to each arrestee would have been prohibitive.[460] But the arrangements were still woefully inadequate in that attorneys were assigned to courtrooms rather than to individual defendants. These attorneys represented all defendants tried in the courtroom to which they were assigned.[461] "While on [sic] attorney was conducting an examination, others were interviewing defendants and preparing their cases. In those instances where defense counsel needed more time to prepare, the court granted adjournment."[462] It is difficult to imagine how an adequate defense could be prepared under such conditions, and thus it seems that "Gideon's Trumpet" blew a sour note in riot-torn Detroit.

One possible solution to this difficult problem is for the local prosecutor to aggressively recruit a large number of volunteer attorneys from the local bar association so that all arrested parties could be adequately represented. Such a plan cannot be too highly recommended and must be finalized long before the city burns.

C. Detention of Rioters

One of the most effective, most widely used, and most objectionable methods of riot control is the incarceration of large numbers of rioters and their leaders until the disorder is suppressed.[463] Most law enforcement officials strongly support such a process.[464] The desired result — keeping the arrested rioters and riot leaders off the streets for the duration of the disturbance — can be accomplished by any one of three methods: (1) bail may be denied to those arrested, (2) an excessively high bail may be set so that the poor would be unable to meet it, (3) the military, when involved, may construe their powers in a riot to include the right to detain dangerous persons without bail.

---

457   E.g., 7,223 in Detroit, Cahalan, supra note 410, at 430; 3,356 in Watts, LOS ANGELES POLICE DEPARTMENT 1965 ANNUAL REPORT 21 (1966); and 400 in Cincinnati, Remarks of Melvin G. Rueger, supra note 435, at 287.
458   Only 30% of those arrested in Detroit had retained counsel, Cahalan, supra note 410, at 433.
459   Id. at 432.
460   Id. at 432-33.
461   Id. at 433.
462   Id.
463   It should be pointed out that the possible long range effect of such tactics might be to foster community resentment and thereby increase the chance of future and more severe disturbances. The National Commission on Civil Disorder reported that the most intensely held grievance of ghetto dwellers was police practices and another listed grievance was discriminatory law enforcement. RIOT COMMISSION REPORT, supra note 2, at 143-44.
464   See Remarks of Brendan T. Byrne, supra note 435 at 283: "Almost everyone agrees on the necessity for high bail during the riot . . . ." Remarks of Melvin G. Rueger, supra note 435, at 287: "The courts generally set high bonds on persons charged. This, of course, kept a large number in custody, thus preventing them from returning to the scene."

1. Denial of Bail

The eighth amendment provides: "Excessive bail shall not be required, nor excessive fines imposed, nor cruel and unusual punishment inflicted."[465] But the amendment does not, and has not been recognized as, granting an absolute right to bail. The Supreme Court in *Carlson v. Landon*[466] said: "Indeed, the very language of the Amendment fails to say all arrests must be bailable. We think, clearly, here that the Eighth Amendment does not require that bail be allowed under the circumstances. . . ."[467] The Eighth Circuit followed that reasoning in *Mastrian v. Hedman.*[468]

> Neither the Eighth Amendment nor the Fourteenth Amendment requires that everyone charged with a state offense must be given his liberty on bail pending trial. While it is inherent in our American concept of liberty that a right to bail shall generally exist, this has never been held to mean that a state must make every criminal offense subject to such a right or that the right provided as to offenses made subject to bail must be so administered that every accused will always be able to secure his liberty pending trial. Traditionally and acceptedly, there are offenses of a nature as to which a state properly may refuse to make provision for a right to bail.[469]

If bail then can legally be denied in certain cases, the question becomes one of whether it can be denied to arrested rioters. Most public officials agree that it is desirable to hold rioters in custody for the duration of the disturbance under the belief that, if released, they would return to the ghetto and resume their participation in the disorder.[470] There is some legal precedent for the denial of bail in cases where the danger to the community would be increased by the accused's release. "If, for example, the safety of the community would be jeopardized, it would be irresponsible judicial action to grant bail."[471] Thus, if the safety of the community does justify a denial of bail and since the eighth amendment precludes excessive bail, one can only conclude, as did Justice Douglas, that it would be unconstitutional to set a bail so high that the defendant could not possibly afford it, but it would be permissible to deny him the right to bail altogether.[472]

Although such may be the current status of the law, its logical absurdity

---

465　U.S. CONST. amend. VIII.

466　342 U.S. 524 (1952).

467　*Id.* at 545-46.

468　326 F.2d 708 (8th Cir.), *cert. denied,* 376 U.S. 965 (1964).

469　*Id.* at 710.

470　*E.g.,* the prosecutor for Wayne County, Michigan, which includes Detroit, said of the situation existing in that city during the riot:

> If each of those arrested had been released on his personal recognizance, there was danger of contempt replacing respect and sober regard for the machinery of law enforcement which might impel him to new acts of lawlessness. What service would it have been to the prisoner or to the community to release one caught *flagrante delicto* looting when the Governor of the State informed the President of the United States that he was not sure that he could maintain law and order in the streets of Detroit? Cahalan, *The Detroit Riot,* 3 THE PROSECUTOR 430, 432 (1967).

471　Carbo v. United States, 82 S. Ct. 662, 666 (1962) (footnote omitted).

472　*See* Rehman v. California, 85 S. Ct. 8, 9 (1964).

was well demonstrated by Justice Burton in a well-reasoned dissent in *Carlson v. Landon.*[473]

> That Amendment clearly prohibits federal bail that is excessive in amount when seen in the light of all traditionally relevant circumstances. Likewise, it must prohibit unreasonable denial of bail. The Amendment cannot well mean that, on the one hand, it prohibits the requirement of bail so excessive in amount as to be unattainable, yet, on the other hand, under like circumstances, it does not prohibit the denial of bail, which comes to the same thing. The same circumstances are relevant to both procedures.[474]

The very concept of holding a person, rioter, or ordinary arrestee in jail because he may commit some crime in the future runs contrary to notions long cherished in our legal system — that future crimes are to be deterred by the threat of future punishment and not by prior incarceration, and that imprisonment should not be imposed on a person without a judicial determination of his guilt.[475] Therefore, such a practice may well constitute a denial of due process of law.[476]

Justice Jackson, sitting as a circuit judge in *Williamson v. United States,*[477] attacked the concept of preventive detention, even in the interest of the national security, by allowing bail to certain convicted communists pending their appeal.

> If I assume that defendants are disposed to commit every opportune disloyal act helpful to Communist countries, it is still difficult to reconcile with traditional American law the jailing of persons by the courts because of anticipated but as yet uncommitted crimes. Imprisonment to protect society from predicted but unconsummated offenses is so unprecedented in this country and so fraught with danger of excesses and injustice that I am loath to resort to it, even as a discretionary judicial technique to supplement conviction of such offenses as those of which defendants stand convicted.[478] (Footnote omitted.)

However, this whole question of denying bail to those arrested during a riot is actually of little practical significance. Only nine states do not provide in their constitutions for a right to bail in all non-capital cases,[479] and, since the Judiciary Act of 1789,[480] bail has been a matter of right in federal non-capital cases.[481] Therefore, prosecutors will usually resort to another technique to hold the arrestees in custody during the riot.

2. Setting of High Bail

Often during a riot, officials of the community have sought to have high

---

473 342 U.S. 524 (1952).
474 *Id.* at 569 (dissenting opinion).
475 Note, *Preventive Detention Before Trial,* 79 Harv. L. Rev. 1489, 1509 (1966).
476 *Id.* at 1498.
477 184 F.2d 280 (2d Cir. 1950).
478 *Id.* at 282-83.
479 Note, *A Study of the Administration of Bail in New York City,* 106 U. Pa. L. Rev. 693, 696 n.11 (1958).
480 Judiciary Act of 1789, ch. 20, § 33, 1 Stat. 91.
481 Fed. R. Crim. P. § 46(a)(1) provides: "A person arrested for an offense not punishable by death shall be admitted to bail."

bails set by the courts in the hope that the indigent rioters will be unable to post the bond. In Detroit the county prosecutor publicly announced that he would ask that a bond of $10,000 be imposed on each person arrested for looting, and he received court reaction favorable to his request.[482] That such a practice was extensively used during the disorder in Detroit was demonstrated in the report of a speech made by John Feikens, president of the Detroit Bar Association, which stated:

> Even though the holocaust caused by the rioting, and despite the understandable near-hysteria in the city that cried out against the prisoners, it had to be remembered that each was entitled to be presumed innocent until proven guilty. Mr. Feikens noted that this principle "bent severely" as judges imposed heavy bail, their motivation being to clear the streets of looters and rioters. No one arrested in the early days of the disturbance was allowed released on personal bond.[483]

Bail has a traditional, legitimate purpose — to assure that the accused will appear for trial — and it can be used for no other end. This was conclusively settled by the Supreme Court in *Stack v. Boyle*[484] where it declared:

> . . . [T]he modern practice of requiring a bail bond or the deposit of a sum of money subject to forfeiture serves as additional assurance of the presence of an accused [at trial]. Bail set at a figure higher than an amount reasonably calculated to fulfill this purpose is "excessive" under the Eighth Amendment. . . .
>   Since the function of bail is limited, the fixing of bail for any individual defendant must be based upon standards relevant to the purpose of assuring the presence of that defendant.[485]

The Constitution does forbid the setting of excessive bail, and under *Stack*, the test for determining whether a particular bail is excessive is by measuring it against the amount of bail reasonably calculated to achieve the purpose for which the bail is used. The only constitutionally acceptable purpose is to assure the accused's presence at trial. When bail is used for any other purpose, including the preventive detention of rioters, it runs contrary to the eighth amendment.[486]

3. Military Detention

It has often been alleged and upheld by the courts that the military, in

---

482   *See* Cahalan, *supra* note 470, at 431; *cf.* Note, *supra* note 475, at 1489.
483   1 BNA CRIM. L. RPTR. 2286 (Aug. 16, 1967).
484   342 U.S. 1 (1951).
485   *Id.* at 5.
486   United States Senator Sam Ervin of North Carolina, commenting on the misuse of bail, has said ". . . where the right to bail does exist, it cannot be denied or abridged by the setting of excessive bail. This alone should preclude the use of high bail to effectuate preventive detention." Ervin, *The Legislative Role in Bail Reform*, 35 GEO. WASH. L. REV. 429, 444 (1967). *See also* Note, *supra* note 479, which says:

> It is fundamental that the state has no right to punish a person until his guilt has been established beyond a reasonable doubt. And there is no support in the law for the proposition that a person may be imprisoned because of the speculative possibility that he may commit a crime. Judges and prosecutors, therefore, should carefully refrain from employing bail to accomplish these illegal ends. Few cases

suppressing domestic violence, may arrest and detain the rioters and their leaders and hold them without bail until the disorder is terminated.[487] The rationale underlying this practice has been simply explained by one authority on martial law:

> Whenever there is a riot or insurrection, there are pretty certain to be ringleaders; once these are apprehended, the back of the disturbance is likely to be broken. Accordingly, commanders ordered into the field to suppress domestic disorders have almost invariably centered their attention on the heads of the offending movement, have arrested them, and have kept them in custody until such time as the disorders subsided and/or the persons detained could be turned over to the civil authorities for trial. In many instances, no trial ever took place; the detention was conceived to be entirely preventive and not at all punitive.[488]

The existing case law does support such action by the military. In *State ex rel. Roberts v. Swope*[489] it was held that the state executive has discretion to order the seizure of persons who stand in the way of troops engaged in restoring order and to authorize their detention until the disorder is terminated.[490] The Colorado Supreme Court upheld such action in *In re Moyer*[491] because the arrest was lawful and the detention was necessary to suppress the insurrection.[492] In *Moyer v. Peabody*,[493] which arose out of the same situation, the Supreme Court of the United States upheld the governor's action in having the National Guard arrest and detain a union president until the labor troubles were over on the rationale that under such riotous conditions ". . . the ordinary rights of individuals must yield to what he [governor] deems the necessities of the moment. Public danger warrants the substitution of executive process for judicial process."[494]

It may well be that when the military is called in, it operates as a super police force ". . . for the restoration of public order; and . . . under this theory the arrest and detention, under the circumstances stated, can be justified and must be upheld."[495] Wiener has pointed out that ". . . even in jurisdictions that never embraced any of the martial law excesses, the principle that the military may temporarily detain ringleaders in riot situations has been sustained."[496] However, there have been no recent decisions on the matter, and it is most doubtful that military detention would be upheld in light of the more modern Supreme Court decisions.[497]

---

of excessive bail ever reach the appellate courts; self-restraint and personal ethics are the only real controls over improper use of bail. *Id.* at 705 (footnotes omitted).
487   F. WIENER, A PRACTICAL MANUAL OF MARTIAL LAW 76 (1940).
488   *Id.* at 66.
489   38 N.M. 53, 28 P.2d 4 (1933).
490   *Id.* at 57-58, 28 P.2d at 6-7. *See also In re* Boyle, 6 Idaho 609, 57 P. 706 (1899), *appeal dismissed,* 178 U.S. 611 (1900); *In re* McDonald, 49 Mont. 454, 143 P. 947 (1914).
491   35 Colo. 159, 85 P. 190 (1904); *cf.* Sterling v. Constantin, 287 U.S. 378 (1932).
492   *In re* Moyer, 35 Colo. 159, 170, 85 P. 190, 194, (1904).
493   212 U.S. 78 (1909).
494   *Id.* at 85.
495   *In re* McDonald, 49 Mont. 454, 462, 143 P. 947, 949-50 (1914).
496   Wiener, *Helping to Cool the Long Hot Summers,* 53 A.B.A.J. 713, 716 (1967).
497   Helman, *Inciting to Riot,* 72 CASE & COMMENT 26, 27 (Nov.-Dec. 1967).

D. Search and Seizure During a Riot

1. The Requirement of a Warrant
    The fourth amendment provides:

> The right of the people to be secure in their persons, houses, papers, and effects, against unreasonable searches and seizures, shall not be violated and no Warrants shall issue, but upon probable cause, supported by Oath or affirmation, and particularly describing the place to be searched, and the persons or things to be seized.[498]

Traditionally, the wording of the amendment has been construed as requiring a warrant in the absence of extreme circumstances.[499] This construction of the amendment reached its high point in *Trupiano v. United States*[500] which held that the police were required to obtain a warrant before conducting a search whenever it was possible to do so.[501] However, this approach was later specifically rejected by the Court in *United States v. Rabinowitz:*[502]

> To the extent that *Trupiano v. United States*, 334 U. S. 699, requires a search warrant solely upon the basis of the practicability of procuring it rather than upon the reasonableness of the search after a lawful arrest, that case is overruled. *The relevant test is not whether it is reasonable to procure a search warrant, but whether the search was reasonable. That criterion in turn depends upon the facts and circumstances — the total atmosphere of the case.*[503] (Emphasis added.)

In later decisions, however, the Court has severely undermined the *Rabinowitz* approach to such an extent that it may have reverted to the *Trupiano* standard. In one of the most recent decisions on the point, *Camara v. Municipal Court*,[504] which overruled *Frank v. Maryland*,[505] Justice White, speaking for the Court, said:

> Nevertheless, one governing principle, justified by history and by current experience, has consistently been followed: except in certain carefully defined classes of cases, a search of private property without proper consent is "unreasonable" unless it has been authorized by a valid search warrant.[506]

The *Camara* court went on to favorably cite from *Johnson v. United States*,[507] a pre-*Rabinowitz* case that struck down a search without a warrant on the ground that the police reasonably could have obtained a warrant where they

---

498   U.S. CONST. amend. IV.
499   McDonald v. United States, 335 U.S. 451, 454 (1948).
500   334 U.S. 699 (1948).
501   *Id.* at 705.
502   339 U.S. 56 (1950).
503   *Id.* at 66.
504   387 U.S. 523 (1967).
505   359 U.S. 360 (1959) (allowing administrative searches without a warrant).
506   Camara v. Municipal Court, 387 U.S. 523, 528-29 (1967). *See also* Chapman v. United States, 365 U.S. 610 (1961); Rios v. United States, 364 U.S. 253 (1960).
507   333 U.S. 10 (1948), cited in Camara v. Municipal Court, 387 U.S. 523, 529 (1967).

smelled burning opium coming from the defendant's hotel room.[508] The part of the *Johnson* opinion cited favorably by the *Camara* court reads: "When the right of privacy must reasonably yield to the right of search is, as a rule, to be decided by a judicial officer, not by a policeman or government enforcement agent."[509]

Some commentators have also interpreted recent decisions of the Supreme Court as indicating that the Court is coming back to *Trupiano:*

> It is apparent that the Supreme Court has in the past regarded the approach later taken in *Rabinowitz* as a backward step in constitutional history and the development of human freedom and there are clear indications that it seems to think so at the present time. An examination of the opinions in *McDonald v. United States* [335 U.S. 451 (1948)], *Johnson v. United States* [333 U.S. 10 (1948)], and *Taylor v. United States* [286 U.S. 1 (1932)] demonstrates clearly that these cases turned upon the availability of, and opportunity to procure, a search warrant. They are still good law today. The very recent case of *Chapman v. United States* [365 U.S. 610 (1961)] is clear evidence of the present Court's intention to revert to the spirit of the *Trupiano* rule, if not to its exact letter.[510] (Footnotes omitted.)

Thus, barring a emergency situation,[511] the police must obtain a search warrant from a magistrate before they may conduct a search of private property.

2. The Area Search

During the civil disorders in Plainfield, New Jersey in 1967, when forty-six semi-automatic rifles were stolen from a nearby firearms plant, large numbers of state policemen and National Guardsmen descended on the Negro section of Plainfield and, without warrants, conducted a house-to-house search for the stolen weapons.[512] Such activities are not unusual during riots[513] since the police officers often wish to search large segments of the rebellious district for weapons, loot, or the ingredients for Molotov cocktails. Because the recent disturbances in this country have occurred in major urban areas with their teeming tenements, massive public housing projects, and other multiple family dwellings, a serious problem confronts the police when they attempt to obtain a warrant to conduct a search in the area. The fourth amendment requires that the warrant state with particularity the place to be searched and the persons or things to be seized.[514] Searches of an area pursuant to a warrant that fails to meet this specificity requirement are necessarily illegal.[515]

---

508 Johnson v. United States, 333 U.S. 10, 15 (1948).
509 *Id.* at 14, cited in Camara v. Municipal Court, 387 U.S. 523, 529 (1967).
510 *E.g.*, Day & Berkman, *Search and Seizure and the Exclusionary Rule: A Re-Examination in the Wake of* Mapp v. Ohio, 13 W. Res. L. Rev. 56, 88 (1961).
511 *See* text accompanying notes 524-39 *infra.*
512 Governor's Select Commission on Civil Disorder, State of New Jersey, Report for Action 150-52 (1968); Note, *Riot Control and the Fourth Amendment*, 81 Harv. L. Rev. 625 (1968).
513 Note, *supra* note 512.
514 U.S. Const. amend. IV. See text accompanying note 498 *supra* for the language of this amendment.
515 *See* Marcus v. Search Warrant, 367 U.S. 717, 739 (1961) (concurring opinion of Justice Black).

The specification of the place to be searched must be sufficiently detailed to make clear the search area in which there is probable cause to believe a crime has been committed; a general or roving search warrant is invalid. Thus a warrant describing an entire building as the place to be searched is invalid where probable cause has been shown only for searching one room or apartment.[516] (Footnotes omitted.)

In the *Camara* decision, the Supreme Court stated that it would continue to forbid any type of sweeping or area search, despite the public interest that may be involved.

. . . [I]n a criminal investigation, the police may undertake to recover specific stolen or contraband goods. But that public interest would hardly justify a sweeping search of an entire city conducted in the hope that these goods might be found. Consequently, a search for these goods, even with a warrant, is "reasonable" only when there is "probable cause" to believe that they will be uncovered in a particular dwelling.[517]

With regard to searches of apartments, tenements, or other multiple family dwellings, the courts have been uniform in holding that probable cause must be shown for each unit to be searched and that a warrant may not be issued for the entire building unless probable cause is separately shown for each individual unit therein.[518]

Federal courts have consistently held that the Fourth Amendment's requirement that a specific "place" be described when applied to dwellings refers to a single living unit (the residence of one person or one family). Thus, a warrant which describes an entire building when cause is shown for searching only one apartment is void.[519]

That the courts will not tolerate the use of area searches as was done in Plainfield was demonstrated by the Fourth Circuit in *Lankford v. Gelston*[520] which enjoined the Baltimore Police Department from indiscriminately searching Negro homes while looking for two brothers who killed one city policeman and wounded another.[521] The court concluded that federal courts, although

---

516   Day & Berkman, *supra* note 510, at 78. *See also* Note, *supra* note 512, at 628.
517   Camara v. Municipal Court, 387 U.S. 523, 535 (1967).
518   *See, e.g.,* United States *ex rel.* Sunrise Prods. Co. v. Epstein, 33 F.2d 982 (E.D.N.Y. 1929); People v. Estrada 234 Cal. App. 2d 136, 44 Cal. Rptr. 165 (1965); People v. Johnson, 49 Misc. 2d 244, 267 N.Y.S.2d 301 (Dist. Ct. Nassau County, 1966); Crossland v. State, 206 P.2d 649 (Okla. Ct. Crim. App. 1958); State v. Costakos, 226 A.2d 695 (R.I. 1967).
519   United States v. Hinton, 219 F.2d 324, 326 (7th Cir. 1955).
520   364 F. 2d 197 (4th Cir. 1966).
521   From December 24, 1964, to January 12, 1965, the Baltimore police conducted 300 such searches of Negro homes looking for the suspects. *Id.* at 199 n.3. The method used in the search was appalling:

Four officers carrying shotguns or submachine guns and wearing bulletproof vests would go to the front door and knock. They would be accompanied or followed by supervising officers, a sergeant or lieutenant. Other men would surround the house, training their weapons on windows and doors. "As soon as an occupant opened the door, the first man would enter the house to look for any immediate danger, and the supervising officer would then talk to the person who had answered the door. Few stated any objection to the entry; some were quite willing to have the premises searched for the Veneys, while others acquiesced because of the show of force." *Id.* at 199.

reluctant to intervene in local law enforcement activities, will nevertheless grant
equitable relief to stop invasions of constitutional rights by local officials.[522] It
is especially significant to note that, in deciding to grant the injunction, the *Lankford* court considered the psychological effects that such police tactics would
have on the ghetto residents.

> Courts cannot shut their eyes to events that have been widely pub-
> licized throughout the nation and the world. Lack of respect for the police
> is conceded to be one of the factors generating violent outbursts in Negro
> communities. The invasions so graphically depicted in this case "could"
> happen in prosperous suburban neighborhoods, but the innocent victims
> know only that wholesale raids do not happen elsewhere and did happen
> to them. Understandably they feel that such illegal treatment is reserved
> for those elements who the police believe cannot or will not challenge them.
> It is of the highest importance to community morale that the courts shall
> give firm and effective reassurance, especially to those who feel that they
> have been harassed by reason of their color or their poverty.[523]

Thus, those charged with riot prevention and riot control should be most reluctant, for both practical and legal reasons, to resort to the sweeping area searches
that were used in Plainfield and condemned in Baltimore.

3. Searches in an Emergency Situation

The primary exception to the warrant requirement applicable in riot conditions[524] is the traditional consideration that justifies searches without a warrant
in an emergency situation.[525] This exception was recognized by Justice Brennan,
speaking for the court in *Warden v. Hayden*,[526] where he said: "The Fourth
Amendment does not require police officers to delay in the course of an investigation if to do so would gravely endanger their lives or the lives of others."[527]

This emergency exception applies ". . . when a police officer obtains certain
knowledge of a grave and pending peril inside a dwelling, which permits of no
delay . . . ."[528] Such a case was demonstrated in *People v. Gilbert*[529] where police
in pursuit of fleeing suspects, who had already mortally wounded one policeman, were allowed to break into the apartment of one of the suspects since he
was armed and dangerous. However, it must be pointed out that, in applying

---

522 *Id.* at 201.
523 *Id.* at 203-04.
524 There are four major exceptions to the warrant requirement: (1) consent, (2) search
incident to an arrest, (3) search based on probable cause that a felony has been committed
(This exception is, of course, based on the *Rabinowitz* approach which later Court decisions
have virtually made meaningless, *see* notes 504-10 *supra* and accompanying text; and has
been specifically rejected for dwellings, *see* cases cited at Day & Berkman, *supra* note 510, at
87 n.193), (4) search in an emergency. Day & Berkman, *supra* note 510, at 80. Since the
emergency situation seems primarily applicable to riot conditions, that is where this discussion
will center.
525 *See* Camara v. Municipal Court, 387 U.S. 523, 539 (1967) (dictum).
526 387 U.S. 294 (1967).
527 *Id.* at 298-99. It might be noted that the emergency situation includes the right to
follow and search a fleeing suspect to avoid the destruction of the evidence, a situation probably
not relevant to riot conditions. *See* Day & Berkman, *supra* note 510, at 80.
528 DeBerry & Mueller, *Pending Peril and the Right to Search Dwellings*, 58 W. Va. L.
Rev. 219, 235 (1956).
529 63 Cal. 2d 690, 408 P.2d 365, 47 Cal. Rptr. 909 (1965), *vacated on different grounds*,
388 U.S. 263 (1967).

this exception, the courts have been very strict in requiring the actual existence of a grave emergency.[530]

As to be expected, this exception does have significant application under riot conditions since ". . . if a policeman sees a sniper or a firebomber in a window of a building he may immediately enter the building to search for both the sniper or bomber and his weapons."[531] The necessity and utility of this exception to law enforcement officers engaged in suppressing a riot are quite obvious.

There has been a long-standing tradition in the law, starting with *Semayne's Case*[532] in 1603 and now generally codified,[533] that a police officer in performing a lawful search of a dwelling must first announce to the occupants his authority and purpose before he may forcibly enter the premises. The federal statute is typical of the law on this point.

> The officer may break open any outer or inner door or window of a house, or any part of a house, or anything therein, to execute a search warrant, if, *after notice of his authority and purpose,* he is'refused admittance or when necessary to liberate himself or a person aiding him in the execution of the warrant.[534] (Emphasis added.)

But this announcement requirement, like the warrant requirement, has recognized an exception in the case of an emergency situation, although this exception has never been codified.[535] If there is imminent danger to the officers or to a third person that would be increased by an announcement of authority and purpose, the officers are excused from making the announcement and are entitled to make immediate forcible entry.[536] But if there is no impending peril to the officers or to others, a forcible entry without a prior announcement of authority and purpose and without a refusal of admittance cannot be sanctioned.[537] Examples of the type of emergencies that justify forcible entry are set out in *Wayne v. United States*:[538]

> Breaking into a home by force is not illegal if it is reasonable under the circumstances. . . . A myriad of circumstances would fall within the terms, "exigent circumstances" referred to in Miller v. United States [357 U.S. 301 (1958)] . . . , the sound of gunfire in a house, threats from inside to shoot through the door at police, reasonable grounds to believe an injured or seriously ill person is being held within.[539]

---

530   *See, e.g.,* McDonald v. United States, 335 U.S. 451, 455 (1948); Ellison v. State, 383 P.2d 716, 720 (Alas. 1963); State v. Rogers, 270 Ohio 2d 105, 198 N.E.2d 796 (C.P. Miami County 1963).
531   Note, *supra* note 512, at 626-27 (footnote omitted).
532   5 Co. Rep. 91a, 91b, 77 Eng. Rep. 194, 195 (K.B. 1603).
533   *See* Miller v. United States, 357 U.S. 301, 308 n.8 (1958); Blakey, *The Rule of Announcement and Unlawful Entry:* Miller v. United States *and* Ker v. California, 112 U. PA. L. REV. 499, 508 (1964).
534   18 U.S.C. § 3109 (1964).
535   *See* Blakey, *supra* note 533, at 508.
536   *E.g.,* People v. Hammond, 54 Cal. 2d 846, 357 P.2d 289, 9 Cal. Rptr. 243 (1960).
537   *E.g.,* United States v. Barrow, 212 F. Supp. 837 (E.D. Pa. 1962).
538   318 F.2d 205 (D.C. Cir.), *cert. denied,* 375 U.S. 860 (1963).
539   *Id.* at 212.

Thus, when the police reasonably believe that a sniper or firebomber, or other rioter intent on inflicting serious bodily harm on the police or on others, is within a dwelling place, the officers may forcibly enter and arrest said person and conduct a search for his weapons even though they do not possess a warrant.

IV. Civil Liability for Riot Damage

At the outset of this Note, it was recognized that the recent disturbing increase in large-scale riots is essentially a socio-economic phenomenon, the intricate causes of which are beyond the scope of legal analysis. Nevertheless, the basic premise of this Note is that when a riot is imminent or in progress, the problem becomes one of immediate and efficient implementation of the state's police power to maintain or re-establish public order. In practice this means principally the promise of criminal sanctions against those who would riot and the imposition of such sanctions against those who have rioted. The emphasis of this Note to this point has been upon the numerous and difficult legal problems that surround the effective use of criminal sanctions to prevent and control riots.

But there is another aspect of large-scale rioting that has yet to be considered — the aftermath. Every year, long after the seething summer nights have passed, more and more American cities carry the scars of untold property damage, and more and more Americans carry scars on their own bodies.[540] However, the real cost of mob violence has a way of escaping most Americans because they tend to view the property damage, injuries, and loss of life in terms of gross figures, failing to recognize that many, if not most, of the scars of mob violence represent personal tragedies to their victims. In recognition of this fact, the emphasis of this Note turns from the criminal sanctions available to society at large for its protection from riots to a consideration of some of the civil remedies available to riot victims against those responsible for their damages.[541]

---

540 See note 1 *supra* and accompanying text.
541 The focus here will be on the liability of those individuals and groups responsible for the riot damage. There are two other possible sources of recovery for the riot victim which initially appear to be much more appropriate for the satisfaction of large damage claims, namely, insurance coverage and liability of the governmental unit.

Under present conditions, however, the chances that a riot victim will have insurance to cover his injuries are becoming increasingly slight. The huge losses that have been suffered by insurance companies as a result of the recent riots have caused the companies to refuse to sell or renew policies to owners of property particularly susceptible to riot damage. The result is an insurance crisis in the urban core of most large American cities. The President's National Advisory Panel on Insurance in Riot-Affected Areas has recently published its report "Meeting the Insurance Crisis of Our Cities," which provides a detailed analysis of the problems and proposes various solutions, including the use of urban area plans and insurance pools, with state and federal backing. The five-part program of the Panel has received approval in the recently published RIOT COMMISSION REPORT, *supra* note 2, at 360-62. *See generally* Comment, *Insurance Protection Against Civil Demonstrations,* 7 B.C. IND. & COM. L. REV. 706 (1966); Note, *Riot Insurance,* 77 YALE L.J. 541 (1968).

Municipal and county liability for riot damage is also fraught with numerous problems. Some fifteen or twenty states presently have statutes that impose some degree of liability on cities or counties. Almost all, however, are severely limited in some way such as a restriction on the amount of damages recoverable, or a requirement of a showing of negligence on the part of the municipality; others cover only property damage or only personal injuries. In the absence of any such statute, the traditional doctrine of governmental immunity remains a substantial barrier to municipal liability despite recent judicial inroads in some jurisdictions.

A. Liability of Persons Who Participate in Mob Violence

It has been said that "[s]trictly speaking, there exists no civil action for riot, rout, or unlawful assembly, but only an action for damages as a result of the trespasses or assaults committed pursuant to the mob enterprise."[542] This absence of a separate legal remedy is reflected in the sparsity of authority that attributes any legal significance at all to the fact that the tortfeasor was a member of a mob.[543] One of the few civil cases that even adverts to "mob action" is *Stevens v. Sheriff*[544] in which the plaintiff sued a number of persons alleging that they assaulted him and destroyed personal property belonging to him. The trial court had instructed the jury that the plaintiff could recover only if he proved his allegation that the defendants constituted a mob. The Supreme Court of Kansas reversed saying:

> The allegation of the petition that the defendants acted as a mob was an immaterial one. It could have been obliterated without destroying or changing the legal effect of the petition. . . .
> . . . . It was apparently used either as a mere epithet or to imply such a concert of action among the defendants as to constitute them joint wrong-doers, and to render each one liable for the acts of any or all of the others. In the latter case it was only repetition, for the specific averment was also made that the defendants acted in concert, and in pursuance and furtherance of a common design.[545]

A defendant who inflicts intentional injuries upon the person or property of another can claim no defense not otherwise available to him simply because he committed the acts during the course of a riot. Therefore, as against the actual perpetrator of an intentional civil injury, the traditional forms of tort liability are adequate to give a riot victim a cause of action.

Realistically, however, the personal injuries and property damage inflicted during the course of a riot result from various degrees of participation by numerous individuals. The plaintiff may be struck by one member of a mob while several others hold him, various items of his property may be destroyed by some members while still others may be shouting threats or giving encouragement to the actors, and finally there may be numerous other persons standing at varying distances from the spectacle experiencing emotions ranging from delight to indignation. The degree to which each of these persons is subject,

---

But even absent these limitations, it is doubtful whether local governments could bear the financial burden of liability for riot damage. *See generally* Note, *Riot Insurance*, 77 Yale L.J. 541 (1968); Sengstock, *Mob Action: Who Shall Pay the Price?*, 44 J. Urban L. 407 (1967).

542   46 Am. Jur. *Riots and Unlawful Assembly* § 18 (1943).

543   An annotation located at .27 A.L.R. 549 (1923), entitled "Civil Liability of Member of a Mob," is apparently the only annotation in the entire ALR series of volumes that treats this topic. Significantly, the annotation is only two and one half pages long and discusses only seven cases, the most recent being a 1922 case. The four volumes of supplemental decisions to the first ALR series, the last volume of which was published in 1967, cite only two additional cases. 2 A.L.R. Blue Book of Supplemental Decisions 67 (1952); 3 A.L.R. Blue Book of Supplemental Decisions 72 (1958).

544   71 Kan. 434, 80 P. 936 (1905).

545   *Id.* at 435-36, 80 P. at 937. *See also* Dickson v. Yates, 194 Iowa 910, 188 N.W. 948 (1922).

or should be subject, to tort liability gives rise to a difficult entanglement of legal theory and factual distinction.

From the viewpoint of the injured plaintiff, what is sought is a device for holding as many of the rioters as possible vicariously liable for the injuries actually inflicted by a few. The usual approach taken by the plaintiffs in these cases is the application of a theory of civil conspiracy.[546] Originally, the writ of civil conspiracy was used against individuals who combined to abuse legal procedure and thus was the forerunner of the modern action for malicious prosecution.[547] Today, however, the civil action for conspiracy has broadened to include any combination of two or more persons to accomplish by concerted action an unlawful purpose, or to accomplish a lawful purpose by unlawful means.[548] It is a rather unusual form of tort remedy in the sense that it is not generally regarded as a substantive tort; in fact, it "cannot be made the subject of a civil action unless something has been done which, absent the conspiracy, would give a right of action."[549] The utility of the civil action for conspiracy is that it extends traditional forms of tort liability "beyond the active wrongdoer to those who have merely planned, assisted or encouraged his acts."[550]

> [T]he major significance of the conspiracy lies in the fact that it renders each participant in the wrongful act responsible as a joint tortfeasor for all damages ensuing from the wrong, irrespective of whether or not he was a direct actor and regardless of the degree of his activity.[551]

The theory of civil conspiracy as a "tort" has met with criticism on the ground that it is a totally unnecessary addition to the law of torts.[552] Its only significant purpose of widening the sphere of available tortfeasors can usually be accomplished just as well by direct factual allegations to the effect that the

---

546 Calcutt v. Gerig, 271 F. 220 (6th Cir. 1921); Weber v. Paul, 241 Iowa 121, 40 N.W.2d 8 (1949); Dickson v. Yates, 194 Iowa 910, 188 N.W. 948 (1922).
547 W. PROSSER, LAW OF TORTS § 43, at 260 (3d ed. 1964).
548 Duplex Printing Press Co. v. Deering, 254 U.S. 443, 465 (1921); Neff v. World Publishing Co., 349 F.2d 235, 257 (8th Cir. 1965). For a comprehensive state-arranged list of cases substantially adopting this definition, as well as other definitions, see 15A C.J.S. *Conspiracy* § 1, n.1 (1967).
549 Middlesex Concrete Prods. & Excavating Corp. v. Carteret Indus. Ass'n, 37 N.J. 507, 516, 181 A.2d 774, 779 (1962). A distinction must be drawn between civil conspiracy and criminal conspiracy. The latter is a substantive criminal act in itself and the conspirators may be guilty even if the conspiracy is thwarted, so long as there was some overt act towards its accomplishment. United States v. Tutino, 269 F.2d 488, 491 (2d Cir. 1959). Likewise, if a criminal conspiracy succeeds, the conspirators may be guilty of the offense of conspiracy as well as the substantive crime. United States v. Palladino, 203 F. Supp. 35, 38 (D. Mass. 1962).
550 W. PROSSER, *supra* note 547, § 43, at 260.
551 Mox, Inc. v. Woods, 202 Cal. 675, 677-78, 262 P. 302, 303 (1927). This proposition is cited with favor in De Vries v. Brumback, 53 Cal. 2d 643, 349 P.2d 532, 536, 2 Cal. Rptr. 764, 768 (1960); *see* Royster v. Baker, 365 S.W.2d 496, 499 (Mo. 1963).
552 Hughes, *The Tort of Conspiracy,* 15 MODERN L. REV. 209 (1952). The author's criticism is qualified by his suggestion that the remedy would not have to be dismissed as superfluous if it were confined to acts that if done by one person would not give rise to civil liability. Relevant here is Dean Prosser's observation that some courts have recognized "that there are certain types of conduct, such as boycotts, in which the element of combination adds such a power of coercion, undue influence or restraint of trade, that it makes unlawful acts which one man alone might legitimately do." (Footnote omitted.) W. PROSSER, *supra* note 547, § 43, at 260. *See, e.g.,* Snipes v. West Flagler Kennel Club, Inc., 105 So. 2d 164 (Fla. 1958).

defendants acted as joint tortfeasors. Even without the theory of civil conspiracy, it is a well recognized principle of tort law that all who command, direct, advise, encourage, or otherwise aid and abet the commission of a tort are jointly and severally liable with the active tortfeasor.[553] Thus, it appears that an allegation that the various defendants formed a conspiracy may be no more necessary for a cause of action against them than was the allegation of the plaintiff in *Stevens v. Sheriff*[554] that the defendants constituted a "mob." In that case, the plaintiff's specific averment that the defendants "acted in concert, and in pursuance and furtherance of a common design,"[555] was sufficient to state a cause of action against all of them in joint tortfeasors.

Whatever legal theory an injured riot victim adopts in hopes of enlarging the class of possible defendants, whether it be by direct allegations that the defendants acted in concert or by alleging a conspiracy, the real difficulty still remains: the factual determination of who is a joint tortfeasor. The rhetoric of joint liability — such phrases as "concerted action," "combination," "participation," "common design," and even "encouragement" and "assistance" — offers little practical aid in determining where the line between liability and non-liability should be drawn with regard to the "members" of a mob or a conspiracy. While several states have passed statutes that apparently eliminate any need for alleging a conspiracy as such in order to hold ". . . each and every person engaged or in any manner participating in the mob or riot"[556] liable for all riot damage, they shed no light on the conduct necessary to make a person present at the riot scene a "participant" in the riot for purposes of complete vicarious liability. In recognition of the problem, the courts have attempted to sharpen the dividing line between liability and non-liability by holding that a participant in a mob or conspiracy need not be an original party,[557] nor need he be present at the actual infliction of the injury or damage,[558] nor is it necessary that he have knowledge of the details of the conspiracy so long as he has knowledge of the common design.[559] This common design is often stressed as the essential element of a conspiracy,[560] but this phrase too is blurred by numerous attempted clarifications. No formal or simultaneous agreement is necessary to establish a conspiracy[561] and in fact it may even be implied from the circum-

---

553   *See* International Bhd. of Elec. Workers, Local 501 v. NLRB, 181 F.2d 34 (2d Cir. 1950), *aff'd*, 341 U.S. 694 (1951); Oman v. United States, 179 F.2d 738 (10th Cir. 1949); Hutto v. Kremer, 222 Miss. 374, 76 So. 2d 204 (1954); Kuhn v. Bader, 89 Ohio App. 203, 101 N.E.2d 322 (1951); W. PROSSER, *supra* note 547, § 43, at 259.
554   71 Kan. 434, 80 P. 936 (1905).
555   *Id.* at 435-36, 80 P. at 937. See text at notes 544 & 545 *supra*.
556   N.J. STAT. ANN. § 2A: 48-5 (1952). For similar language, see PA. STAT. ANN. tit. 16, § 11823 (1956) and S.C. CODE ANN. § 16-109 (1962).
557   Calcutt v. Gerig, 271 F. 220, 223 (6th Cir. 1921).
558   *Id. See also* De Vries v. Brumback, 53 Cal. 2d 643, 349 P.2d 532, 2 Cal. Rptr. 764 (1960).
559   Hux v. Butler, 220 F. Supp. 35, 41 (W.D. Tenn. 1963), *rev'd on other grounds*, 339 F.2d 696 (6th Cir. 1964); Bedard v. La Bier, 20 Misc. 2d 614, 616-17, 194 N.Y.S.2d 216, 220 (Sup. Ct. 1959).
560   Neff v. World Publishing Co., 349 F.2d 235, 257 (8th Cir. 1965); Rettinger v. Pierpont, 145 Neb. 161, 195, 15 N.W.2d 393, 411 (1944). Also see cases cited in note 559 *supra*.
561   Interstate Circuit, Inc. v. United States, 306 U.S. 208, 227 (1939); Otto Milk Co. v. United Dairy Farmers Cooperative Ass'n, 261 F. Supp. 381, 385 (W.D. Pa. 1966); John Wright & Associates, Inc. v. Ullrich, 203 F. Supp. 744, 750 (D. Minn. 1962), *aff'd*, 328 F.2d 474 (8th Cir. 1964).

stances. In the case of *Calcutt v. Gerig*,[562] the court stated the generally accepted view:

> While perhaps there is no proof in this record of any preliminary meeting of these plaintiffs in error, or of a definite plan or agreement entered into by them to injure plaintiff in his person or property or deprive him of his lawful rights as an American citizen, yet such proof is not essential to the establishing of a conspiracy, and indeed would be wholly impossible in the great majority of cases of this character for the evident reason that conspirators do not, as a rule, invite the public into their confidence or advise the contemplated victim or victims in reference to such preliminary matters. . . . It is sufficient if the proof shows such a concert of action in the commission of the unlawful act or such other facts and circumstances from which the natural inference arises that the unlawful overt act was in furtherance of a common design, intention, and purpose of the alleged conspirators to commit the same.[563]

On the other hand, the courts recognize the need for keeping the civil remedies of conspiracy and joint liability within reasonable — and constitutional — limits. Thus, while an agreement may be inferred from the circumstances, "[m]ere association does not constitute a conspiracy."[564] Likewise, mere suspicion or knowledge of another's independent acts, or even acquiescence in or approval of them, without some form of cooperation or agreement to cooperate, is not sufficient to constitute one a joint tortfeasor or a party to a conspiracy.[565]

Despite these judicial attempts to clarify the nature of liability for conspiracy or concert of action, the results are far from satisfying. A workable criterion for determining the liability or non-liability of any given "member" of a riot or conspiracy must depend, as in so many other areas of law, upon the facts of the individual case. An examination of the factual situations involved in the relatively few cases that have dealt with the liability of members of a mob,[566] whether such liability is based on conspiracy or directly upon a finding of concerted action, reveals a similarity which is disturbingly absent in the large-scale riots that cities have been experiencing recently. The typical situation presented by the cases is a relatively small group of angry citizens who converge on the plaintiff's house to force him to leave town[567] or to cancel a judgment he had recovered from one of them,[568] or who are intent on destroying his stock of liquor and cigars,[569] preventing him from putting on his traveling minstrel

---

562   271 F. 220 (6th Cir. 1921).
563   *Id.* at 222.
564   Hoffman v. Herdman's Ltd., 41 F.R.D. 275, 277 (S.D.N.Y. 1966) and cases cited therein at n.3.
565   Harris v. Capitol Records Distrib. Corp., 64 Cal. 2d 454, 413 P.2d 139, 145, 50 Cal. Rptr. 539, 545 (1966); Aaron v. Dausch, 313 Ill. App. 524, 535, 40 N.E.2d 805, 810 (1942); American Security Benevolent Ass'n, Inc. v. District Ct. of Black Hawk County, 147 N.W.2d 55, 63 (Iowa 1966).
566   See note 543 *supra.*
567   Saunders v. Gilbert, 156 N.C. 463, 72 S.E. 610 (1911).
568   Weber v. Paul, 241 Iowa 121, 40 N.W.2d 8 (1949).
569   Stevens v. Sheriff, 71 Kan. 434, 80 P. 936 (1905).

show,[570] or tarring and feathering him for unpatriotic conduct during a war.[571] In all of these cases, two factors are present: first, the size of the mob is not overwhelming and second, it is possible to speak of a common design to inflict injury upon a definite individual or group of individuals for preconceived, and to a certain extent rational, reasons. The effect was to give the respective courts patterns of conduct that could be reasonably evaluated in the light of the admittedly vague standards of "concert of action," "participation," and "activity in furtherance of a common design."

But the recent mob violence seems to be a different kind of social phenomenon. It is characterized by irrationality and hysteria rather than by common design or purpose. It is rarely directed against any particular individual, but rather against society itself; and, for most of the participants, it is a matter of being caught up in a human juggernaut rather than acting in furtherance of a common plan. The old standards may still prove to be useful in finding joint liability for those whose actual conduct or encouragement contributes immediately to the particular injury and also in exonerating those whose participation is limited to physical presence along with mere knowledge, acquiescence, or approval. But unlike in the earlier cases, there exist today numerous individuals whose boisterous allegiance to the ultimate group goals of social and economic betterment inspires the more militant members of the group to acts of destruction. As yet, there is no indication in the courts of any trend to extend the scope of joint liability to include this intermediate group of "rioters," even in those jurisdictions that have adopted statutes purporting to make any person in any way participating in a riot jointly liable for all resulting damage.[572] This notable lack of any movement to expand the liability of riot participants may simply reflect recognition on the part of plaintiffs and their lawyers that it is quite futile to attempt to satisfy judgments against rioters, regardless of the number that are joined as defendants. On the other hand, it is fair to speculate that if riot damage continues its upward spiral, while the availability of riot insurance to property that is more susceptible to mob violence continues to decrease,[573] greater attention may be given to holding as many rioters as possible jointly liable for the damage they collectively cause.

B. Liability of Persons Who Incite Mob Violence

In light of what has been said regarding the civil liability of participants in a riot, the need to devote separate attention to the civil liability of those whose words and actions have the effect of inciting a riot[574] may not be clear. To be sure, the general principle of tort liability that one who counsels, incites, encourages or otherwise aids and abets a third party in the commission of an intentional tort is treated as a principal is adequate to hold the inciter of a

---

570 Calcutt v. Gerig, 271 F. 220 (6th Cir. 1921).
571 Walker v. Kellar, 226 S.W. 796 (Tex. Civ. App. 1920).
572 See note 556 *supra* and accompanying text.
573 See note 541 *supra*.
574 This broad phrase was purposely chosen to include both intentional incitement to riot and speech which, under the circumstances, merely has the tendency to incite a riot and in fact does. Each type of speech will be considered separately.

riot jointly liable for all the resulting riot damage.[575] Likewise, incitement alone is sufficient to make a person a member of a conspiracy and thereby render him civilly liable for the wrongs committed by the more active conspirators.[576] However, there are enough significant differences between the person whose words incite others to riot and the actual participant in a riot to warrant separate treatment of the problems involved in the civil liability of the inciter. First of all, there is a chronological difference in that, although his civil liability cannot arise until an injury has occurred, the inciter's role has been completed and he may not even be present during the riot itself.[577] Secondly, his responsibility may be fixed more readily than that of other individual participants because his conduct is, to a variable extent, isolated both in time and kind, with the result that he is less likely to remain anonymous. Finally, and most importantly, the use of language that has the effect of inciting a riot, especially if incitement was not the intention of the speaker, raises significant first amendment problems that do not exist with respect to the riotous activity itself.[578]

1. Intentional Incitement

As is the situation with regard to the civil liability of rioters, there are few reported cases that find civil liability for riot damage on the part of those who intentionally incite a riot[579] — probably in recognition of the fact that payment of a judgment by the inciter of a riot is generally as unlikely as by the rioters themselves. The tort case against the party who intends to incite a riot, however, seems to be as strong as that against the active participants in the riot. One court has stated:

> It would seem almost unnecessary to say that persons responsible for mob violence cannot escape liability for the necessary and natural consequences thereof. It would be just as reasonable to say that a man might start a fire, and then by retiring to some distant spot avoid responsibility for the destruction wrought by the conflagration he initiated.[580]

---

575   See note 533 *supra* and accompanying text.
576   Calcutt v. Gerig, 271 F. 220, 223 (6th Cir. 1921).
577   In criminal actions involving a riot, the courts are careful to note that the crimes of inciting a riot and participating in a riot are separate and distinct offenses.
> Inciting to riot is not a constituent element of riot; they are separate and distinct offenses. * * * One may incite a riot and not be present or participate in it, or one may be present at a riot, and by giving support to riotous acts be guilty of riot, yet not be guilty of inciting to riot. State v. Cole, 249 N.C. 733, 740-41, 107 S.E.2d 732, 738, *cert. denied*, 361 U.S. 867 (1959), quoting from Commonwealth v. Safis, 122 Pa. Super. 333, 340, 186 A. 177, 180 (1936).

578   Although a riot may be both a form of assembly and a form of expression, the first amendment only protects "the right of the people *peaceably* to assemble, and to petition the Government for a redress of grievances." U.S. Const. amend. I (emphasis added).
579   The standard definition of the crime of incitement to riot is
> such a course of conduct, by the use of words, signs or language, or any other means by which one can be urged on to action, as would naturally lead, or urge other men to engage in or enter upon conduct which, if completed, would make a riot.

Commonwealth v. Hayes, 205 Pa. Super. 338, 341, 209 A.2d 38, 39 (1965); *accord*, State v. Cole, 249 N.C. 733, 107 S.E.2d 732, *cert. denied*, 361 U.S. 867 (1959); 77 C.J.S. *Riot* § 1 (1952). Although no case has been found that has considered the question, there is no apparent reason why this description of criminal incitement to riot could not be applied to tortious incitement to riot, with the added stipulation that the riot must actually occur and the plaintiff suffer injury as a result.
580   Calcutt v. Gerig, 271 F. 220, 223 (6th Cir. 1921).

It is generally recognized that the fact that injury or damage is actually inflicted by a third person who himself commits a tortious or criminal act does not relieve the instigator of equal liability for the tort. If the instigator "intends to cause a third person to do a particular act in a particular manner, he is subject to liability for any harm to others caused by that act, although the third person's act is negligent or even criminal."[581] This principle is widely accepted and applied in almost all areas of intentional tort liability: a person who encourages or incites another to commit assault and battery on a third person,[582] to libel or slander him,[583] or to falsely imprison him[584] is jointly liable with the perpetrator for all the resultant damages. Clearly, therefore, on the basis of ordinary principles of tort liability, a person who intentionally incites a riot which results in injury to an innocent party should bear joint liability with the rioters.

One possible barrier to the civil liability of one who intentionally incites a riot is the fact that his utterances may be protected by the first amendment guarantee of freedom of speech. However, this contention hardly seems to be a plausible one in view of the numerous cases upholding criminal convictions of those whose speech constituted a clear and present danger of inciting riotous or seditious conduct,[585] even though the threatened violence did not materialize. The contention becomes even weaker in a tort action when an actual riot has resulted from the inciter's speech and the plaintiff has suffered injury during this intended riot. Likewise, first amendment rights are not sufficient to protect the speaker from civil remedies when he has used speech to inflict intentional harm on the plaintiff. The typical example, of course, is civil liability for libel and slander[586] where the injury caused to the plaintiff is the direct result of the speech alone. It is inconceivable that speech, operating in conjunction with an intended separate tortious invasion of the plaintiff's interests, could give the speaker first amendment protection.[587] One court has put the inevitable conclusion this way: "Nobody doubts that, when the leader of a mob already ripe for riot gives the word to start, his utterance is not protected

---

581 RESTATEMENT (SECOND) OF TORTS § 303, comment c, at 94 (1965).
582 Thompson v. Johnson, 180 F.2d 431 (5th Cir. 1950); Hargis v. Horrine, 230 Ark. 502, 323 S.W.2d 917 (1959); Duke v. Feldman, 245 Md. 454, 226 A.2d 345 (1967); Pike v. Eubank, 197 Va. 692, 90 S.E.2d 821 (1956).
583 Kilian v. Stackpole Sons, 98 F. Supp. 500 (M.D. Pa. 1951); Greer v. Skyway Broadcasting Co., 256 N.C. 382, 124 S.E.2d 98 (1962); Bebout v. Pense, 35 S.D. 14, 150 N.W. 289 (1914).
584 Palmentere v. Campbell, 344 F.2d 234 (8th Cir. 1965); Miller v. Stinnett, 112 App. D.C. 329, 257 F.2d 910 (10th Cir. 1958); Knupp v. Esslinger, 363 S.W.2d 210 (Mo. App. 1962).
585 See notes 52-60 supra and accompanying text.
586 The Supreme Court has said that ". . . it must be emphasized that malicious libel enjoys no constitutional protection in any context." Linn v. United Plant Guard Workers of America, Local 114, 383 U.S. 53, 63 (1966). See also Curtis Publishing Co. v. Butts, 388 U.S. 130, rehearing denied, 389 U.S. 889 (1967).
587 The tendency is exactly the opposite — to give greater protection to "pure speech" than to "speech-in-action":
    We emphatically reject the notion urged by appellant that the First and Fourteenth Amendments afford the same kind of freedom to those who would communicate ideas by conduct such as patrolling, marching, and picketing on streets and highways, as these amendments afford to those who communicate ideas by pure speech. Cox v. Louisiana, 379 U.S. 536, 555 (1965).
See also NAACP v. Overstreet, 221 Ga. 16, 142 S.E.2d 816, cert. granted, 382 U.S. 937 (1965), cert. dismissed as improvidently granted, 384 U.S. 118, rehearing denied, 384 U.S. 981 (1966).

by the [First] Amendment."[588] But whether the inciter merely gives the word to start or whether he also assists in the ripening process, he should bear the consequences of his tortious conduct without protection from the first amendment.

2. Words or Conduct Unintentionally Resulting in Mob Violence

Where any group of people in a common situation views its lot as one of social and economic subordination, as in the case of racial minorities, or as one of authoritarian oppression, as in the case of certain elements of the younger generation, it may take far less than direct and intentional incitement to impel the group to violent rebellion. The power of suggestion,[589] or even the mere act of calling the group together for the purpose of "discussion" may be entirely sufficient to spark an explosion. What then is the liability of the individual who, while avoiding actual incitement, reminds a "mob already ripe for riot" of their common miseries, or who calls for a "peaceful" demonstration at a time and place, and under circumstances that would indicate to a reasonable man that it is substantially certain that mob violence will ensue and innocent persons will be injured? In terms of criminal liability, the question has apparently been resolved in favor of the agitator on first amendment grounds;[590] civil liability is another question. There are at least three grounds upon which the civil liability of the riot agitator or demonstration organizer could be based: 1.) ordinary principles of negligence, 2.) violation of state law, and 3.) a kind of strict liability for setting in motion forces that erupt into mob violence. Each will be treated separately in terms of its basic elements, followed by a consideration of the possible limitations imposed on all three by the first amendment.

With reference only to general principles of tort liability for negligence, an individual who addresses a crowd with words that are not intentionally designed to incite it to violence, but that should appear to a reasonable man destined to have that effect, may be exposing himself to civil liability for resulting injuries. This may also be true with regard to the individual who assembles the crowd initially, even for peaceful and legal purposes, where it is entirely likely that, given the time, place, and all the circumstances, violence is likely to erupt. The basis for these conclusions lies in the principle that an actor whose conduct creates a known or knowable unreasonable risk of harm to another by the acts of third persons will not be relieved of liability because of those intervening acts.[591] For the purpose of determining whether the actor should

---

588 United States v. Dennis, 183 F.2d 201, 207 (2d Cir. 1950), aff'd, 341 U.S. 494 (1951).
589 Consider, for example, the following words of H. Rapp Brown, spoken at Cambridge, Maryland, on the night of July 25, 1967, before a group assembled in the street:

> You see that school over there . . . . Y'all should have burned that school a long time ago. You should have burned it to the ground. Ain't no need in the world, in 1967, to see a school like that sitting over there. You should have burned it down and then go take over the honkey's school.

Soon after those words were spoken violence erupted and during the night the fifty-year-old, all-Negro Pine Street Elementary School, to which Brown was referring, "was indeed burned to the ground." Gottschalk, *Just How Free Should Free Speech Be?* Wall Street Journal, October 19, 1967, at 16, col. 4 (Eastern ed.).
590 See notes 105-08 *supra* and accompanying text.
591 Barclay Kitchen, Inc., v. California Bank, 208 Cal. 2d 347, 25 Cal. Rptr. 383 (Dist.

recognize that his conduct involves a foreseeable risk of violence by third persons, he is required to know ". . . the qualities and habits of human beings . . . and the qualities, characteristics, and capacities of . . . forces in so far as they are matters of common knowledge at the time and in the community."[592] The *Restatement (Second) of Torts* makes it clear that this applies not only to the ordinary qualities and habits of the majority of human beings, but also

> . . . if the known or knowable peculiarities of even a small percentage of human beings, or of a particular individual or class of individuals, are such as to lead the actor to realize the chance of eccentric and improper action, he is required to take this chance into account if serious harm to a legally important interest is likely to result from such eccentric action . . . .[593]

Thus, an individual's conduct may be held to create an unreasonable risk of harm where he brings into contact with third persons ". . . a person whom the actor knows or should know to be peculiarly likely to commit intentional misconduct, under circumstances which afford a peculiar opportunity or temptation for such misconduct."[594] The application of these principles in a riot context indicates that an agitator who merely tells an already angry crowd what it wants to hear or a person who organizes a "peaceful" demonstration under obviously volatile circumstances may be held accountable for the always present militant minority who can be expected to use the assembly as an occasion for violence. It is no defense for the agitator that the foreseeable acts of the rioters are criminal acts,[595] that the precise manner of the damage done or the identity of the actual victims was not foreseeable,[596] or that the police were negligent in failing to control and disperse the mob or in failing to adequately protect the injured persons.[597] The only defense apparently available is that the risk created by the agitator's conduct was not an unreasonable one, as where the activity was of "such preeminent social utility as to justify the serious character of risk involved therein."[598] What this means in terms of first amendment

---

Ct. App. 1962); Torrack v. Corpamerica, Inc., 51 Del. 254, 144 A.2d 703 (Super. Ct. 1958); Johnson v. Clement F. Sculley Constr. Co., 255 Minn. 41, 95 N.W.2d 409 (1959); RESTATEMENT (SECOND) OF TORTS §§ 302-302B (1965).

592   RESTATEMENT (SECOND) OF TORTS § 290(a) (1965).

593   *Id.* § 290, comment *c*, at 48.

594   *Id.* § 302B, comment *e*(D), at 91. *See* Shafer v. Keeley Ice Cream Co., 65 Utah 46, 234 P. 300, 38 A.L.R. 1523 (1925).

595   Barclay Kitchen, Inc. v. California Bank, 208 Cal. 2d 347, 25 Cal. Rptr. 383 (Dist. Ct. App. 1962); Torrack v. Corpamerica, Inc., 51 Del. 254, 144 A.2d 703 (Super. Ct. 1958); W. PROSSER, *supra* note 547, § 51, at 313-14.

596   "The defendant need not foresee the precise injury or the exact manner in which it occurs. . . . It is sufficient if the result is within the ambit of risk created by defendant." Barclay Kitchen, Inc. v. California Bank, 208 Cal. 2d 347, 25 Cal. Rptr. 383, 388 (Dist. Ct. App. 1962). "It is sufficient [to establish defendant's liability] that he should have foreseen that his negligence 'would probably result in injury of some kind to someone. . . .' " Brown v. National Oil Co., 233 S.C. 345, 105 S.E.2d 81, 84 (1958); *accord,* Mathews v. Porter, 239 S.C. 620, 124 S.E.2d 321, 324 (1962).

597   SEE RESTATEMENT (SECOND) OF TORTS § 290, comment *n*, at 53 (1965) which provides in part:

> [An actor] . . . is not, with a few exceptions, entitled to expect that a risk which is involved in his conduct will be prevented from taking effect in harm to others by the positive action of a third person. And this is true even though the third person is not only able to prevent the harm but under a duty to do so.

598   RESTATEMENT (SECOND) OF TORTS § 290, comment *c*, at 48 (1965).

rights will be extensively considered in a later section of this Note.[599]

A second possible ground for finding tort liability on the part of an agitator or individual who causes the formation of a peaceful demonstration that erupts into violence is based on the violation of a statute. As a general rule, the courts look upon the standard of conduct embodied in a statute as a standard required of a reasonable man, so that a violation of the statute may expose the violator to civil as well as criminal liability.[600] It is probably safe to say that all courts recognize, however, that not every violation of a statute constitutes *actionable* negligence; the violation must be a proximate cause of the plaintiff's damages[601] and must also be an unexcused violation.[602] In determining whether the violation of the statute constitutes negligence, the courts will usually look into the purposes of the statute to determine whether the injured party was a member of the class for whose benefit the statute was enacted and whether the injury caused by the defendant's act was the type of injury sought to be avoided by the legislation.[603] However, once the statute is found to comprehend both the plaintiff and his injury, the courts divide sharply as to the operative effect to be given to the defendant's violation. The majority view is that the statutory violation amounts to negligence per se and is therefore binding on a jury,[604] while a significant minority hold that it is only evidence of negligence that the jury is free to reject.[605] Whichever approach is followed, the effect is clear with respect to the individual whose conduct is found to be an unintentional but proximate cause of a riotous disturbance: if he has failed to comply with any constitutional statutes or ordinances[606] aimed at preserving the public order, such as those requiring the securing of a parade permit and the notification of police officials of a planned march,[607] the violation could be viewed as at least some evidence of negligence in a damage action arising out of any violence that may be attributed in part to the statutory violation. This is not to say, how-

---

599 See notes 612-74 *infra* and accompanying text.

600 Some of the courts adopt the legislative standard only out of deference and respect for the legislature. *See, e.g.,* Tamiami Gun Shop v. Klein, 116 So. 2d 421 (Fla. 1959); Rudes v. Gottschalk, 159 Tex. 552, 324 S.W.2d 201 (1959). Other courts take the view that the legislative standard is binding upon them. *See, e.g.,* Lynghaug v. Payte, 247 Minn. 186, 76 N.W.2d 660 (1956); Scott v. Smith, 73 Nev. 158, 311 P.2d 731 (1957), *overruled on other grounds* in Maxwell v. Amaral, 79 Nev. 323, 383 P.2d 365 (1963).

601 Kaplan v. Philadelphia Transp. Co., 404 Pa. 147, 171 A.2d 166 (1961); Smith v. Virginia Transit Co., 206 Va. 951, 147 S.E.2d 110 (1966).

602 RESTATEMENT (SECOND) OF TORTS § 288 A (1965); W. PROSSER, LAW OF TORTS § 35, at 198-202 (3d ed. 1964); *see* New York Central RR. v. Glad, 242 Ind. 450, 179 N.E.2d 571 (1962).

603 Elder v. Fisher, 217 N.E.2d 847 (Ind. 1966); Kalkopf v. Donald Sales & Mfg. Co., 33 Wis. 2d 247, 147 N.W.2d 277 (1967); W. PROSSER, *supra* note 602, § 35, at 193-98.

604 W. PROSSER, *supra* note 602, § 35, at 202. *See, e.g.,* Foster v. Harding, 426 P.2d 355 (Okla. 1967); Alex v. Armstrong, 215 Tenn. 276, 385 S.W.2d 110 (1964); Bock Constr. Co. v. Dallas Power & Light Co., 415 S.W.2d 227 (Tex. Civ. App. 1967).

605 W. PROSSER, *supra* note 602, § 35, at 202; *see, e.g.,* Aravanis v. Eisenberg, 237 Md. 242, 206 A.2d 148 (1965); Peterson v. Skiles, 173 Neb. 470, 113 N.W.2d (1962).

606 Some courts that hold that violation of a statute is negligence per se take the view that violation of an ordinance or traffic law is only evidence of negligence. But the prevailing view is that a violation of an ordinance is not given a different effect from that accorded a violation of a statute. *See* W. PROSSER, *supra* note 602, § 35, at 203 & n.81.

607 For a discussion of these statutes or ordinances and their constitutionality, see notes 114-21 *supra* and accompanying text.

ever, that statutory compliance automatically rules out the presence of ordinary negligence.[608]

A third possible theory for civil liability of the agitator or organizer of a peaceful demonstration that nonetheless results in violence is a kind of strict liability based on the fact that the purpose of the demonstration was unlawful or even the very fact that it has resulted in actual violence. The leading recent case on both these points is the recent Georgia decision in *NAACP v. Overstreet.*[609] The plaintiff-owner of a grocery store had been accused of beating and discharging a fourteen-year-old Negro employee for alleged stealing. The officers of the local chapter of the NAACP responded by organizing a group to picket the plaintiff's store for the purpose of publicizing a boycott of his business. Despite the "peaceful" purpose that the picketing was intended to accomplish, violence soon erupted; a large hostile crowd gathered, the plaintiff's employees and customers were abused and threatened, bricks and rocks were thrown through windows, at one point a shot was fired, and the plaintiff's business suffered serious economic losses. He sued the individual officers, the local NAACP chapters, and the national NAACP organization for damages and recovered a judgment of $85,793, including $50,000 in punitive damages. The basis of the court's decision was twofold: First, since the legality of civil rights picketing depends on the presence of a genuine civil rights issue, the purpose here was unlawful because the picketing was to punish the plaintiff for his alleged assault and battery. Second, since the picketing was not peaceful, it thereby became unlawful. On this latter point, the fact that the acts of violence may have been committed by members of the crowd attracted by the picketers rather than the picketers themselves was held to be of no consequence because the jury was justified in finding that "the presence of the pickets brought about . . . violence . . . ."[610] The soundness of the case has been severely criticized, especially on first amendment grounds,[611] a matter to be considered below in a broader context, and there are as yet no cases that follow its bold initiative in establishing an almost strict liability for violence caused by the very act of carrying on a civil rights demonstration. Whatever its soundness, however, for the present the case must be reckoned with as a sword of Damocles suspended over the head of any individual who would organize even a peaceful demonstration.

The foregoing discussion of some of the possible grounds for holding one whose conduct unintentionally causes a riot civilly liable for the resulting damage has been purposely framed solely in terms of traditional concepts of common-law tort liability and state-created legal rights. It is apparent, however,

---

608 RESTATEMENT (SECOND) OF TORTS § 288 C (1965): "Compliance with a legislative enactment or an administrative regulation does not prevent a finding of negligence where a reasonable man would take additional precautions."
609 221 Ga. 16, 142 S.E.2d 816, *cert. granted,* 382 U.S. 937 (1965), *cert. dismissed as improvidently granted,* 384 U.S. 118, *rehearing denied,* 384 U.S. 981 (1966). The holding in this case may be restricted to its facts, *see* notes 667-74 *infra* and accompanying text.
610 142 S.E.2d at 825.
611 NAACP v. Overstreet, 384 U.S. 118 (1966) (dissenting opinion of Justice Douglas), *noted in* 13 How. L.J. 193 (1967) *and* 27 OHIO ST. L.J. 361 (1966); Comment, *Civil Suits and Civil Rights: Recovery of Police Expenses,* 115 U. PA. L. REV. 238, 260-63 (1966). The decision, however, has been approved in one commentary. 37 MISS. L.J. 481 (1966).

that the ultimate success of any of these theories of liability depends upon its
compatibility with the first amendment guarantees of freedom of speech and
assembly as defined by the United States Supreme Court. The position of the
Court with respect to its jealous guardianship of first amendment rights is indicated by the language in *New York Times Company v. Sullivan*[612] regarding
civil liability for libel:

> In deciding the question now, we are compelled by neither precedent nor
> policy to give any more weight to the epithet "libel" than we have to
> other "mere labels" of state law . . . . Like insurrection, contempt, ad-
> vocacy of unlawful acts, breach of the peace, obscenity, solicitation of
> legal business, and the various other formulae for the repression of expres-
> sion that have been challenged in this Court, libel can claim no talismanic
> immunity from constitutional limitations. It must be measured by stan-
> dards that satisfy the First Amendment.[613] (Footnotes omitted.)

The Court, however, has made it clear that it views its duty as going beyond
the mere elaboration of constitutional principles. When construction of first
amendment rights is at issue, the scope of review extends to an independent
examination of the whole record to assure that the principles are constitutionally
applied as well.[614] In short, it can be expected that any state court decision
that finds a person civilly liable when his words or actions unintentionally result
in mob violence will be subject to final scrutiny by the Supreme Court, however sound the decision may be in terms of state law principles.

It may be argued that the Supreme Court would be without jurisdiction
to review such civil liability cases because the state action required by the fourteenth amendment is lacking.[615] The Court, however, has soundly rejected the
argument that merely because the law suit is between private parties, state
action is necessarily absent. The Court's position is that the enforcement of
any right by the state's judicial machinery can supply the necessary state action
to bring the fourteenth amendment into operation and thereby provide the basis
for federal jurisdiction.[616]

A related argument also designed to avoid federal jurisdiction is that since
a civil suit involves only private persons and a private quarrel, any constitutional
questions presented are incidental and too insignificant to warrant Supreme

---

612   376 U.S. 254 (1964).
613   *Id.* at 269. For a similar view, expressed with regard to traditional agency concepts,
see Justice Douglas' dissenting opinion in NAACP v. Overstreet, 384 U.S. 118, 124 (1966).
614   New York Times Co. v. Sullivan, 376 U.S. 254, 285 (1964); *see* Edwards v. South
Carolina, 372 U.S. 229, 235 (1963).
615   U.S. CONST. amend. XIV, § 1 provides in part:
> No *State* shall make or enforce any law which shall abridge the privileges or immu-
> nities of citizens of the United States; nor shall any *State* deprive any person of
> life, liberty, or property, without due process of law; nor deny to any person within
> its jurisdiction the equal protection of the laws. (Emphasis added.)
This necessity for state action as a prerequisite of federal power to protect the individual
from violation of his constitutional rights has recently been seriously questioned by a majority
of the Supreme Court in United States v. Guest, 383 U.S. 745 (1966). For an evaluation
of this position in *Guest*, in terms of its historical soundness, see Avins, *Federal Power to
Punish Individual Crimes Under the Fourteenth Amendment: The Original Understanding*,
43 NOTRE DAME LAWYER 317 (1968).
616   Shelley v. Kraemer, 334 U.S. 1 (1948).

Court review. However, in *New York Times Company v. Sullivan*[617] the Court recognized that many of the criminal-law safeguards, such as the requirement of an indictment, proof beyond a reasonable doubt, and double jeopardy protection, are not available in a civil action — a fact that results in ". . . a form of regulation that creates hazards to protected freedoms markedly greater than those that attend reliance upon the criminal law."[618] Accordingly, the Court concluded that since the defendant's alleged libel was constitutionally beyond the reach of the state's criminal libel statute, it must likewise be beyond the reach of its civil law of libel.[619] Although the Court in *Sullivan* was dealing with a libel action, its reasoning would apply with equal strength to the case of an individual whose conduct unintentionally sparks a riot; the mere fact that the suit is a civil rather than a criminal action will not discourage review by the Court of first amendment issues affecting the liability of the defendant.

Granting, then, that the limiting effect of first amendment rights would apply with similar force in the area of civil liability, it is necessary to confront the crucial issue: Is it an infringement of an individual's first amendment rights of free speech and peaceful assembly to hold him civilly liable for damages caused by mob violence where his acts were the unintentional though foreseeable cause of the violence? As of this writing, the Supreme Court has not been confronted by this issue, nor apparently has any other court of record. However, the first amendment rights of free speech and peaceful assembly have generated a body of law that should readily permit the distillation of principles and the construction of analogies.

In its role as final arbiter of the balance between first amendment rights and a state's duty to protect domestic tranquillity,[620] the Supreme Court has adopted the basic approach that complete freedom of speech is the rule, while instances of unprotected speech, for which the speaker may be subjected to potential criminal or civil liability, are exceptions. In *Chaplinsky v. New Hampshire*[621] the Court stated:

> There are certain well-defined and narrowly limited classes of speech, the prevention and punishment of which have never been thought to raise any Constitutional problem. These include the lewd and obscene, the profane, the libelous, and the insulting or "fighting" words — those which by their very utterance inflict injury or tend to incite an immediate breach of the peace.[622] (Footnotes omitted.)

The rationale of the Court in holding that these specified forms of speech are not protected by the first amendment is that they

---

617 376 U.S. 254 (1964).
618 *Id.* at 278, quoting from Bantam Books, Inc. v. Sullivan, 372 U.S. 58, 70 (1963).
619 New York Times Co. v. Sullivan, 376 U.S. 254, 277 (1964).
620 In the heat of the debate over the degree of preeminence to be accorded first amendment rights, there is a tendency to forget that the Preamble to the Constitution recites that it was established to secure the "domestic Tranquility" as well as the "Blessings of Liberty."
621 315 U.S. 568 (1942).
622 *Id.* at 571-72. When *Chaplinsky* was decided in 1942, it was true that libelous utterances raised no "Constitutional problem." However, since the Court's adoption in *New York Times Company v. Sullivan* of a standard of liability for libel of public officials based on malice, libel has become a fertile source of constitutional controversy. *See* notes 644-60 *infra* and accompanying text.

are no essential part of any exposition of ideas, and are of such slight social value as a step to truth that any benefit that may be derived from them is clearly outweighed by the social interest in order and morality.[623]

The approach of the Court thus seems to be that these categories of speech are unprotected because they are bad in and of themselves, without regard to the specific intention of the speaker or any harmful consequences that may result.[624] The states may accordingly prohibit or punish their very utterance.[625]

If speech having a tendency to incite a riot could be included with these other categories of unprotected speech, the speaker could be subjected to criminal liability without showing that he intended to incite a riot or that one actually occurred or was even imminent under the circumstances. It could then be argued that, by analogy, there is no constitutional necessity for *intentional* incitement in order to establish civil liability so long as the utterances constituted incitement in fact and caused injury to the plaintiff. The language in *Chaplinsky* to the effect that "fighting" words include utterances that "tend to incite an immediate breach of the peace"[626] would seem to support the conclusion that the category of fighting words may be broad enough to include incitement to riot. However, even before *Chaplinsky*, the Court had already given a clear indication that it would not look upon incitement to riot as a category of speech in itself prohibited. In *Cantwell v. Connecticut*[627] the Court stated:

> No one would have the hardihood to suggest that the principle of freedom of speech sanctions incitement to riot . . . . When clear and present danger of riot, disorder, interference with traffic on the public streets, or other immediate threat to public safety, peace, or order, appears, the power of the State to prevent or punish is obvious.[628]

While the first part of the above quoted material indicates that speech constituting incitement to riot is not constitutionally protected, the remainder makes it clear that the non-protection arises not from the speech itself, but from its probable effect under the specific circumstances. The loss of constitutional protection does not result because the utterances are necessarily "no essential part of any exposition of ideas" or of little "social value as a step to the truth,"[629] but because they actually created an imminent threat of a substantial breach of the public peace.

Whether, in addition to the clear and present danger of disorder, it must be shown that the speaker actually intended to incite a riot was not directly considered by the Court. However, the following statement in the *Cantwell* opinion may be enlightening.

> One may . . . be guilty of [breach of the peace] if he commits acts or makes

---

623   *Id.* at 572.
624   *See* C. PRITCHETT, CIVIL LIBERTIES AND THE VINSON COURT 65 (1954).
625   Chaplinsky v. New Hampshire, 315 U.S. 568, 572 (1942). *See* Roth v. United States, 354 U.S. 476 (1957); Fox v. Washington, 236 U.S. 273 (1915).
626   Chaplinsky v. New Hampshire, 315 U.S. 568, 572 (1942).
627   310 U.S. 296 (1940).
628   *Id.* at 308.
629   Chaplinsky v. New Hampshire, 315 U.S. 568, 572 (1942).

statements *likely* to provoke violence and disturbance of good order, even though no such eventuality be intended. Decisions to this effect are many, but examination discloses that, *in practically all,* the provocative language which was held to amount to a breach of the peace consisted of profane, indecent, or abusive remarks *directed to the person of the hearer.*[630] (Emphasis added.)

The Court seems to be implying that no intent is required only if the language constituting the breach of the peace consists of fighting words — speech that is in and of itself unprotected. But if the speech is capable of conveying truth or exposing an idea, there may be a requirement for an intent to incite the violence.

Eleven years later in *Feiner v. New York,*[631] the Court upheld the defendant's conviction for violating a statute prohibiting speech or conduct which occasions, or by which the actor intends to incite, a breach of the peace. Quoting from *Cantwell,* the Court relied essentially on the power of the state to respond to an immediate threat to the public peace with prevention or punishment.[632] But, in addition, the Court relied on the finding of the state courts that Feiner's conduct under the circumstances amounted to intentional incitement of a breach of the peace.[633] It seems, therefore, that the Court has taken the position that the state has the power to prevent or punish a speaker whose words are tending to provoke a breach of the peace, provided the "speaker passes the bounds of argument or persuasion and *undertakes* incitement to riot. . . ."[634] (Emphasis added.) Since one of the recognized functions of speech is to invite dispute, it cannot be prohibited or punished when it merely "induces a condition of unrest, creates dissatisfaction with conditions as they are, or even stirs people to anger."[635]

Thus, the Court relied on the absence of any actual incitement to violence in *Cox v. Louisiana*[636] where the defendant had been convicted for disturbing the peace under a statute that prohibited ". . . congregating with others 'with intent to provoke a breach of the peace, *or under circumstances such that a breach of the peace may be occasioned . . . .* ' "[637] (Emphasis added.) The conviction was reversed ". . . as the statute is unconstitutional in that it sweeps

---

630   Cantwell v. Connecticut, 310 U.S. 296, 309 (1940).
631   340 U.S. 315 (1951).
632   *Id.* at 320.
633   *Id.* at 319-20. In People v. Feiner, 300 N.Y. 391, 91 N.E.2d 316 (1950), the New York Court of Appeals said that
        [d]efendant, at the very least, knew of the condition [of the crowd] and was heedless of the potential evil consequences. More, as found by the trial court, he deliberately continued in a vein calculated to precipitate those consequences. *Id.* at 400,
91 N.E. 320. For another portion of this opinion indicating the New York courts found Feiner guilty of intentionally provoking a breach of the peace, see the Supreme Court's opinion in Feiner v. New York, 340 U.S. 315, 319 n.2 (1951).
634   Feiner v. New York, 340 U.S. 315, 321 (1951). In this regard, consider the following statement of the court in Allen v. District of Columbia, 187 A.2d 888 (D.C. App. 1961).
        The appellant's conduct, and not the crowd's reaction to it, must be the starting point, for "the measure of the speaker is not the conduct of his audience." . . . Audience reaction, and the immediacy of disorder, become significant elements of proof only after the speaker "passes the bounds of argument or persuasion and undertakes incitement to riot." *Id.* at 889.
635   Terminiello v. Chicago, 337 U.S. 1, 4 (1949).
636   379 U.S. 536 (1965).
637   *Id.* at 551.

within its broad scope activities that are constitutionally protected free speech and assembly."[638] It seems that each case must still be examined on its own facts to determine whether the speaker was undertaking incitement or merely inducing unrest.

Viewing this position of the Court that some intention to incite a riot is necessary to sustain a conviction together with the Court's statement in *Sullivan* that what a state may not constitutionally bring about by means of a criminal statute is likewise beyond the reach of its civil law, the inference can be drawn that an intention to incite is a necessary element of civil liability for riot damage, regardless of the degree of foreseeability of the violence.[639] However, this analogy between civil liability and criminal liability with regard to the inhibiting effect of the first amendment is far from perfect.

First, in all of those cases[640] in which the Court indicated a need for intent to incite violence as a prerequisite to the state's right to punish the speech, no violence in fact occurred. Where there is no violence *and* no intent to incite violence, the imposition of criminal sanctions upon speech that does not of itself fall into one of the prohibited categories such as obscenity or fighting words has all the appearances and connotations of a prior restraint.[641] On the other hand, in any civil action for damages, violence has necessarily occurred and injuries have been suffered. The speaker is not, therefore, being silenced or punished for his speech in itself or even for any threatened violence, but rather he is only being held accountable for injuries in fact resulting from his speech. To hold a speaker liable for such injuries, even though unintentional, may be no more of an unreasonable limitation on the right of free speech than to designate certain categories as unprotected per se and punishable by the state regardless of the intention of the person who uttered them.

The second factor that points up the difficulty in drawing an easy analogy between criminal and civil liability in this area of free speech is that while the criminal action is based on a violation of legitimate state interests, a civil action is based on an invasion of the personal rights of the plaintiff. In effect, the preeminence of first amendment rights in a civil action is determined by a balancing process between competing individual rights where in fact the "substan-

---

638 *Id.* at 552.
639 Proving the subjective intent of an individual is often extremely difficult. It is therefore possible that the Court would consider a degree of foreseeability equivalent to substantial certainty sufficient to indicate an intention to incite violence. On the other hand, because of the vagueness of "substantial certainty," the Court may not be willing to accept such indirect proof of intent where first amendment rights are at stake.
640 *E.g.*, Cox v. Louisiana, 379 U.S. 536 (1965); Feiner v. New York, 340 U.S. 315 (1951); Cantwell v. Connecticut, 310 U.S. 296 (1940). *See also* Allen v. District of Columbia, 187 A.2d 888 (D.C. App. 1963).
641 The term "prior restraint" or "previous restraint" has long been one of the watchwords used by the Supreme Court in its role as interpreter and guardian of first amendment rights. Its meaning of the expression is evident from the following statement of Blackstone quoted in Near v. Minnesota, 283 U.S. 697 (1931), concerning one of the first amendment rights — freedom of the press:

> The liberty of the press is indeed essential to the nature of a free state; but this consists in laying no *previous* restraints upon publications, and not in freedom from censure for criminal matter when published. Every freeman has an undoubted right to lay what sentiments he pleases before the public; to forbid this, is to destroy the freedom of the press; but if he publishes what is improper, mischievous or illegal, he must take the consequences of his own temerity. *Id.* at 713-14.

tive evil . . . rises far above public inconvenience, annoyance, or unrest."[642]
And so, while the Supreme Court should exercise the same degree of watchfulness against invasions of free speech and assembly in civil as well as in criminal actions, it by no means follows that the same standard of intentional abuse should apply.

On its face, the legal analogy that seems most appropriate to the solution of the conflict between the demonstration organizer's rights of free speech and the rights of the riot victim who has suffered personal injury or property loss is the standard used by the Court to solve the conflict of similar competing personal rights involved in civil libel suits. In *Sullivan*[643] the task of the Court was ". . . to determine for the first time the extent to which the constitutional protections for speech and press limit a State's power to award damages in a libel action brought by a public official against critics of his official conduct."[644] Stressing the fact that it was a public official who was the object of the alleged libel, the Court held that the first amendment requires a rule that

> . . . prohibits a public official from recovering damages for a defamatory falsehood relating to his official conduct unless he proves that the statement was made with "actual malice" — that is, with knowledge that it was false or with reckless disregard of whether it was false or not.[645]

By requiring actual malice as a necessary element of a successful libel action, the Court seemed to adopt a standard similar to the one applied in constitutionally permissible convictions for incitement to riot and related crimes — the necessity for deliberate or malicious abuse of first amendment rights. However, the Court failed to give any indication whether "actual malice" was to be the only acceptable constitutional standard in all libel suits or only those involving public officials.[646] Subsequent decisions of the state and lower federal courts,[647] and even of the Supreme Court itself,[648] left doubts as to whether the *Sullivan* standard would be broadly applied in all libel actions.

---

642   Terminiello v. Chicago, 337 U.S. 1, 4 (1949).
643   New York Times Co. v. Sullivan, 376 U.S. 254 (1964).
644   *Id*. at 256.
645   *Id*. at 279-80.
646   We have no occasion here to determine how far down into the lower ranks of government employees the "public official" designation would extend for purposes of this rule, or otherwise to specify categories of persons who would or would not be included. . . . Nor need we here determine the boundaries of the "official conduct" concept. *Id*. at 283 n.23.
647   For an extensive list of these cases, see Curtis Publishing Co. v. Butts, 388 U.S. 130, 134 n.1 (1967).
648   In Garrison v. Louisiana, 379 U.S. 64 (1964), the Court applied the *Sullivan* standard in reversing the conviction of the appellant for his allegedly libelous attacks on the integrity and honesty of eight local judges. The Court found "no difficulty" in extending this standard even though the state court had found that the attacks were not directed at any official conduct of the judges. *Id*. at 76.
      In Rosenblatt v. Baer, 383 U.S. 75 (1966), the Court found that a former supervisor of a public recreation area was a "public official" and that his libel judgment against a newspaper columnist would have to be reversed for failure to apply the *Sullivan* standard. The Court, however, added an interesting footnote hinting that society's strong and pervasive interest in preventing and redressing attacks on reputation might preclude application of the *Sullivan* standard where the libeled person is not a public official:
            It is suggested that this test might apply to a night watchman accused of stealing state secrets. But a conclusion that the *New York Times* malice standards

But it was not until *Curtis Publishing Company v. Butts*[649] that the Court was squarely presented with the issue of whether or not actual malice or its alternate, reckless disregard of the truth, is a constitutionally required element of a civil libel action brought by a person who was a public figure but not a public official. The Court was being asked to balance the interest of the individual in his reputation against freedom of the press, as it was asked to do in *Sullivan,* but with some critical differences: gone was the significant interest of the public in scrutinizing the official conduct of its own servant;[650] gone also was the danger that a recovery by the plaintiff would be viewed as a "vindication of governmental policy."[651] The issue, stated most narrowly, was whether the absence of these elements from the publishers' side would unbalance the scales of justice in favor of the individual's rights so as to require a less vigorous standard of actionable libel than actual malice. Although the Court affirmed a judgment in favor of the plaintiff for $460,000, it could not resolve this issue; there was no majority opinion. Nonetheless, the plurality opinion[652] of Justice Harlan, joined by Justices Clark, Fortas, and Stewart, represents a definite retreat from an across-the-board application of the actual malice standard of *Sullivan.* The thesis of the opinion was that "the rigorous federal requirements of *New York Times* are not the only appropriate accommodation of the conflicting interests at stake."[653] In deciding upon an appropriate standard, the opinion said:

---

apply could not be reached merely because a statement defamatory of some person in government employ catches the public's interest; that conclusion would virtually disregard society's interest in protecting reputation. The employee's position must be one which would invite public scrutiny and discussion of the person holding it, entirely apart from the scrutiny and discussion occasioned by the particular charges in controversy. *Id.* at 86 n.13.

Finally in Time, Inc. v. Hill, 385 U.S. 374 (1967), the Court found the *Sullivan* standard applicable to a damage suit brought by a private individual whose personal life had been exposed to the public view by a magazine review that had falsely stated that a certain play was based on events involving him. Significantly, however, the suit was brought under a state invasion of privacy statute and was not a libel suit. In fact, the false account portrayed the plaintiff in a favorable light. The Court expressly cautioned against reading the case as an extension of the *Sullivan* standard to all libel actions:

We find applicable here the standard of knowing or reckless falsehood, not through blind application of *New York Times Co. v. Sullivan,* relating solely to libel actions by public officials, but only upon consideration of the factors which arise in the particular context of the application of the New York statute in cases involving private individuals. This is neither a libel action by a private individual nor a statutory action by a public official. Therefore, although the First Amendment principles pronounced in *New York Times* guide our conclusion, we reach that conclusion only by applying these principles in this discrete context. *Id.* at 390-91.

649   388 U.S. 130, *rehearing denied,* 389 U.S. 889 (1967). The case was argued with Associated Press v. Walker and the opinion is written for both cases. Walker sued the Associated Press for alleged libel arising out of a dispatch which stated that he, a politically prominent figure but not a public official, had encouraged and led a violent mob against federal marshals on the University of Mississippi campus. The jury found this account to be false and awarded him a damage verdict which the Supreme Court reversed unanimously, five justices applying the *Sullivan* standard and four applying the gross negligence standard of Justice Harlan.

650   *See* Rosenblatt v. Baer, 383 U.S. 75, 86 (1966).

651   Curtis Publishing Co. v. Butts, 388 U.S. 130, 154 (1967).

652   The opinion represents an elaboration of the views expressed by Justice Harlan in his opinion, concurring in part and dissenting in part, in Time, Inc. v. Hill, 385 U.S. 374, 402-11 (1967). See note 648 *supra.*

653   Curtis Publishing Co. v. Butts, 388 U.S. 130, 155 (1967).

We are prompted, therefore, to seek guidance from the rules of liability which prevail in our society with respect to compensation of persons injured by the improper performance of a legitimate activity by another. Under these rules, a departure from the kind of care society may expect from a reasonable man performing such activity leaves the actor open to a judicial shifting of loss.[654]

Justice Harlan concluded that

> . . . a "public figure" who is not a public official may . . . recover damages for a defamatory falsehood whose substance makes substantial danger to reputation apparent, on a showing of *highly unreasonable conduct constituting an extreme departure from the standards of investigation and reporting ordinarily adhered to by responsible publishers.*[655] (Emphasis added.)

Central to the opinion was the belief that application of the *Sullivan* standard to all defamation suits brought by public figures would give first amendment rights a much greater weight than is necessary to maintain their ordained primacy. As preferred rights,[656] they must be allotted sufficient "breathing space"[657] so that they may be enjoyed without fearful reliance on a narrow and indefinite boundary between protected and unprotected utterances. But to hold that the breathing space should extend all the way to intentional or even reckless abuse is to needlessly stifle the breathing space that other valuable individual rights need in order to survive. A far more reasonable approach would be to protect false defamatory utterances so long as they are made innocently or negligently but to withdraw protection when they are made in a grossly negligent manner. In short, Harlan's opinion in *Butts* displays an implicit faith in the proposition that the concept of the reasonably prudent man has a place in the world of first amendment rights.[658]

In many respects, the constitutional issue to which Harlan's opinion is addressed resembles the issue that would face the Court in a civil action against an individual whose conduct has unintentionally, but foreseeably caused personal injury or property damage through mob violence. Both situations involve

---

654　*Id.* at 154.

655　*Id.* at 155.

656　"When we balance the Constitutional rights of owners of property against those of the people to enjoy [first amendment rights] . . . we remain mindful of the fact that the latter occupy a preferred position." Marsh v. Alabama, 326 U.S. 501, 509 (1946) (footnote omitted).

657　This phrase, first used by the Court in NAACP v. Button, 371 U.S. 415, 433 (1963), caught the fancy of the Court and has received heavy play in the recent cases dealing with freedom of the press. Time, Inc. v. Hill, 385 U.S. 374, 388, 407 (1967); Curtis Publishing Co. v. Butts, 388 U.S. 130, 148 (1967); New York Times Co. v. Sullivan, 376 U.S. 254, 272 (1964).

658　This terminology is borrowed from Kalven, *The Reasonable Man and the First Amendment: Hill, Butts, and Walker,* in 1967 THE SUPREME COURT REV. 267, 301, 303 (Kurland ed.). This article is an excellent consideration and evaluation of the positions taken by the Justices in the three cases. The author states his suspicion that ". . . properly viewed, there is in the world of the First Amendment no place for 'the reasonable [*sic*] prudent man.' " *Id.* at 303. This suspicion is based on the author's conclusion that since in both *Butts* and *Walker* five Justices applied the *Sullivan* standard, this standard has been applied across the board to civil actions involving public figures. He views the apparent victory of the Harlan standard in *Butts* as a fluke, occasioned when Chief Justice Warren concurred in the result reached by .Harlan, but did so by applying the "reckless disregard of the truth" standard of *Sullivan.* *Id.* at 307.

essentially the same conflict between first amendment rights and legitimate state enforced rights. Both situations also entail the balancing of first amendment interests not against the state's own broad interest in preserving public order, but rather against compensation for actual injuries inflicted on other individuals. And finally, the feeling expressed in Harlan's opinion that the fact that an activity is a ". . . legitimate, protected and indeed cherished activity does not mean, however, that one may in all respects carry on that activity exempt from sanctions designed to safeguard the legitimate interests of others,"[659] applies as well to freedom of speech and assembly as to freedom of the press. Whether the Court would find Harlan's theory persuasive in a case involving grossly negligent activity or speech resulting in mob violence is, of course, highly speculative. But two things are clear: 1) Although Justice Harlan's opinion in *Butts* adopting the gross negligence standard was not a majority opinion, the case resulted in the affirmance of a $460,000 judgment even though everyone, including Butts' own counsel,[660] agreed that the *Saturday Evening Post* was not guilty of actual malice under the *Sullivan* standard. 2) There is a valid analogy between unintentional libel and unintentional causation of a riot.

The four opinions in *Butts* represent the Court's most recent consideration of the problem of balancing first amendment rights against other individual rights in the context of civil liability. Of the four, the Harlan opinion takes the most liberties with the traditional sanctity of such rights, a position that clearly stops short, however, of saying that mere negligence in the exercise of such rights destroys their preferred status. The conclusion seems inevitable, therefore, that the first amendment would ordinarily provide full protection from civil liability for an individual who calls a demonstration or who addresses (as opposed to "incites") an assemblage in the streets even if it is reasonably foreseeable that violence will erupt. The lesson of *Edwards v. South Carolina*[661] and *Cox v. Louisiana*[662] is that an initially peaceful protest march during daylight hours at the site of a public building[663] is an exercise of first amendment rights "in their most pristine and classic form,"[664] even though there is the ever-present danger of violence. To hold that the organizers of such demonstrations or the persons who address them must suffer the risk of extensive tort liability would surely drain all the oxygen from the breathing space that the rights of free speech and assembly need to survive.

On the other hand, it would seem that there should be some limits imposed on the exercise of these first amendment rights. Suppose, for example, a protest march is arranged to take place on a steaming July night in the midst of an urban ghetto where the atmosphere is already highly charged by recent violent outbreaks. Add the fact that the organizers have deliberately called it on

---

659 Curtis Publishing Co. v. Butts, 388 U.S. 130, 150 (1967).
660 *Id.* at 156 n.20.
661 372 U.S. 229 (1963).
662 379 U.S. 536 (1965).
663 *But see* Adderley v. Florida, 385 U.S. 39 (1966), where the Court, in upholding convictions, distinguished conduct in violation of a state malicious trespass statute from the non-trespassory conduct involved in *Edwards* and *Cox*.
664 Edwards v. South Carolina, 372 U.S. 229, 235 (1963).

such short notice as to make adequate police supervision impossible.[665] In this situation, violence is not only foreseeable; it is substantially certain. This situation seems to be tailor-made for the application of the "grossly negligent" standard espoused by Harlan's opinion in *Butts*.

The second ground that was previously considered as a possible basis for the tort liability of one whose conduct or words unintentionally result in mob violence was the violation of a statute designed to protect the public safety. If, even under the Harlan standard, negligence alone is not sufficient to deprive the exercise of a first amendment right of its protected status, it is initially hard to conceive of a statutory violation, whether it be considered evidence of negligence or even negligence per se, serving as a constitutionally acceptable basis of civil liability. At the same time, however, the Supreme Court has upheld the constitutionality of criminal convictions arising out of such violations.[666] By arguing from analogy, it may be possible to sustain a conclusion that when such a statute is violated and the violation results in injuries within the contemplation of the statute, there would be no constitutional barrier to a civil action against the violator, a result achievable without reliance on the gross negligence standard of Harlan's opinion in *Butts*. This position is somewhat weakened by the absence of traditional criminal law safeguards from the civil proceeding and by the threat of a substantial and indeterminate judgment. The Harlan standard might prove to be the best route after all if the statutory violation could be coupled with enough other factors so that the totality of evidence would establish gross negligence.

The final ground considered above with respect to the tort liability of one who organizes a demonstration that unintentionally erupts in violence was a kind of strict liability found in *NAACP v. Overstreet*[667] However, if negligence is not sufficient to deprive one of first amendment protection, a fortiori, any kind of strict liability standard would seem to be equally impotent. But before such a conclusion need be drawn, analysis of the *Overstreet* case may reveal that its value as precedent in the area of civil liability for group action is limited by its own facts.

---

665 In this regard, consider the following statement of Chicago's former Superintendent of Police, O. W. Wilson:

> During the Summer of '66 there were several civil rights groups which conducted marches into areas of Chicago where a majority of the residents were not sympathetic with the view of the marchers. I believe that it was the aim of these marchers to subject themselves to violence. If the marches were conducted without incident, nothing would be gained. The violence which occurs is in fact their bargaining wedge. If violence occurs, they can make demands upon the city administration and in return for the granting of those demands agree to end the marches and thereby the violence. Otherwise they have no bargaining power. For this reason, those in charge of the marches do not really want adequate police protection and control, although they say they do.
>
> At first, the leaders of the marches agreed to notify the police sufficiently in advance of the march so that the police might mobilize an adequate force to control the onlookers, hecklers, and other trouble makers. Only twice, however, were we notified.

Wilson, *Civil Disturbances and the Rule of Law*, 58 J. CRIM. L.C. & P.S. 155, 159 (1967).
666 Cox v. New Hampshire, 312 U.S. 569 (1941) (conviction of defendants upheld for violation of state statute requiring parade permits).
667 221 Ga. 16, 142 S.E.2d 816, *cert. granted*, 382 U.S. 937 (1965), *cert. dismissed as improvidently granted*, 384 U.S. 118, *rehearing denied*, 384 U.S. 981 (1966).

It is significant that the violence in *Overstreet* resulted during picketing of a single identified business establishment rather than during a public demonstration. Although the Supreme Court has held that, since picketing is a form of expression, a state cannot constitutionally impose a blanket prohibition on all picketing, it added the proviso that, because picketing was also a form of action, the states could regulate and even forbid it where it posed an imminent threat to the public peace or threatened lives and property.[668] In *Hughes v. Superior Court*[669] the traditional criteria for state regulation of picketing received the Court's approval: "Picketing is not beyond the control of the State if the manner in which picketing is conducted or the purpose which it seeks to effectuate gives grounds for its disallowance."[670] *Overstreet* rests principally on this power of the states to control picketing when it is used for an illegal purpose, which in this case was the malevolent infliction of harm on the legitimate business interests of the plaintiff.

> Where, as alleged here, the sole purpose of the picketing of plaintiff's place of business was to injure and damage his business, as punishment of him for the alleged beating of a negro boy who worked for him, the picketing is unlawful and not protected under the free speech provisions of the Federal and State Constitutions.[671]

Only after grounding the decision on this constitutionally firm foundation did the court imply that the defendants would be liable even if the violent acts were solely the deeds of the sympathetic crowd attracted by the picketing.[672] It would be a mistake, therefore, to read this implication of absolute liability for the resulting violence as a separate and self-sufficient grounds for liability in the absence of an illegal purpose. Where a defendant's conduct constitutes a malicious and unexcused interference with the plaintiff's legitimate business interests, as was found in *Overstreet*, the resulting liability is absolute in the same sense that liability flowing from any other intentional tort is absolute.[673] Therefore, the prominence of the intentional "business tort" basis for liability makes it an inapplicable precedent for any type of strict liability for violence resulting from the conduct or organization of a *public* demonstration, except perhaps when the very purpose of the demonstration is to arouse mob violence. So long as the purpose of a public demonstration is an essentially peaceful one,

---

668   Thornhill v. Alabama, 310 U.S. 88, 105 (1940).
669   339 U.S. 460 (1950).
670   *Id.* at 465-66.
671   NAACP v. Overstreet, 221 Ga. 16, 142 S.E.2d 816, 824, *cert. granted,* 382 U.S. 937 (1965), *cert. dismissed as improvidently granted,* 384 U.S. 118, *rehearing denied,* 384 U.S. 981 (1966). The Georgia Supreme Court concluded that this was not a case of legitimate civil rights picketing:
> First, there is no allegation that the plaintiff practised racial discrimination nor any facts alleged from which such conclusion could be drawn. . . . The sole reason alleged for the picketing was the alleged assault and battery upon the 14 year old negro boy who worked for the plaintiff. It is not alleged that plaintiff was charged with beating the boy because he was a negro. 142 S.E.2d at 823.
672   142 S.E.2d at 825.
673   The essence of a so-called "business tort" is an intentional interference with legitimate business interests of another with a *purely* malevolent motive. Thus, the tort does not arise where the individual is acting in his own business interests or other legitimate interests. *See* W. Prosser, Law of Torts § 124, at 978 (3d ed. 1964).

such as the publicizing of grievances and the petitioning for their redress, the purpose itself comes within the protection of the first amendment.[674]

C. Liability of Organizations for Incitement by Their Agents

1. The Nature of the Vicarious Liability

It is apparent that the problems involved in obtaining a judgment against an individual whose conduct unintentionally causes a riot are more complex than those involved in prosecuting a successful damage action against the actual rioters. What is more disturbing, however, is that the likelihood of the extra effort paying off in terms of recovery on the judgment is probably only slightly better in most situations. The greatest advantage that may be gained by succeeding in a cause of action against the individual who occasions a riot is the possibility of enforcing the judgment against an organization that he may be representing. In order for this endeavor to be successful, it must be shown that the individual's activities were sponsored by, or carried on under, the authority of the organization; that is, an agency relationship must be established.

The *Overstreet* case[675] represents a recent and apparently successful example of a national political organization being held liable for the actions of its local officers. The plaintiff joined the national NAACP, a New York corporation, as a party defendant in his damage action, alleging that one of the individual defendants, an officer of the local (Savannah) branch of the NAACP, was " '. . . acting in and for the services [of the national NAACP corporation] as its agent, employee, and servant, within the scope of said agency, employment and service.' "[676] In answering the crucial question " . . . whether there is evidence that the defendants Law or Jaudon were acting as agents of said [organizational] defendants . . . ,"[677] the Georgia Supreme Court followed a two step process. It first reviewed various facts about the relationship between the national and the local chapters, from which it concluded that there existed a close affiliation between the two bodies.[678] Then, in view of this affiliation, the court took the simple but effective approach that

> [i]f Law originally acted without authority and assumed to act for them without authority, they had the option to repudiate or ratify the act,

---

674 Cox v. Louisiana, 379 U.S. 536 (1965); Edwards v. South Carolina, 372 U.S. 229 (1963).
675 See text at notes 609-11 *supra* for a summary of the facts of *Overstreet.*
676 NAACP v. Overstreet, 384 U.S. 118, 120 (1966) (dissenting opinion of Justice Douglas).
677 NAACP v. Overstreet, 221 Ga. 16, 142 S.E.2d 816, 825-26, *cert. granted,* 382 U.S. 937 (1965), *cert. dismissed as improvidently granted,* 384 U.S. 118 (1966).
678 The court substantiated its finding of affiliation as follows:
     The Savannah Branch used the corporate name, N.A.A.C.P., and held itself out as representing the national corporation. The national corporation gave orders and counsel to its local representatives at annual conventions; the locals were affiliated with the national organization and under its corporate charter, were units thereof; one paying dues to the local N.A.A.C.P. also became a member of the national N.A.A.C.P.; members of the local were members of the national N.A.A.C.P. and a portion of the dues went to the N.A.A.C.P. corporation. These facts evidence that the locals are within the framework of the national organization and are used in furtherance of the latter's business and interest. 142 S.E.2d at 826.

but they were required to do one or the other. And where, as here, they never repudiated the act, they are deemed to have affirmed it.[679]

The deftness with which this fatal one-two punch was administered caught not only the NAACP off guard, but apparently also a majority of the United States Supreme Court. The Court granted certiorari on the specific question of whether the national organization had been deprived of "due process of law under the fourteenth amendment by being held liable in damages for acts performed without its knowledge and by persons beyond its control,"[680] but, for unexplained reasons, the writ was then dismissed as improvidently granted.[681] Four Justices dissented in an opinion written by Justice Douglas that took the position that such a manipulation of agency concepts and terms poses as definite a threat to the first amendment rights of freedom of association as forced disclosure of political associations[682] and guilt by association.[683] After stating that "agency" and "affiliation" are mere labels without "talismanic significance," the dissenting opinion concluded that the first amendment forbids the imposition of liability on a national political association because of the misconduct of a local branch without proof that the national organization specifically authorized or ratified the conduct for which liability is sought to be imposed. "A *general* finding of 'agency' or 'affiliation' is not enough."[684] Not only did the corporate NAACP here not authorize the picketing of the plaintiff's store, but it was not even aware of this action until it received secondhand the service of process made on the individual defendants.

The proposal by Justice Douglas that a national principal be liable for a local agent only when the "conduct for which liability is sought to be imposed" is specifically authorized or ratified would be a just and effective standard in situations like that presented in *Overstreet* where the "demonstration" itself was illegal, that is, was conducted for an illegal purpose. But what about the situations in which a demonstration, legal in purpose, erupts into violence through the gross negligence of those authorized by the organization to conduct it? As discussed earlier,[685] if the gross negligence standard of individual liability proposed by the Harlan opinion in *Butts* were applied to find the agents personally liable, could the organization escape liability because it specifically authorized

---

679   *Id.*
680   382 U.S. 937 (1965).
681   384 U.S. 118, *rehearing denied,* 384 U.S. 981 (1966).
682   DeGregory v. Attorney General of N.H., 383 U.S. 825 (1966); Gibson v. Florida Legislative Investigation Comm., 372 U.S. 539, 543-46 (1963); NAACP v. Alabama, 357 U.S. 449, 462-63 (1958).
683   Schware v. Board of Bar Examiners, 353 U.S. 232, 245-46 (1957). *See also* Elfbrandt v. Russell, 384 U.S. 11 (1966); Aptheker v. Secretary of State, 378 U.S. 500 (1964); Wieman v. Updegraff, 344 U.S. 183 (1952).
684   NAACP v. Overstreet, 384 U.S. 118, 125 (1966) (dissenting opinion) (footnote omitted). Justice Douglas felt that the affiliation standard approved in *Overstreet* in reference to a political organization is the same kind of standard that once burdened labor unions with liability for all the violence of their scattered affiliates. *Id.* at 124; *see* the *Danbury Hatters' Cases,* Lawlor v. Loewe, 235 U.S. 522 (1915); Loewe v. Lawlor, 208 U.S. 274 (1908). Congress came to the unions' rescue with section 6 of the Norris-LaGuardia Act, 29 U.S.C. § 106 (1964), which requires a finding of "clear proof of actual participation in, or actual authorization of, . . . or . . . ratification of" the local union activities before the national organization can be held liable. *See* United Mine Workers v. Gibbs, 383 U.S. 715 (1966).
685   See text accompanying notes 649-58 *supra.*

a peaceful demonstration and not "the conduct for which liability is sought to be imposed"? If "specifically authorized conduct" is read in its strictest sense, liability should not be imposed on the organization in this situation. Such a result would have the anomalous effect of creating a higher degree of first amendment protection for the organization itself when its agent, though acting within the scope of his authority, has been guilty of gross misconduct — a result certainly at odds with the basic agency doctrine of respondeat superior. Perhaps such an exception can be justified on the theory that while gross negligence might be the point at which the first amendment rights of the *individual* are outweighed by the property or personal rights of another individual, there is no comparable balancing point at which such property or personal rights of an individual outweigh the first amendment rights of an *association* of individuals.

On the other hand, this view seems not only unnecessary but equally as unjust, in the opposite direction, as the affiliation theory used by the state court in *Overstreet*. If the organization has authorized the demonstration and placed its agents in charge of its conduct, it has the ability to exert control over the qualifications and reputation of its agents and thus maintain some control over the circumstances. To absolve it of liability in this situation would be to encourage irresponsibility in the choice and control of persons whose every word and act carries the potentiality of dynamite. Furthermore, if actual intent to cause violence were the standard of organizational liability, the practical task of proving intent by producing some kind of resolution or similar evidence would create an impossible burden of proof and bestow veritable tort immunity on the most militant of organizations.

Whether the Douglas standard raises more problems than it solves and what refinements it ought to undergo are not pressing questions under the present state of the law. Regardless of its apparent constitutional inadequacies, the decision of the Georgia Supreme Court in *Overstreet* stands by judicial default: a political organization is liable for the misconduct of persons affiliated with it but acting beyond its control and knowledge.

2. Unincorporated Organizations

It may happen that the organization sought to be held liable for riot damage is not a corporate entity as was the NAACP in *Overstreet*, but rather an unincorporated nonprofit association.[686] In this situation, not only are the problems of finding substantive liability more complicated, but there are additional problems of enforcing the liability once it is found. Initially, it should be emphasized that the same constitutional limitations on the agency relationship should be applied to unincorporated associations as to incorporated ones. Whether a group of individuals united for a common legal purpose is recognized by a

---

686 The ordinary definition of an "association" is a body of persons united for the prosecution of a common enterprise without a corporate charter but using corporate methods and forms. *See* Hecht v. Malley, 265 U.S. 144, 157 (1924). A "non-profit" association is to be distinguished from a business association such as a partnership where the common enterprise is for the purpose of making a profit.

state as a corporate body would not seem to bear on the value or extent of the constitutional protection accorded it.[687]

The general rule with respect to liability is that an unincorporated association is held to the same standard of care as any other group and is liable for the tortious conduct of its servants or agents committed during the prosecution of the association's business.[688] Some courts have insisted upon the additional requirement that an agent, especially one who is not a servant, must be under the actual control of the association at the time of his tortious conduct.[689] At least one jurisdiction has distinguished between unintentional and intentional acts of the agent, saying that while the former are governed by the general agency rules of scope of employment,[690] the latter must be specifically authorized or ratified before the association can be held liable.[691]

If an unincorporated association is liable for the authorized acts of its agents, logic suggests that it should be subject to suit and required to satisfy a judgment against it. However, the vague legal status of associations both at common law and under the many different state statutory schemes of today often does not admit of logical conclusions.[692] The common-law rule, and thus the rule today in the absence of statute, is that in actions at law[693] an association cannot sue or be sued in its own name because it is not a legal person distinct from its members;[694] rather the action must be brought by or against all the members jointly.[695] The obvious impracticality of such a rule led to widespread statutory modification of the rule so that now procedural statutes in most states provide for class action suits[696] or suits brought in the association name.[697] In New York, suit against an association may be brought against an officer of the association;[698] while in Iowa a class action is essential, but the association may be joined as a

---

687 Justice Douglas' dissenting opinion in *Overstreet* makes no attempt to distinguish the corporate from the non-corporate, political organization with respect to the agency standard he believes to be constitutionally required. 384 U.S. 118 (1966) (dissenting opinion).
688 Feldman v. North British & Mercantile Ins. Co., 137 F.2d 266, 268 (4th Cir. 1943); Ketcher v. Sheet Metal Workers' Int'l Ass'n, 115 F. Supp. 802, 811 (E.D. Ark. 1953); Weese v. Stoddard, 63 N.M. 20, 312 P.2d 545, 547 (1956).
689 Cox v. Government Employees Ins. Co., 126 F.2d 254 (6th Cir. 1942); Mercury Cab Owners' Ass'n v. Jones, 79 So. 2d 782 (Fla. 1955), aff'd, 95 So. 2d 29 (Fla. 1956); Jopes v. Salt Lake County, 9 Utah 2d 297, 343 P.2d 728 (1959).
690 Torres v. Lacey, 5 Misc. 2d 11, 159 N.Y.S.2d 411, *modified on other grounds*, 3 App. Div. 2d 998, 163 N.Y.S.2d 451, *reargument denied*, 4 App. Div. 2d 831, 166 N.Y.S.2d 303 (1957).
691 Kirby v. Dubinski, 39 Misc. 2d 1064, 242 N.Y.S.2d 543 (1963).
692 *See* H. OLECK, NONPROFIT CORPORATIONS, ORGANIZATIONS, AND ASSOCIATIONS § 225-26, at 465-73 (2d ed. 1965). For an excellent general analysis of the procedural problems relating to unincorporated associations, see Brunson, *Some Problems Presented by Unincorporated Associations in Civil Procedure*, 7 S.C.L.Q. 394 (1955).
693 At early common law, there could be no suit by or against an association as an entity. But the class action suit was allowed much earlier in equity than at law and in fact became the model for the class action suit at law in the case of associations. *See* Brunson, *supra* note 692, at 395-99.
694 Morris v. Willis, 338 S.W.2d 777 (Mo. 1960); Teubert v. Wisconsin Interscholastic Athletic Ass'n, 8 Wis. 2d 373, 99 N.W.2d 100 (1959); Brunson, *supra* note 692, at 396-97.
695 Brunson, *supra* note 692, at 398 and cases cited there at note 15.
696 *E.g.*, OHIO REV. CODE ANN. § 2307.21 (Page 1954); WIS. STAT. ANN. § 260.12 (1957). *See also* FED. R. CIV. P. 23.
697 *E.g.*, GA. CODE ANN. § 3-118 (1962); MINN. STAT. ANN. § 540.151 (Supp. 1967). *See also* FED. R. CIV. P. 17(b).
698 N.Y. GEN. ASS'NS LAW § 12 (McKinney 1942), § 13 (McKinney Supp. 1967).

party.[699] Numerous other variations have existed and still do: permitting an association to be sued but not to sue in its common name,[700] or allowing suits of an equitable nature against it in its common name only if it is a business association but not if it is a nonprofit association.[701] The general rule is that these statutory procedures are not considered to be exclusive remedies, so that in a jurisdiction permitting suit against an association as an entity, a class action may also be brought or even a joinder of all the members as at common law.[702]

Many times the procedural device permitting a specified form of suit or specified joinder of plaintiffs or defendants will, as a practical matter, determine and limit the sources from which a judgment can be recovered. For example, in states where an association is not suable as an entity, it has been held that the assets of the association cannot be reached since the members are jointly liable as individuals.[703] Conversely, where statutes exist making an association a suable entity, the courts have held that their effect,[704] or even their purpose,[705] is to make the assets of the association available to satisfy adverse judgments. The courts in Ohio have taken the position that where a plaintiff sues an association under an entity statute, he is limited to recovery from the assets of the association, even though initially he could have brought a class action suit and recovered against the individual members.[706]

In those situations where a plaintiff chooses or is required to use a class action device against an association, the procedural rule may unsettle the substantive liability in certain situations by causing some courts to hold that only those association members who actually participated in the activity that caused the injury can be held liable.[707] Other jurisdictions have disagreed with this view, especially in the labor area, and have found all the members can be liable on a civil conspiracy theory.[708]

In addition to these problems of proper parties and enforcement of judgments in litigation involving voluntary nonprofit associations, there are often

---

699   Boyer v. Iowa High School Athletic Ass'n, 258 Iowa 285, 138 N.W.2d 914 (1965).
700   PA. R. CIV. P. 2152, 2153. See generally Brunson, supra note 692, at 401-10.
701   N.J. STAT. ANN. § 2A:64-6 (1952). See generally Brunson, supra note 692, at 401-10.
702   Lyons v. American Legion Post No. 650 Realty Co., 172 Ohio St. 331, 175 N.E.2d 733 (1961); H. OLECK, supra note 692, § 225, at 467.
703   Benz v. Compania Naviera Hidalgo, S.A., 233 F.2d 62 (9th Cir. 1956), aff'd, 353 U.S. 138 (1957); Florio v. State, 119 So. 2d 305, 80 A.L.R.2d 1117 (Fla. Dist. Ct. App. 1960).
704   United Mine Workers of America v. Coronado Coal Co., 259 U.S. 344 (1922); RESTATEMENT OF JUDGMENTS § 78, comment c, at 352 (1942) provides:
        In states in which suit can be maintained against an unincorporated association in its business name, judgment can be rendered which is valid against the assets of the association. . . . Whether the judgment is effective to bind personally the members of the association over whom the court has jurisdiction depends upon whether the judgment is directed against the members or merely against the assets of the organization.
705   Donnelly v. United Fruit Co., 40 N.J. 61, 190 A.2d 825 (1963).
706   E.g., Miazga v. International Union of Operating Eng'rs, 2 Ohio St. 2d 49, 205 N.E.2d 884 (1965); Lyons v. American Legion Post No. 650 Realty Co., 172 Ohio St. 331, 175 N.E.2d 733 (1961).
707   Barry v. Covich, 332 Mass. 338, 124 N.E.2d 921 (1955); Lyons v. American Legion Post No. 650 Realty Co., 172 Ohio St. 331, 175 N.E.2d 733 (1961); see Martin v. Curran, 303 N.Y. 276, 101 N.E.2d 683 (1951).
708   Ketcher v. Sheet Metal Workers' Int'l Ass'n, 115 F. Supp. 802 (E.D. Ark. 1953); Hall v. Walters, 226 S.C. 430, 85 S.E.2d 729, cert. denied, 349 U.S. 953 (1955).

problems of jurisdiction, venue, and process — matters equally subject to the
vagaries of state law.[709] In the context of this topic on civil liability of organizations for riot damage, it is not possible to cover in detail all the procedural
problems that could arise when the organization sought to be held is unincorporated. Rather it is hoped that this brief discussion will serve to emphasize
that not all problems of organizational liability involve unsettled constitutional
issues. Much of the complexity in the area is essentially procedural; the solutions
in any particular case must be sought in the appropriate statutory and decisional
law of the forum jurisdiction.

3. Charitable Immunity

Whether the organization sought to be held liable for riot damage is incorporated or not, there is one other doctrine of local law that bears some mention, namely, the once vigorous doctrine of charitable immunity.[710] The time
was when practically all the states accorded charitable organizations some degree
of immunity from tort liability for the acts of their servants.[711] Today in more
than half of the states the doctrine has been repudiated,[712] and in the rest of the
states, it is being increasingly subjected to inroads and exceptions.[713] Where
the doctrine still survives in one form or another, however, it could conceivably
be pleaded as a defense by organizations whose agents and servants are responsible for mob violence.

The availability of this defense depends first of all upon the ability of the
organization to bring itself within the legal status of a "charitable" organization.
One of the standard descriptions of a charitable organization is that " . . . it has
no capital stock and no provision for making dividends or profits, but derives
its funds mainly from public and private charity, and holds them in trust to be
expended for charitable and benevolent purposes."[714] Charitable purposes, in
turn, are said to include the relief of poverty, the advancement of education
or religion, the promotion of health, governmental or municipal purposes, and

---

709   See generally Brunson, supra note 692, at 411-19.
710   The doctrine applies or does not apply regardless of whether the charitable organization is incorporated or not. Farrigan v. Pevear, 193 Mass. 147, 78 N.E. 855 (1906).
711   In an exhaustive analysis of the doctrine in President and Directors of Georgetown
College v. Hughes, 130 F.2d 810 (D.C. Cir. 1942), Justice Rutledge recognized that
although it had already been "devoured in 'exceptions,' " charitable immunity was still the
rule in almost all the states. Id. at 817.
712   Dean Prosser in the 1964 edition of his treatise on tort law lists nineteen states that
have repudiated charitable immunity; they are Alaska, Arizona, California, Delaware, Florida,
Iowa, Kansas, Kentucky, Michigan, Minnesota, Montana, New Hampshire, New York, North
Dakota, Oklahoma, Oregon, Utah, Vermont, and Wisconsin. W. PROSSER, LAW OF TORTS
§ 127, at 1023-24 (3d ed. 1964). As of March 1968, the following states may be added
to the list: Idaho (Bell v. Presbytery of Boise, 421 P.2d 745 (Idaho 1966)); Illinois (Darling v. Charleston Community Memorial Hosp., 33 Ill. 2d 326, 211 N.E.2d 253 (1965));
Nebraska (Meyers v. Drozda, 180 Neb. 183, 141 N.W.2d 852 (1966)) (nonprofit charitable
hospitals); Nevada (NEV. REV. STAT. § 41.480 (1965)); Pennsylvania (Flagiello v. Penn.
Hosp., 417 Pa. 486, 208 A.2d 193 (1965)); Washington (Friend v. Cove Methodist Church,
Inc., 65 Wash. 2d 174, 396 P.2d 546 (1964)); West Virginia (Adkins v. St. Francis Hosp.,
149 W. Va. 705, 143 S.E.2d 154 (1965)).
713   See text at notes 720-26 infra.
714   Town of Cody v. Buffalo Bill Memorial Ass'n, 64 Wyo. 468, 492, 196 P.2d 369, 377
(1948).

other purposes the accomplishment of which is beneficial to the community.[715] The courts are in substantial agreement regarding these definitions as well as the abstract standards to be applied in determining the charitable status of organizations. For example, it is generally held that an organization's charter or articles of incorporation are only prima facie evidence of its charitable nature, so that evidence as to its actual operation may be introduced to establish otherwise.[716] Likewise, there is substantial agreement that the fact that the organization is a nonprofit one is not conclusive for its charitable status,[717] nor is the fact that it may receive some form of compensation for its services conclusive against charitable status.[718]

But, despite the consensus on the general characteristics of charitable organizations, the cases clearly reveal that different courts often achieve opposite results in applying the standards to similar organizations.[719] It would therefore be futile to attempt to propose a single test for determining whether an organization responsible for riot damage would or would not qualify for charitable immunity. This is especially true because the organizations that could conceivably be responsible for mob violence do not fall into a well defined category; the numerous civil rights organizations differ greatly from each other as to purposes and activities and, as a group, they differ greatly from various other political groups, and even more so from student organizations and clubs.

Simply qualifying as a charity, however, under whatever standards the court may apply or whatever evaluation of the facts the court may make, does not mean that the organization can automatically claim charitable immunity under all circumstances. Almost all the states that still recognize some form of charitable immunity will protect the charity only when the claim against it arises out of an actual charitable activity.[720] Following this view, numerous courts have held that when the charitable organization engages in primarily commercial activities such as running a bingo game,[721] a parking lot,[722] or an office building,[723] it cannot claim charitable immunity from injuries arising from these activities, even though the profits are to be used ultimately for charitable purposes. Likewise, it can be argued that an organization that otherwise qualifies as a charity should not be able to claim immunity with respect to activities such as demon-

---

715   Boyd v. Frost Nat'l Bank, 145 Tex. 206, 196 S.W.2d 497, 502 (1946). *See also* RESTATEMENT (SECOND) OF TRUSTS §§ 368-74 (1959).
716   Krpan v. Otis Elevator Co., 226 F. Supp. 293 (E.D. Pa. 1964); Barrett v. Brooks Hosp., 338 Mass. 754, 157 N.E.2d 638 (1959); Hodgson v. William Beaumont Hosp., 373 Mich. 184, 128 N.W.2d 542 (1964). *But see* Oak Park Club v. Lindheimer, 369 Ill. 462, 17 N.E.2d 32 (1938) (certificate of incorporation is controlling for tax purposes).
717   Krpan v. Otis Elevator Co., 226 F. Supp. 293 (E.D. Pa. 1964); Bush v. Aiken Elec. Cooperative, Inc., 226 S.C. 442, 85 S.E.2d 716 (1955).
718   *See* Duncan v. Steeper, 17 Wis. 2d 226, 116 N.W.2d 154, 157 (1962), and authorities cited therein.
719   *E.g., compare Appeal of* Subers, 173 Pa. Super. 558, 98 A.2d 639 (1953) *with* Neptune Fire Engine & Hose Co. v. Board of Educ., 166 Ky. 1, 178 S.W. 1138 (1915), *overruled on other grounds in* Greene v. Stevenson, 295 Ky. 832, 175 S.W.2d 519 (1943).
720   *E.g.,* Blatt v. Geo. H. Nettleton Home for Aged Women, 365 Mo. 30, 275 S.W.2d 344 (1955); Eiserhardt v. State Agricultural & Mechanical Soc'y, 235 S.C. 305, 111 S.E. 2d 568 (1959).
721   Blankenship v. Alter, 171 Ohio St. 65, 167 N.E.2d 922 (1960).
722   Eiserhardt v. State Agricultural & Mechanical Soc'y, 235 S.C. 305, 111 S.E.2d 568 (1959).
723   Gamble v. Vanderbilt Univ., 138 Tenn. 616, 200 S.W. 510 (1918).

strations, marches, and picketing, even though they may indirectly further admittedly charitable purposes and goals. Such activities may not be commercial enterprises in the same sense as a bingo game or a publishing house, but they are equally as non-charitable and even more likely to adversely affect the interests of third persons.

There are other limitations often imposed on charitable immunity that may affect the availability of the defense to an organization responsible for mob violence. For example, several jurisdictions that hold charitable organizations immune from the tortious conduct of their servants will nonetheless find the organization liable where it has been negligent in hiring or retaining an employee.[724] Where this exception is recognized, it seems evident that an organization may lose its charitable immunity for entrusting the conduct of a demonstration to an agent who it knows is likely to incite violence. Other courts limit immunity to cases where the person suing is a beneficiary of the charitable activities of the organization, but allow others to recover.[725] In these states, the organization responsible for the violent demonstration would have to establish that the injured person was a beneficiary of the demonstration in order for the organization to qualify for immunity. It is difficult to imagine such a finding unless perhaps the injured person may have requested or approved of or participated in the demonstration. Finally, some states, especially those basing immunity on a trust fund theory, hold that the organization is freed from liability only to the extent that its trust funds may not be made subject to judgment; but where it has other funds available, usually in the form of liability insurance, it may be held liable up to the policy limits.[726]

There is no doubt that the law of charitable immunity today is undergoing rapid changes — all tending toward an eventual elimination of the doctrine altogether or at least a confinement of it to its narrowest limits. Whether an organization that would otherwise be liable for mob violence could escape that liability by claiming charitable immunity is a question apparently not yet considered by any court.[727] But if such a case should arise, it is predictable that the pronounced trend away from charitable immunity will motivate most courts that still recognize the doctrine to seize upon one of the available exceptions

724   Southern Methodist Univ. v. Clayton, 142 Tex. 179, 176 S.W.2d 749 (1943); Hill v. Lehigh Memorial Hosp., 204 Va. 501, 132 S.E.2d 411 (1963).
725   Viosca v. Touro Infirmary, 170 So. 2d 222 (La. App. Ct. 1964); Peacock v. Burlington County Historical Soc'y, 95 N.J. Super. 205, 230 A.2d 513 (1967).
726   Michard v. Myron Stratton Home, 144 Colo. 251, 355 P.2d 1078 (1960); YMCA v. Bailey, 112 Ga. App. 684, 146 S.E.2d 324 (1965); ME. REV. STAT. ANN. tit. 14, § 158 (Supp. 1967).
727   It may perhaps be worthy of noting that in the Overstreet case, discussed at length above, there is no indication that a charitable immunity defense was raised at all by the NAACP, although the doctrine is still recognized in Georgia and although the organization could possibly qualify as charitable for purposes of tort immunity. See Justice Douglas' dissenting opinion in NAACP v. Overstreet, 384 U.S. 118, 120 (1966) where he recognized that the NAACP is "a nonprofit corporation . . . for the purpose of promoting equality of treatment for Negro citizens," citing NAACP v. Alabama, 357 U.S. 449, 451-52 (1958). In short, it was at least arguable that the NAACP in Overstreet could have pleaded itself as a charitable corporation. Why it was not attempted is, of course, speculation, but it is possible that the NAACP attorneys recognized that even if they could establish the organization as a charitable one, they would still have the problem of showing that the picketing was a charitable activity, almost certainly an impossibility in view of the violence that erupted and the fact that the picketing itself was found to be illegal.

as grounds for denying charitable immunity to an organization otherwise responsible for mob violence.

Conclusion

The entire area of law applicable to a riot situation is currently a topic of vital concern for this nation. There are strong indications that the long, hot summers of civil unrest in the cities will continue, at least, in the immediate future. For this reason, the solution of the legal problems that were considered in this Note will continue to plague the courts and other law enforcement agencies in the years to come. Since the root causes of the recent urban ghetto riots are basically social and economic inequalities, the legal system alone cannot effect a total remedy for the riot problem. However, until the causes of riots are eliminated from our society, it remains the burden of the legal system to restore and maintain law and order. It is to this latter objective that this Note is directed.

James P. Gillece, Jr.[728]
John A. Macleod[729]
Gerald J. Rapien[730]
John P. Rittinger[731]

---

[728]   Text accompanying notes 361-539 *supra.*
[729]   Text accompanying notes 173-360 *supra.*
[730]   Text accompanying notes 540-727 *supra.*
[731]   Text accompanying notes 1-172 *supra.*